More Praise for
Cyber-Safe Kids, Cyber-Savvy Teens

"Nancy Willard's book promotes a safe and enriching online experience for young people. . . . We rely on Willard's insights to help parents understand how young people use new technologies—including social networking and e-commerce sites—and teach children how to protect themselves online."

—Nancy Kranich, past president, American Library Association

"Nancy Willard has written a terrific book. I found it to be well-researched, thoughtful, and filled with sound, practical advice. Written in a clear, down-to-earth style, it will be an indispensable tool for parents who are struggling to raise their children in the midst of this pervasive new digital media culture."

—Kathryn C. Montgomery, professor of communication, American University, and author, *Generation Digital: Politics, Commerce, and Childhood in the Age of the Internet*

"This is sound, much-needed parenting advice for Web 2.0—what I'd call the kid-driven Web. Never has parental engagement (rather than control) been more important, and it's tough to be involved without being informed. *Cyber-Safe Kids, Cyber-Savvy Teens* covers all the angles, from parenting strategies to what children do and face on the social Web. I highly recommend it."

—Anne Collier, editor, *Net Family News*, coauthor, *MySpace Unraveled*, and codirector, BlogSafety.com

"Nancy's unique background in law, education, technology, and parenting are evident in the book's practical, sensible, and highly specific advice for teaching kids to anticipate, avoid, and deal with risky online situations. This book should be required reading for every adult responsible for both a child and a browser."

—Linda Starr, curriculum and technology editor, *Education World*

"Nancy Willard combines her considerable expertise in law, technology, and parenting to create this important and accessible guide. For many parents, myself included, the Internet can be a foreign sea and helping children navigate it safely can be confusing and frightening. Nancy uses a commonsense approach in teaching both children and young adults to avoid a comprehensive range of potential Internet hazards—from social networking to cyberbullying to accessing adult materials. For any adult who wants to help students learn safe and ethical online behaviors, this book is a must-read."

—Doug Johnson, director of Media and Technology, Mankato Schools, Minnesota, and author, *Learning Right from Wrong in the Digital Age*

"*Cyber-Safe Kids, Cyber-Savvy Teens* is a comprehensive and practical book for parents on how to monitor, guide, and effectively communicate with their children regarding the Internet. Such guidance is critical in order to parent effectively today."

—Patti Agatston, prevention specialist, Cobb County School District, Georgia

Cyber-Safe Kids, Cyber-Savvy Teens

•

Helping Young People
Learn to Use the Internet
Safely and Responsibly

Nancy E. Willard

John Wiley & Sons

JB JOSSEY-BASS

Published by Jossey-Bass
A Wiley Imprint
989 Market Street, San Francisco, CA 94103-1741   www.josseybass.com

Jossey-Bass books and products are available through most bookstores. To contact Jossey-Bass directly, call our Customer Care Department within the U.S. at 800-956-7739, outside the U.S. at 317-572-3986, or fax 317-572-4002.

Jossey-Bass also publishes its books in a variety of electronic formats. Some content that appears in print may not be available in electronic books.

Library of Congress Cataloging-in-Publication Data
Willard, Nancy E.
 Cyber-safe kids, cyber-savvy teens: helping young people learn to use the Internet safely and responsibly / Nancy E. Willard.—1st ed.
     p. cm.
 Includes bibliographical references and index.
 ISBN 978-0-7879-9417-4 (cloth)
 1. Internet and children. 2. Internet and teenagers. 3. Internet—Safety measures.
 4. Parenting. I. Title.
 HQ784.I58W55 2007
 025.04—dc22   2006100388

Cover image credits: Abstract lines © Kemie/istockphoto; Network © Mark Evans/ istockphoto; Teen Girl with Laptop and Headphones courtesy Stockbyte Royalty Free; all other images courtesy Corbis.

Printed in the United States of America
FIRST EDITION
HB Printing   10 9 8 7 6 5 4 3 2 1

Contents

Part Two: Foundational Issues

Part Three: Influences on Online Decision Making

Part Four: Specific Risks and Concerns

Part Five: Accenting the Positive

To my extraordinary children,
Jordan, Allegra, and Bakul,
who enrich my life and provide me with
opportunities to learn new things every day

Acknowledgments

Thanks to:

All of the wonderful educators and librarians who participate on the WWWEDU, LM-Net, and EdTech mail mailing lists, who are always willing to provide me with their insight and feedback on issues related to Internet use, and who put up with my occasional *8-0 [=[ ] (me on a soapbox—look at this sideways) email messages when I am feeling especially passionate about a certain matter under discussion.

The great folks who meet or provide feed service at Fifth Street Public Market, Eugene, Oregon—where most of this book was written. Thanks for the great coffee, food, conversation, and support.

Anne Collier and Larry Magid, managers of the Web site BlogSafety and authors of *MySpace Unleashed,* Larry Rosen of California State University, Stephen Carrick-Davies of Childnet International in Great Britain, Rod Nockles and Martin Chambers of NetAlert in Australia, and the many excellent staff members of the American Library Association—all of whom are committed to collaborative efforts to address youth risk online concerns.

The fine folks at Research Press, who have published my book for educators, *Cyberbullying and Cyberthreats: Responding to the Challenge of Online Social Aggression, Threats, and Distress,* and who introduced me to the fine folks at Jossey-Bass.

The fine folks at Jossey-Bass: Kate Bradford, Connie Santisteban, David Horne, Elizabeth Forsaith, Natalie Lin, and Jennifer Wenzel, and my indexer Susan Edwards, who have brought this book into reality.

Introduction

Some young people, especially teens, appear to believe that the online world is their personal playground—with no need for parental attention or guidance. The Internet provides wonderful opportunities and is clearly an important vehicle for information sharing and communication that is enhancing our society. But there are dark sides to this wonderful resource that can present risks and concerns for the well-being of young people.

To effectively negotiate cyberspace and avoid the risks and areas of concern, young people need parents. When they are younger, they need parents to establish safe online places where they will be protected from possible harm. They need parents to say, "No, you may not do that, because it is just not safe." As they grow, they need parents to help them gain the knowledge, skills, and values to consistently make safe and responsible choices online. During this time, they also need parents to remain "hands-on"—paying attention—until they have successfully shown that they will consistently exercise their knowledge and skills in a way that demonstrates respect for themselves and others.

This is a book for parents and other adults who work with young people, and it is divided into five major sections:

- Part One, "Internet Parenting Strategies," includes a brief introduction to the risks and concerns of the online world and offers a wide range of strategies that parents and others can use to help young people gain the knowledge, skills,

and values that support safe and responsible online choices.
This section also provides strategies to help ensure that
parents remain engaged.

- Part Two, "Foundational Issues," addresses the Internet
  use issues that underlie the more specific risks and concerns.
  These foundational issues include the wide appeal of social
  networking sites, the commercial aspects of the Internet,
  privacy, Internet addiction and multitasking, information
  literacy, and stranger literacy.

- Part Three, "Influences on Online Decision Making,"
  delves more deeply into a broad range of issues that are
  important to understand in the formation of an effective
  Internet parenting approach. This includes insight into
  brain development, how technology can interfere with
  responsible decision making, social-influence techniques,
  "at risk" young people, and strategies that parents can use
  to empower children to make good choices.

- Part Four, "Specific Risks and Concerns," provides an in-
  depth discussion of specific risks and concerns, including
  online pornography, cyberbullying, cyberthreats, violent
  gaming, gambling, hate groups, sites that support self-harm,
  computer security concerns, and more, with recommendations for actions parents can take to address the risk or
  concern and on how to give your child the knowledge,
  skills, and values that can empower him or her to make
  the right choices online.

- Part Five, "Accenting the Positive," provides suggestions
  on ways in which you can encourage your child to engage
  in online activities that will enrich his or her life.

- The appendices provide a template for a "Parent-Teen
  Internet Use Agreement" and an overview of Internet
  technologies and activities. If you are not an experienced
  Internet user, you might want to read the overview first.

Many of the topics addressed in this book are interrelated, so concepts that are briefly referenced in one chapter either have been or will be addressed in full in another chapter.

Some Words About Words

These days, with the explosive growth in various wireless digital devices that can access the Internet, it is getting pretty hard to define where the Internet begins and where it ends. Whenever the terms *Internet* or *online* are used in this book, consider these to be very expansive terms that encompass all of the current and emerging information and communication technologies. The word *parent* is used to refer to any adult who has a parent-like relationship with a child.

Cyber-Safe Kids, Cyber-Savvy Teens and BlogSafety

The Cyber-Safe Kids, Cyber-Savvy Teens Web site at http://cskcst .com has been created to provide additional material to support the mission of this book. This Web site will provide additional informational resources, as well as links to other sites that can provide helpful information.

The author is also a member of the advisory board for BlogSafety. The BlogSafety Web site, located at http://blogsafety.org, offers a forum for parents to engage with other parents and professionals in order to ask questions and discuss issues. Please join us.

Part One

•

INTERNET PARENTING STRATEGIES

Of Fenced Play Yards and Hands-On Parenting

EFFECTIVE REAL-WORLD PARENTING ONLINE

P arents already know how to raise children and teens to make safe and responsible choices. When children are younger, we keep them in safe places—such as fenced play yards—and carefully monitor their activities. We teach important safety skills and expectations for responsible behavior, especially when we are together in public places. Setting limits and imposing discipline helps to enforce these expectations.

As children grow, we allow them more freedoms, under conditions that support safe and responsible behavior. We continue to discuss behavioral expectations and impose limits. We also remain "hands-on"—asking questions such as Where are you going? What are you doing? Who are you doing it with? How long will you be gone? And, yes, sometimes we find it necessary to impose a negative consequence for failure to abide by our expectations.

Unfortunately, it is difficult for many parents to apply these real-world parenting strategies to their children and teens' use of the Internet. Even relatively Internet-savvy parents can get lost in Internet "kidzones." Parents may not even know what online dangers to watch out for, or how these dangers might appear on the Internet. Parents may believe that by installing filtering software they have done all that is necessary to protect their children. Or they may think that Web sites are effectively "babysitting" their children. Some parents think—or their teens have convinced them—that it is necessary and appropriate to respect their children's privacy online and fail to understand that the online sites on which their children are posting material are very public and present some significant risks. Or parents may think that because their children are sitting in the family room using the computer, they are safe and all is well.

Having grown up with technology, children and teens have no fear when it comes to exploring new technologies and online activities. And they have lots more time to explore the nooks and crannies of cyberspace. Your child already is, or can be expected to become, very adept at computer technology. Children can quickly leave their parents behind in embracing emerging online technologies and activities.

As savvy as children and teens may be about the Internet, there are still many things they do not know about life and about making safe and responsible choices. Sometimes they take risks. Sometimes they fail to recognize the possible negative consequences of certain actions. There are dangerous strangers online, who might seek to seduce or manipulate your child. As a parent, you are still the "life experiences" and "risk management" expert. An effective parent-child partnership to address Internet issues is essential.

It appears, however, that many young people, especially teens, are not telling their parents or any other adults about problems or difficulties they encounter online. This includes disturbing online situations that involve sexual solicitations or cyberbullying. The disinclination to report online concerns to adults appears to reflect a concern on the part of young people that adults do not understand the teen online world, will likely overreact to any reported concern, will not know how to respond effectively to such concerns, and may make the situation worse if they do try to help. Most significantly, young people fear that if they report a disturbing online situation to a parent or other adult, the most likely response will be to restrict their access or prevent involvement in desired online activities. As parents and other adults gain greater understanding of the teen online world and knowledge of how to respond effectively to concerns without overreacting, this can create the conditions necessary for young people to feel that it is safe to report disturbing online situations.

The same "real-world" parenting approach discussed earlier is necessary to guide children's use of the Internet. When children are younger, they are at a developmental stage during which they should use the Internet in very protected "safe places," with very simple rules. Parents essentially must keep them in safe fenced play yards online. As children grow, there comes a time when their explorations on the Internet will expand, but parents must remain by their side, holding their hand, imparting knowledge and skills, discussing safe and responsible choices, and monitoring their online activities. Eventually, older teens and young adults must have the knowledge, skills, and values to be able to consistently make good choices on their own.

·2·

Danger Signs on the Information Highway

OVERVIEW OF ONLINE
RISKS AND CONCERNS

This chapter contains a brief outline of the risks and concerns associated with young people and online activities to provide an overall context for the information presented in the remaining chapters in Parts One, Two, and Three. All of the risks and concerns mentioned briefly in this chapter are discussed in-depth in Part Four.

When the Internet first burst into public awareness, the initial concerns expressed about young people and online activities were about pornography, predators, and privacy. These concerns are still present, but additional risks and areas of concern have appeared or have been more clearly recognized. These risks and areas of concern can be divided into two basic categories: safety risks, involving situations in which an individual or group engages in activities that present danger to a young person, and responsible use concerns, involving situations in which young people engage in activities that are unsafe, irresponsible, harmful, or even illegal.

You may at some point in this chapter have the thought, That's it. It is too dangerous. I am not allowing my child to go online unless I am sitting in a chair right nearby. As much as you may want to delay, limit, or prohibit your child from going online, sooner or later—and probably sooner—your child will be an active participant in cyberspace. Your child must have the knowledge, skills, and values to make safe and responsible choices in this environment. This is a reality you cannot ignore.

Risky Sexual Activities

Risky sexual activities include situations in which individuals present safety risks to young people and situations in which young people themselves engage in behavior that causes concern.

Pornography and Sexual Materials

One concern about online pornography and other sexual materials is accidental premature exposure to these materials by younger children and accidental access by teens. We can presume that many, if not most, teens will be inclined to spend some time looking at online erotica. This is an issue that families will handle differently in accord with their family values. The more significant problems for all parents of teens are online activities that go beyond normal sexual curiosity to excessive, addictive access, especially access to pornographic material that involves violence or is child pornography.

Adult Sexual Predators

Adult sexual predators seduce young people who they contact through public online communication services with the objective of arranging for a sexual liaison or obtaining child pornography. Unfortunately, sometimes teens engage in unsafe or irresponsible behavior that is highly likely to attract the attention of these adult sexual predators. It appears that some adult sexual predators seek more naïve and innocent young people, whereas others simply troll for teens who welcome such contacts.

Self-Produced Child Pornography

Some teens provide sexually explicit pictures and videos of themselves online. They may be seduced into this activity by adult pornographers. Other teens appear to be exchanging images to earn money, receive gifts, or gain attention. And still others create and share sexually explicit materials in the context of online relationship building. They do not appear to recognize that any sexual image provided to someone electronically, even in the context of a private relationship, can easily be disseminated further. Many of these teens apparently also do not realize that the production or dissemination of a sexual image of a minor—even if done by that minor—is a crime.

"Hook-ups"—Sex Without Commitment

Teens are using the Internet to arrange for sexual involvement with other teens for "hook-ups," which is slang for sex without commitment. This behavior emulates the behavior of some adults involved in matchmaking sites. In the context of these activities, they may post sexually suggestive or provocative material in their profiles, blogs, or Web pages.

Sexual Harassment

Teens may receive unwanted sexual communications, including harassment or sexual propositions, through email or messaging from other teens or from adults. Teens also send unwanted sexual communications to other teens and to adults.

Cyberdating

Cyberdating is a phenomenon that has become an accepted social activity. Parents can expect that teens, especially older teens, will form romantic relationships with people they meet online. While there are risks associated with the formation of such relationships, there also can be advantages, because the early stages of such relationships involve a substantial amount of communication.

Cyberbullying

"Cyberbullying" is being cruel to others by sending or posting harmful material or engaging in other forms of social cruelty using the Internet or other digital technologies, such as cell phones. Young people may be the target of cyberbullying from others or may engage in such harmful behavior. Direct cyberbullying involves repeatedly sending offensive messages. More indirect forms of cyberbullying include disseminating denigrating materials or sensitive personal information or impersonating someone to cause harm. Cyberbullying may escalate to cyberstalking. The harmful impact of cyberbullying may be even greater than in-person bullying because online communications can be very vicious and ongoing, the cyberbully can be anonymous, and harmful material can be widely disseminated.

Unsafe Online Communities

Young people who are attracted to unsafe online communities are often "at risk" to begin with. Young people who are depressed and do not have healthy "real world" relationships that provide them with the attention they need may seek new friends in online communities in which they are welcomed and feel supported. Unsafe online communities support a range of self-harm activities, including suicide, cutting, anorexia, and drug use, as well as other risky behaviors. When "at risk" young people become involved in these groups, they feel that they finally have found acceptance and take the perspective that "what the group thinks is what I think." This can lead to the adoption of even more harmful attitudes and involvement in extremely dangerous activities.

Hate Groups, Gangs, and Other Troublesome Groups

Hate groups, gangs, and other troublesome groups are another form of unsafe online community. These groups attract troubled and angry "at risk" teens. Hate groups and gangs tend to be well-established, have adult leadership, and engage in activities specifically intended to recruit new members, especially young people. The concern is that these groups can combine the aspects of dangerous online communities and seduction techniques similar to those used by sexual predators. Other, informal groups are formed by angry and troubled young people who use the Internet to vent their anger and discuss plans for revenge.

Cyberthreats

Cyberthreats can be direct threats or distressing material that provides clues that a person is emotionally upset and may be considering harming someone or committing suicide. Unfortunately, young people also sometimes post threats or distressing material as a "joke." This kind of online "joke" can have very serious ramifications.

Gaming

Many young people, especially boys, are highly attracted to gaming environments. Online games have a variety of formats: one person against a machine, two or more players located anywhere in the world playing against each other, and rich simulated gaming communities in which players create long-standing "characters" that interact with other game "characters" in endless simulated activities within a mythical environment. Two key concerns related to gaming are gaming addiction and involvement in excessively violent games.

Gambling

Research consistently has shown that underage involvement in gambling is associated with other social and emotional difficulties and is a predictor for gambling addiction problems in adulthood. There are many ways that young people can become involved with gambling online: so-called "risk-free" gambling-type games are popular on sites targeting teens and younger children. Online gaming activities may offer the opportunity to win cash prizes. Teens who have access to a credit card—theirs or their parent's—may be able to participate in online gambling casinos hosted in countries that have few legal controls on gambling activities.

Hacking and Hacker Tribes

Since the dawn of the computer age, technically sophisticated young people have engaged in hacking. Although these activities are considered illegal, most young people engaged in hacking have no intention to cause harm by their explorations. Online hacker communities are very prevalent. More recently, the criminal element has embraced hacking as a means of committing other crimes, especially those involving identity theft. Computer security criminals appear to be recruiting young hackers to be the "ground forces" in vast criminal hacking enterprises.

Plagiarism

Plagiarism involves presenting material created by someone else as your own. Plagiarism may be inadvertent or intentional. Inadvertent plagiarism generally involves incorporating material written by others into one's work without proper quotations or citations. Intentional plagiarism includes taking large portions of material written by others or submitting an entire document written by someone else as an original work. Students can find or even purchase papers online that they may turn in as their own work. Engaging in plagiarism can result in failed grades and possibly other sanctions.

Copyright Infringement

Copyright laws, standards, and expectations are undergoing significant changes to address the opportunities and challenges of new technologies. These technologies allow more people to disseminate their own creative works, but they also make it easier for other people to inappropriately make copies of someone's creative work.

Technical Security Concerns

Technical security concerns arise from wide dissemination of many forms of "malware," short for "malicious software," that can infect a computer—including viruses, Trojan horse attacks, worms, spyware, and the like. Many online activities that are attractive to young people can increase vulnerability to security risks. That neat new computer game your child just downloaded for free might contain spyware that will infect your computer and result in identity theft.

Spam

All Internet users are, unfortunately, well aware of the concerns related to unwanted email communications. This spam may include inappropriate sexual content, advertisements for sexual products, or scams, including identity theft scams. Sometimes young people may unknowingly sign up to receive advertising email.

Scams

Parents may think that identity theft is a concern for adults, not teens—because teens generally have not established a credit history. Unfortunately, identity theft is also happening to young people.

They may not even know their identity has been stolen until they try to get a driver's license or a college loan and find that someone has already stolen their identity and destroyed their credit. Other concerns include fraudulent offers to assist in obtaining college scholarships and scams related to purchasing products online, lotteries, or business opportunities.

· 3 ·

Internet Use for
Different Ages

GUIDELINES FOR CHILDREN,
EARLY TEENS, AND OLDER TEENS

The conditions under which your child uses the Internet, and the rules or guidelines for such use, must be age-based. Your child's ability to engage in safe and responsible behavior will increase with maturity. However, the risks and concerns also increase with age.

First, consider the end objective: at around the age of eighteen, most children likely are headed off to college or trade school and most likely will be living on their own. Children headed for a college dorm room or apartment with other students will be immersed in an environment of young people who are all feeling their first real adult-like freedom and are making extensive use of the Internet. No one will be supervising your child. There certainly is no ability to implement "parental controls" on your child's computer. You will not be readily available for in-person consultation—and your child may be very unlikely to want to discuss online activities with you anyway. Ideally, therefore, by the age of sixteen, your child should have all of the necessary knowledge, skills, and values to make safe and responsible choices online. This will allow for two years of "fine-tuning" just to be sure all of the lessons have been successfully learned.

Let's start with some general guidance:

- Keep the computer in a more public area of your house—at least until your child is around the age of sixteen (more on this later). This will allow you to periodically check over the shoulder of your child to see what is happening online, assess whether or not any online experiences might be affecting him or her emotionally, and foster ongoing conversations about Internet activities.

- Establish standards regarding use of the computer when you are not present in the home that are appropriate for your child's age and risk factors. Also, set limits on late-night use. You can use time-management software to ensure compliance with these standards, if necessary.

- Be a part of your child's online experience. This means more than simply monitoring. Find out where your child likes to go and why. Explore the Internet together. Ask to meet your child's new online friends. Discuss situations that come up and how your child has addressed the situations.

- Encourage high-quality online activities. The Internet provides access to an incredible range of quality information resources and the ability to create solid friendships with people in other parts of the world. But the primary ways in which young people use the Internet are for surfing, gabbing, and gaming. Clearly some level of surfing, gabbing, and gaming can be fun and enjoyable—but these activities really do not do all that much to improve the quality of one's life. Strive to engage your child in online activities that will enrich his or her life.

- Communicate with your child electronically. Send your child a daily email message. Install instant messaging (IM) on your computer, and IM with your child. Use these times to make positive statements to your child—reinforcing achievement and providing encouragement. It is entirely possible that when you communicate like this online, your child will temporarily forget that you are a parent and be willing to engage in substantive discussions.

- Make sure you have a good understanding of security issues and have implemented technologies that control spam and prevent the display of pop-up advertisements.

Guidelines for Younger Children— Under Age Eight

The childhood years are "magical years," when children believe in the tooth fairy and other such imaginary creatures. Children who believe in magical creatures are simply incapable of understanding how the Internet functions or of independently making safe decisions online. Children of this age should use the Internet only in very safe places, with simple rules. It is your full responsibility as a parent to make sure they are safe online.

You could use parental controls offered by online services to establish a safe place, but consider this: these "child safe portals" have been established by companies that are seeking to attract children and their parents. They market their child safe portals to parents as "safe places." But these sites are also in business to make a profit. So in addition they are promoting advertising possibilities within these environments to companies marketing products or services to children. The degree of advertising will vary. Check these portals carefully and make a decision on the degree to which you find this level of advertising to your child acceptable.

A better alternative is to create a safe place by bookmarking Web sites you think are appropriate for your child and making it easy for him or her to access these special bookmarked sites. Using this strategy, you can ensure that the Web sites fully meet your values and standards—not that of an online portal company. If your child wants to go to a new site, you can look for the site together and, if you deem it appropriate, you can add this to your child's special bookmarks.

Childhood is the time to start encouraging more high-quality online activities. Find the great sites for children provided by non-commercial art, science, and history organizations. Try to steer your child to enrichment sites and sites that will engage him or her in creative activities, not simply sites that have advertisements and games.

If you think it necessary for your child to use email, establish an email account with strict limits on who can send messages to this account.

The three simple rules for younger children are as follows:

- "Never type your name, address, or phone number online. Always use your computer username." Because your child may not be able to fully distinguish between educational software that is on your computer and online activities, it is best to require the use of a computer username for all computer activities.

- "If something 'yucky' comes up on the screen, turn off the screen like this [show your child how to turn off the screen] and come and get me. You won't get in trouble." If something yucky does come up, this instruction provides your child with a simple and rapid response that should limit exposure. Turning off the screen but leaving the site where it is will allow you to determine how your child might have gotten to a bad site. Turn this into a positive experience for your child by praising your child for the prompt and appropriate response.

- "Only go to the sites that we have bookmarked. If you want to go to a new site, we will look for it together." Use these searches as a "teachable moment" to talk with your child about safe searching and the values that you are using to make a determination of appropriateness. If a new site requires registration, use this as an opportunity to teach your child how to safely register without disclosing personal contact information.

Your child will suffer no loss if you choose not to allow or encourage any Internet use at this age. Let your child spend a small amount of time using high-quality educational software. Then invite some "real world" friends over to play, and bring out the paints, building blocks, or a soccer ball. These activities are much more helpful for your child's development.

Guidelines for Older Children— Ages Eight to Ten

Ages eight to ten are those precious years between the "magical years" and the era of "raging hormones." Many older children will want to engage in greater explorations of the Internet. They do not have the insight necessary to be left entirely on their own, but they also do not need constant "over the shoulder" supervision. They can begin to practice decision making on their own, under your guidance.

Older children generally are still responsive to adult instruction and are willing to follow "rules." These years are an important age to use every available opportunity to talk about issues of safe and responsible Internet use. Values discussed and lessons learned at this age can carry into the teenage years.

Help your child establish a safe Internet environment of favorite bookmarked sites, with a requirement that you are consulted before he or she searches for sites outside of this environment. This will provide an opportunity to practice safe searching skills. This is an important time for teachable moments about safe searching. Provide guidance on safe search strategies, discuss the possible risks that may emerge in the context of conducting a search, watch as your child demonstrates good decision making, and acknowledge good choices.

Your child likely will begin to use the Internet for class projects, such as writing papers, during this time. Many schools are now providing access to online educational research resources. These research resources include Web sites that offer high-quality material in an age-appropriate manner. Ask your child's teacher how you can access these resources from home.

A firm rule should be established that your child should not register on any site without first checking with you and getting your permission. This will provide the opportunity for teachable moments about the protection of personal information and safe ways to register on sites. Most important, make sure that your child knows never to give a full name, address, or phone number. Teach your child how to safely fill out a registration form without disclosing any personal information that could lead to unwanted advertisements or inappropriate contact.

Many Web sites have a minimum age limit of thirteen. By the age of nine or ten, many children will have discovered or have been clued in by friends that it is possible to lie about one's age and register on these sites. These sites are not safe places for younger children. Pay close attention to the sites your child has included on the collection of bookmarked sites and regularly review the history file to make sure that he or she has not registered on a site for older users without asking for your prior permission.

Continue the use of a safe, supervised email account, making sure your child knows that you have full access to email communications. If your child wants to engage in instant messaging, be sure that his or her IM contacts are limited to known friends and that strict limits are placed on the addition of any other IM contacts without your review and approval.

It is time to start educating your child about how to close inappropriate windows that may pop up on the screen or to get out of inappropriate sites. The first lesson that must be imparted is to never click in an unwanted window. To close a window or get out of a bad site, click on the red close button on the far left corner of the window. If this does not work, your child should turn off the screen and get your assistance.

The other very important rule that should be introduced at this age is to never click on a link unless you are quite sure you know where that link will take you. Absolutely never click on a link in an email message, a pop-up advertising window, or a banner advertisement on a Web site. Clicking on one of these links could result in the display of pornographic material or the download of some form of "malware."

These years are an important time to encourage use of the Internet as a research tool for school projects and independent, high-quality explorations—rather than just as a surfing, gabbing, and gaming environment. Establish strict time limits and continue to encourage and facilitate lots of non-screen-time activities with "real world" friends.

Guidelines for the Tweens—
Ages Eleven to Twelve

Tweens tend to think of themselves as teens and begin to act like teens. The tween years are frequently the beginning of the most tumultuous years in a child's life. In these years, there is often a greatly expanded interest in online activities. With this expanded interest and activity come expanded technical skills. The tween years are the time when many parents may begin to feel left behind when it comes to Internet skills—if not, just wait until the teen years.

In many communities, there is a shift to a middle school environment at around age eleven. Children leave the safe comfort of the primary or elementary school environment and are grouped together with other students who are at varying levels of physical, emotional, and sexual development. Any visit to a middle school will validate the perception that young people enter as children and leave as teens. Generally accompanying this change in school environments is a tremendous desire to act and be perceived as a "teen."

As was noted before, the vast majority of Web sites with teen-oriented activities, including the popular social networking environments, have an age limit of at least thirteen or older. This age limit presents significant challenges for parents of middle school children who are younger than thirteen. You can expect that your eleven-year-old knows how to register on these sites with a falsified age over thirteen. There is significant social pressure on all middle school students to become part of these online communities.

It is really preferable that young people wait until they are through the middle school developmental shifts before they start to participate in these communities. The major contest of wills that you will have at this age will be grounded in the fact that some of the parents of your child's friends might not be setting the same standards about involvement in these communities or simply may not be paying attention to what their children are doing online. When you seek to impose such standards, you will be faced with such arguments as "It's not fair, [child's name]'s parents think it is okay do this" or "Everyone else at school is on [name of site]."

The best strategy for addressing this challenge is to form a partnership with the parents of your child's best friends. Find a way to foster electronic communication within this safe group of friends— and no further.

Guidelines for Early Teens— Ages Thirteen to Fifteen

Early teens likely will be seeking full engagement online. They are now at an age when they can register on most social networking sites, as well as many other sites. In many respects, on the Internet your thirteen-year-old child is considered to be an adult. Your early teen will have greater involvement in online communities that include older teens and young adults. Essentially, all of the risks and concerns that are addressed in Part Four of this book are highly relevant to this age period. Parents must grapple with their early teen's desire for greater freedom and technical ability to gain such freedom, with the concurrent danger that early teens are highly vulnerable online.

Raging hormones, rapidly changing bodies, emerging sexuality, and changes in brain functions all contribute to a challenging time during this age period. Most early teens are sorting out their identity, social status, and relationship interests—which can lead to many different kinds of interactions with friends and other peers. Many of the risks and concerns related to Internet use are directly tied to this search for identity and status.

If you have not formed a partnership with the parents of your child's friends prior to this time, consider doing so now. When early teens start to participate in online social networking sites, the safest approach to implement is to use the privacy features to create a safe enclave for your child and your child's friends—with parental oversight. Used wisely, the privacy features can allow your child to explore social networking with close friends, with much lower risk. Pay close attention to the friendship links on your child's profile, as well as those on the profiles of your child's friends.

In the early teen years there is a significantly increased danger related to risky sexual situations and activities, including seduction by online sexual predators and interest in looking at online pornography. It is absolutely essential that you have in-depth discussions about these issues prior to allowing any activity in environments in which your child is more likely to come in contact with adults who are potentially unsafe or teens who are making unsafe decisions. You may think your seventh-grade daughter is too young for a discussion about sexual predators, and then find that she has established a profile on a social networking site in which she has posted provocative pictures of herself in a bathing suit.

Just to make things even more complicated, this period of time is when young people begin to have a much greater interest in personal privacy. As much as early teens might protest, parents must insist on their right and responsibility to effectively supervise and monitor Internet use. This especially includes all public activities within a social networking site even if your child has implemented privacy protection. Now is the time to make a deal: as your child demonstrates to you an understanding of potential risks and concerns, effective decision-making strategies, and a personal commitment to values and standards for Internet use, you will back off on your supervision and monitoring of online activities. But it is unlikely that you will be backing off until around the age of sixteen. Your child's right to privacy must be earned through the demonstration of a consistent pattern of making good online choices!

Absolutely *do not* let your early teen talk you into allowing a computer with Internet access disappear into a bedroom. If ever there is a time when you need to be able to easily check on your child's online activities, this is it.

The "Parent-Teen Internet Use Agreement" included in Appendix A provides a vehicle for discussing issues that your child will face with the greatly expanded level of access and for your child to enunciate personal standards for online activities. Embrace this developmental period as the time when your child is taking important steps toward adulthood—including the development of personal values and standards. Emphasize the importance of acting in accord with values and standards in all aspects of life—including online.

Guidelines for Older Teens— Ages Sixteen to Eighteen

Your timeframe is now down to a few short years before your child will leave home for work or college. This is the period of time when you will seek to shift full responsibility to your child for making good choices online.

Many, if not most, older teens will be actively involved on social networking sites. This involvement will include far more expansive activities than deemed appropriate for early teens. These activities are likely to bring your teen into greater contact with young adults, who may be exploring their freedom in ways that are entirely inappropriate for teens—and are also quite likely to be inconsistent with your family values for adult behavior. Your older teen's online activities will provide ongoing opportunities to witness behavior choices of others and to decide whether or not those behavior choices are in accord with personal values and standards.

The only way to address Internet use concerns with older teens is through collaboration. Teens think that they know much more about the Internet than their parents—and they are likely right. But still this does not mean that they yet fully comprehend all of the concerns, or the potential consequences of risky actions. Their personal identity, including personal values and standards, is still under development. Although they do not yet have sufficient cognitive development to consistently recognize and address the issues that will emerge related to Internet risks and concerns, their capabilities in this regard are improving. Expect that your child will act in accord with agreed-upon values and standards and hold him or her accountable for decisions that are contrary to such values and standards.

If you are concerned about any particular aspect of your child's Internet use, ask him or her to describe the risk or concern and to outline decision-making strategies, values, and standards related to this concern. If you have any concerns about the basis of your child's knowledge, strategies, values, or standards, ask penetrating questions. By asking questions you can help your child gain a deepened personal understanding and commitment to making good choices.

Provide your child with the opportunity to earn the right to have a computer with Internet access in the bedroom around the age of sixteen—if, and only if certain expectations have been met related to grades, work, chores, and time with family and friends. Revisit the points outlined in the "Parent-Teen Internet Use Agreement." The objective of this strategy is to provide your child with two years of comparative freedom online, while you are still able to pay attention and provide a sounding board for decision making. You also can impose necessary consequences, such as moving the computer back to the family room, if your child's behavior does not meet certain expectations.

Maintaining open communications is essential during this time period. One of the most effective ways to do this is by communicating electronically with your child. With any luck, your child may simply begin to think of you as an online friend, with whom it is safe to freely share thoughts and information. Establishing warm and supportive online communications with your child during this period will support the continuation of such online communications as he or she makes the transition into college and the adult world. This will provide the opportunity for frequent and substantive involvement as your child faces the challenges of young adulthood.

Too Hard, Too Soft, Just Right

PARENTING STYLES AND EFFECTIVE INTERNET PARENTING

G oldilocks knew. One chair was too hard. One chair was too soft. But one chair was just right. Interestingly, the same can be said about parenting styles, especially parenting approaches to the Internet. One style is too hard. One style is too soft. One style is just right.

Common Parenting Styles

The research on parenting styles conducted by Diane Baumrind has significant relevance to the subject of effective parenting strategies to encourage safe and responsible use of the Internet by children and teens.[1] Through a series of research investigations, Baumrind identified three basic parenting styles. Only one style was found to foster responsible decision making, high social competence, internalized self-control, and strong healthy values. While each style has some variations, the three primary styles of parenting identified by Baumrind were authoritarian parenting, permissive parenting, and authoritative parenting.

Authoritarian Parenting

They are obedience- and status-oriented, and expect their orders to be obeyed without explanation.[2]

Authoritarian parents are "father knows best"-style parents. Authoritarian parents focus on strong parental control. They establish absolute standards of behavior—standards that are not to be questioned or negotiated. They are highly demanding, expect prompt obedience, and use punishment techniques that enforce their status as "boss." They expect their children to accept their judgments, values, and goals without questioning. Obedience is a virtue, as is respect for authority, respect for work, and respect for the preservation of order and traditional structure. Authoritarian parents do not encourage their children to engage in problem solving, but expect their children to consult them for guidance. They are less likely to use more supportive approaches, such as affection, praise, and rewards, with their children. They exert external control and do not foster internalized control.

Children from authoritarian families tend to perform moderately well in school and do not generally demonstrate problem behavior. They also tend not to engage in antisocial behaviors, such as drug use, alcohol use, and gang involvement. But they have poorer social skills, lower self-esteem, and higher levels of depression. Girls raised by authoritarian parents tend to become highly compliant. They are easily frustrated and tend to give up or look to others for assistance when faced with any challenges. Boys tend to become quite authoritarian themselves and can become hostile when frustrated. Children of authoritarian parents lack the internalized control to independently make good choices when they are in situations in which no one is telling them what they should do.

Permissive Parents

They are nontraditional and lenient, do not require mature behavior, allow considerable self-regulation, and avoid confrontation.[3]

Permissive parents are the "find your own way" or "I'm too busy"-style parents. Permissive parents are highly indulgent and place relatively few demands on their children. They accept their child's impulses, desires, and actions—even when such actions fall outside of accepted standards. They generally do not monitor their children's behavior effectively and are likely to be inconsistent in responding to misbehavior. Some permissive parents appear to have made a conscious decision to let their children find their own path. They specifically do not seek to shape or alter the behavior of their children for fear that this might damage their child's natural development and creativity. Other permissive parents are simply not paying attention, not involved. Permissive parents do not exert external control, nor do they foster the development of internalized control.

Although children raised by permissive parents tend to be friendly and sociable, they also tend to lack knowledge of appropriate behaviors for ordinary social situations and take too little responsibility for their own misbehavior. Such children are likely to be focused on meeting their own needs, rather than considering the needs of others. They tend to have poor emotional control and can become rebellious when faced with expectations that they comply to certain standards. They also tend to become engaged in antisocial behaviors. Children of permissive parents have no internalized control to support responsible decision making, because no standards and reasons for the standards have ever been articulated for them.

Authoritative Parents

They monitor and impart clear standards for their children's conduct. They are assertive, but not intrusive and restrictive. Their disciplinary methods are supportive, rather than punitive. They want their children to be assertive as well as socially responsible, and self-regulated as well as cooperative.[4]

Authoritative parents take the perspective that their job is to empower their children to independently make good choices.

Authoritative parents are warm and responsive. They seek to nurture their children's social competence and independent, responsible decision making. They set high standards for behavior but seek to impart these standards through ongoing discussions about values and reasons for rules. They provide guidance in the thinking strategies necessary to decide how to apply these standards in specific situations. When it is necessary to impose discipline in response to misbehavior, they do so in a way that helps their children understand the harm or potential harm associated with the misbehavior and that allows the child the opportunity to cure any harm. They engage in discussions about important issues and demonstrate respect for their children's perspectives. They reinforce appropriate behavior and provide support during times of stress or challenge. Authoritative parents foster the development of internalized control based on values, standards, and effective decision-making strategies.

Children of authoritative parents have been found to have greater social competence and social and emotional well-being. They do well in school and do not engage in antisocial behaviors. They demonstrate self-confidence and have high self-esteem. These children are assertive, socially responsible, cooperative, and self-regulated. They resist negative peer pressure and demonstrate effective engagement with friends. They have strong values and standards, engage in effective decision-making, and have internalized control.

Parenting Styles and the Internet

Let's consider how these different types of parenting styles might be reflected in Internet parenting strategies.

Children of Authoritarian Parents Online

If authoritarian parents allow their children to go online, they will seek to maintain a significant amount of control. However, whether they are successful in achieving such control may be a question. For authoritarian parents, the Internet represents the epitome of an environment that lacks structure and control. Authoritarian parents who allow their children to go online likely will rely on parental empowerment tools, including child safe portals or filtering software. In fact, some providers of Internet filtering software promote the use of software for the entire family, perhaps tapping into a fear among authoritarian parents that they themselves may lack sufficient personal control to avoid going to some kinds of sites.

Placing significant reliance on the use of parental controls may end up backfiring, because such reliance often leads to false security. Rebellious children of authoritarian parents are likely to be able to find ways around the filter to seek out the "forbidden fruits." Authoritarian parents may also use monitoring technologies in a surveillance manner—"I don't trust you"—that is not related to any concerns or misbehavior on the part of their child.

The rules for Internet use provided to children by authoritarian parents are likely to be simplistic and lack the essential information necessary to understand the reasons and values that underlie the rules or how to apply the rule in new situations. Children are expected to stay in safe places and to consult with their parents for guidance in dealing with any situation that might present itself when online.

Children of authoritarian parents are unlikely to gain the knowledge and skills necessary to independently make safe and responsible choices online. They are at significant risk of making very bad choices when they are not being closely supervised. The perception of invisibility when using the Internet reduces concerns about detection and punishment by an adult. A child of an authoritarian parent who gains free and open access to the Internet likely will not have developed sufficient internalized controls and effective decision-making skills to independently make safe and responsible choices.

Children of authoritarian parents may also be more susceptible to seduction by dangerous strangers. These children are taught to obey and never question demands placed on them by an adult—any adult. It is very likely that dangerous strangers are able to recognize this behavior when they are seeking to groom a child who has authoritarian parents and will use this insight to seek compliance on the part of the child by assuming the role of an "authority."

Children of Permissive Parents Online

Unfortunately, according to surveys that ask questions about parental supervision of Internet use, permissive Internet parenting is a far too common approach. Classic permissive parents are likely to take the approach that their child or teen must have the freedom to explore this wonderful new world, and that any interference on their part would violate the privacy of their child or teen. Other parents may simply be too busy with their own lives to pay proper attention to what their children are doing online.

If you want to see how teens with permissive parents are using the Internet simply spend some time exploring some of the profiles on social networking sites. You will find ample evidence of the unfortunate results of permissive parenting.

Children of Authoritative Parents Online

The only approach to parenting that will effectively empower children and teens to make safe and responsible choices online is the authoritative approach. This approach provides the foundation for all of the guidance set forth in this book.

·5·

Filtering Follies and Other Myths

TECHNOLOGY "QUICK FIXES" LEAD TO FALSE SECURITY

The initial concerns about Internet use and children were related to easy access to pornography. So-called parental empowerment tools—parental controls and filtering software—were developed and promoted as the "solution" to protecting children on the Internet. There are ways in which technologies can be used to create a safer online environment. The biggest problem with the promotion of protection technologies is that these technologies will never be totally effective. The false security and resulting complacency that has been generated through a decade of promotion of filtering software is at the heart of the current concerns related to the behavior of teens on social networking sites.

In 2002, the U.S. National Academy of Sciences released an extensive report titled "Youth, Pornography, and the Internet."[1] In the preface to the report, the chair of the committee that investigated this issue, Dick Thornburgh, noted

> It is the hope of the committee that this report will be seen as comprehensive and authoritative, but I believe it is bound to disappoint a number of readers. It will disappoint those who expect a technological

"quick fix" to the challenge of pornography on the Internet. . . . It will disappoint parents, school officials, and librarians who seek surrogates to fulfill the responsibilities of training and supervision needed to truly protect children from inappropriate sexual materials on the Internet.

The Internet industry and government policymakers were very interested in creating the perception that concerns related to Internet use by young people had been adequately addressed so that the growth of the Internet could continue. Filtering and child safe portals were promoted to alleviate parental fear. The result of this promotion has been the misperception that all parents need to do is to configure the protection tool correctly and their child will magically be protected and learn to make safe and responsible choices online. Schools also have placed significant reliance on filtering software and often fail to recognize the need for more effective education and supervision. Of most significance, the false security and resulting complacency have led to a failure to ensure that young people have the knowledge, skills, and values necessary to independently make good choices online.

Underblocking

In 2002, the Kaiser Family Foundation did an analysis of many of the most common filtering systems.[2] They found that while individual performance varied, it generally was possible get to approximately 10 percent of the sites that had pornography. So let's translate this into "kid time." A 10 percent failure rate means that about one in ten sites containing pornography are accessible. With a failure rate like this, a determined teen using an unsupervised computer will have no difficulties accessing inappropriate material.

If you are using a parental empowerment tool, such as filtering software or a child safe portal, run some tests on its accuracy— without your child in close proximity. Pick some appropriate search key words, such as *XXX, porn,* or *hot teen sex.* Check how many sites in both the search returns and the advertisements you can get to. Check on the first three pages of the search returns, then go to the thirtieth page of search returns and check the next three pages from there.

Bypassing

There are easy ways for teens to circumvent or bypass filters. Search for "bypass, Internet, filter" to find more information. Teens can find many proxy sites on the Internet that allow them to bypass a filter. If your child has some friends who do not have Internet filtering on their home computer, they can easily turn their computer into a proxy for your child to use. Young people can also seek access to blocked sites through a "cached" site. They can use foreign word equivalents for the inappropriate material they want to access.

They also can simply get access to the Internet through a computer that does not have filtering.

Overblocking

Filters block sites based on the values and standards of the companies that create the filters. These values and standards may or may not be in accord with your family's values and standards. The filters also often accidentally block access to perfectly appropriate sites. You may not consider this to be an exceptionally high concern, because it generally is possible for you to override the filter. But if young people are frequently blocked from accessing material they think they should have the ability to access, this leads to efforts to bypass the filter. Overblocking, especially bias-based blocking of controversial information, is a significant concern when public institutions, such as schools and libraries, are forced to use these filtering products.

Technologies to Protect Teens
on Social Networking Sites

In a predictable manner, as concerns about teen behavior on social networking sites have emerged, policymakers are promoting technology protection tools to address these concerns. Whenever a technology protection tool is recommended, look carefully at how effective this tool might be.

Age Verification

Some policymakers are calling for the social networking sites to implement age verification. Sites that responsibly seek to serve only adult users have effectively implemented age verification. There are technologies and processes that are capable of accurate age verification—for adults.

But effective age verification is totally dependent on the ability of adults to provide evidence of their age through some form of government or business-issued identification, such as voter's registration, driver's license, or credit card. There are no similar forms of independent identity and age verification for young people. There are also many concerns associated with any approach that would create a mechanism for identity and age verification of young people—not the least of which is identity theft.

Privacy Features

Some social networking sites have implemented privacy-protection capabilities that users can use to cloak their profile and discussion groups. These technologies can be used to enhance safety. But they also raise concerns of false security. Teens are most concerned about parental intrusion into their online activities. They can use the privacy protections to block parental review. Parents may think that because their child has implemented privacy protection, their child is safe. But behind the veil of privacy, their child may have invited unsafe strangers to be friends, be engaged in or be the target of cruel cyberbullying, or be engaged in other unsafe or irresponsible behavior.

Effective Use of Technology Protection Tools

There is certainly a role for some technology protection tools, especially for younger children. Technologies to address computer security and provide spam control clearly are necessary. Parents may also make effective use of time-limiting software and monitoring software. But no parent should ever expect that any technology protection device can absolve them of the need to teach their child to independently make safe and responsible choices and of the need to remain vigilant in monitoring their child's online activities until they are sure that their child is doing so. The best "filtering software" will be the "software" that resides within the "hardware" that sits on your child's shoulders.

· 6 ·

I'm Your Parent.
It's My Responsibility

SUPERVISING YOUR
CHILD'S ONLINE ACTIVITIES

Make it your business to know what your child is doing online. Every news story that reports some kind of a bad incident happening to a child online—a teen who has run off with a predator, a teen who has committed suicide in the face of cyberbullying, teens who were arrested and charged with attempted murder because they were planning a school attack online—all have one element in common: a lack of parental attention to what was happening online.

Consider the analogy to teaching a child to cross a busy street. At first, you will hold that child's hand. This is accomplished online by ensuring that your young child or tween uses the Internet in a carefully controlled safe manner. Fortunately, children and tweens generally are not concerned about privacy. They should have no expectation of privacy for their online activities whatsoever. All of their activities should be under your open and direct supervision, including communication activities. You likely will not have any complaints about this. Children and tweens expect their parents to be involved in their affairs.

The next stage in teaching children to cross the street safely involves standing by their side. Supervising and monitoring your child's online activities is equivalent to standing by your child's side when crossing a busy street. This is a necessary safety step until you are absolutely sure that your child knows how to cross the street safely. It is also important to consider speeding cars and drivers who run through red lights, which are the "real world" equivalent to unsafe strangers online. In addition to following safety rules, such as watching the signal to "cross," it is also important to recognize that others might not follow safety rules, so additional steps to protect your safety are important—such as also looking both ways before you cross the street.

When your teen child starts to actively engage in online communications in which contact with strangers is possible, especially on social networking sites, this is the time to be by your child's side. Many times, online dangers will not be as obvious to your child as are speeding cars or drivers who might run a red light. Unfortunately, the time when your child will want to engage in expanded online activities and will be exposed to more risks is precisely the time when he or she will also want more privacy.

Teens do have a higher interest in personal privacy—which is justified. But the early teen years are also the time when your child will not have the cognitive development necessary to consistently make safe and responsible choices online. Teens are not cognitively able to effectively and consistently perceive the connection between online actions and consequences. Further, there are strong social pressures that support bad choices as well as the presence of dangerous adults or other teens who are not making good choices in online environments.

The presence of dangerous adults and teens in online environments can provide a justification for the need for monitoring that does not suggest that you distrust your child's decision making. You can indicate that you generally trust your child to make good choices—or to want to make good choices—but that because there are potential dangers online that he or she might not be prepared to recognize, it is necessary that you remain closely involved.

Limited Expectation of Privacy

The best standard to set for teens is a standard of "limited expectation of privacy." You will regularly review all of your child's public online activities. This includes what your child is posting on public sites, even if your child is using privacy protection features, and the history of your child's online activities as revealed through the browser history file. But you will review personal communications only if you have reason to believe that there are any concerns. Your child should be able to earn the right to greater privacy by demonstrating consistent responsible behavior—but never "absolute privacy" for as long as your child is a minor or using a computer in your home. Here is some language you can adapt to describe this privacy standard to your child:

> It is my job to make sure that you are making safe and responsible choices online. Too many teens are not making good choices online. I am really not as concerned about your choices as I am about some of the dangers out there that you may simply not fully recognize or know how to deal with. So until I am quite sure that you are making good choices and know how to recognize and respond to dangers presented by others, it is necessary for me to pay close attention to what you are doing. As you demonstrate to me through your choices that you understand and recognize the dangers, you have good strategies to deal with these dangers, and you are using good values and standards to guide your online choices, I will be able to back off of my supervision and allow you to have more privacy. But you will never have total privacy because my job as a parent is to pay attention to what you are doing, including what you are doing online.
>
> So for now, you should understand that I am going to regularly review all of your public postings online. This

includes postings on social networking sites, even if you are using privacy protection features to prevent access by strangers. What you post on these sites and in these communities is public or could easily be made public, so I am not invading your privacy when looking at what you are posting. I need to know all of the sites that you are registered on and your username and password on these sites. I also will regularly check the history file to find out where you are going online.

I will review your personal communications only if I have specific concerns or suspicions about your Internet use. The things that will create such concerns or suspicions include

- You are spending too much time online or you are using the Internet late into the night.
- You are evasive and unwilling to talk with me about your online activities and friends.
- I receive a report of possibly inappropriate online behavior or other concern from someone else.
- I find material you have posted publicly that raises concerns.
- Your grades go down or you start to develop any attitude problems.
- There is any effort to restrict my ability to review your online activities, computer files, and the like.

Using Monitoring as a "Teachable Moment"

The best way to approach monitoring is to make it such a natural and enjoyable experience that your child does not even recognize that what you are doing is monitoring. Ideally, your child will regularly invite you to see recent online postings and meet new online friends. Whenever you visit your child's "online house," make yourself such a pleasurable guest that you are invited back frequently.

Have you made a practice of posting your child's artwork on the refrigerator; copying your child's latest, greatest essay to send to grandma; cheering wildly when your child makes a soccer goal; and expressing delight when introduced to a new friend of your child? Demonstrating the same level of delight and enthusiasm for your child's online accomplishments will encourage him or her to invite your attention.

Finding out what your child is posting online and who he or she is communicating with will provide you with an excellent opportunity to learn more about your child. Your review of online activities presents the best possible "teachable moment" to address important knowledge, skills, and values with your child. Let your child use this review as an opportunity to demonstrate to you the knowledge, skills, and values associated with safe and responsible Internet use.

A very helpful parenting technique is to track the number of times you say positive things to your child. Use this technique when you are reviewing your child's online activities and presence. Make it a mental goal that during your review you will make at least ten positive comments about your child's activities and choices online. Watch your child's expression of pride when you make such comments. The more you can make your child feel that these review sessions are an opportunity to shine, the better. Ideally, your child will get to the point of wanting to encourage your review.

Another effective way to establish monitoring on social networking sites is simply to become one of your child's "friends." Your child may not want you to be really obvious about this. This is the age when your child generally wants you to walk ten feet behind, preferably on the other side of the hall, whenever you visit school. You can create a "persona" the age of your child and use a graphic image instead of your picture. You can then regularly visit your child's profile and send very positive private messages. With any luck, your child will simply begin to consider you a favorite online friend.

The younger your child is, the easier it will be to set up a situation in which your monitoring and review of online activities is expected. If your child is a teen and you have not, prior to reading this book, paid close attention to what he or she is doing online, you may have greater difficulties. You might want to give your child the opportunity to remedy any concerns prior to your review. Should you always have your child present when you review online activities? This likely depends on your child. It may be wise to do the review both with and without your child present, especially at the beginning.

Technical Monitoring

It is possible to install monitoring software on your child's computer that will enable you to easily monitor absolutely everything that your child does online. Monitoring software provides an excellent way to retain and review private communications, including synchronous communications for which there is generally no permanent record.

The use of this software raises trust concerns. It is best not to rely on such software unless you really think it necessary—basing your decision on the online behavior of your child, the quality of your relationship with your child, and your ability to be present when your child is online. The best use of monitoring software is as a deterrent to misuse or a logical consequence to inappropriate online behavior, not as a surveillance tool.

When and how might you use monitoring software?

- *Stage 1 Approach.* If you have a trusting communicative relationship with your child and generally are restricting Internet use when you are not present, there is no need for monitoring software.

- *Stage 2 Approach.* If you generally cannot be present when the Internet is used or if there are any "tensions" in your relationship with your child and there are some concerns about your child's online behavior, use of monitoring software may be justified. If your child is "at risk" in any way, you might want simply to establish a technical environment that allows you the immediate ability to review all Internet use—just in case.

- Install the monitoring software.
- Inform your child that monitoring software has been installed and demonstrate its capabilities.
- Tell your child that you will use the monitoring system to review online activities only when there are other indicators of concerns, such as those described earlier.

- *Stage 3 Approach.* If your child has engaged in significantly unsafe or irresponsible behavior, a regular in-depth review of all public and private online activities is warranted. This is a very appropriate "logical consequence" in response to evidence of your child's inappropriate behavior. This approach will be far more effective than limiting Internet access because it allows you to turn the situation into teachable moments to help your child learn to make better choices.

  - Install the monitoring software.
  - Inform your child that monitoring software has been installed and demonstrate its capabilities.
  - Regularly review all online activities, public and private, until your child has regained your trust. Establish what conditions will be necessary for your child to regain your trust. Allow your child to "earn" the privilege of a reduction to a Stage 2 approach.
  - Make sure you also restrict access at other locations such as the houses of your child's friends and the public library. Alert your child's school to your concerns and request that your child's Internet access be curtailed or closely monitored.

- *Stage 4 Approach.* If you have concerns or suspicions that your child might be communicating with a sexual predator, or any other kind of dangerous online stranger, or if you fear that your child has become involved in any dangerous online groups, including hate groups, gangs, or groups supporting suicide or self-harm, this may be the time for surreptitious use of monitoring software to obtain necessary evidence of these concerns without your child's knowledge.

- Install the monitoring software.
- *Do not* inform your child that monitoring software has been installed. A child who is involved in a dangerous situation who knows that monitoring software has recently been installed could warn the predator or other dangerous person, or run off to join this person or group.
- Obtain professional assistance to address any concerns that are revealed. If no concerns are revealed, drop back to a Stage 2 approach.

·7·

A Community
of Parents

COLLABORATING WITH
OTHER PARENTS

Children and teens are most likely to spend the greatest amount of time online engaged in communication with other children and teens who are their friends within the local community—their local group of friends. Savvy parents can leverage this knowledge by collaborating with the parents of their children's friends to address Internet use issues. This approach is especially important in the teen years, when the influence of peers is so strong.

If you are seeking to ensure that your child is off the Internet by 10:00 P.M., but the parents of your child's friends allow their children to be online until midnight or do not know that their children are online until midnight, it is going to be very difficult for you to get your child off-line and to bed. If you have significant concerns about your child's involvement on a certain online social networking site, seeking to get your child to disassociate from this site when your child's best friends are also members of the site can result in a significant "battle of wills" that you are very likely to end up losing.

But if you and all of the other parents of your child's friends are agreed that Internet use will end at 10:00 P.M., if you have achieved consensus on approved online communities and activities, and if all parents agree to periodically review Internet activities, your efforts to manage and monitor your child's Internet use will be significantly easier.

Invite the parents of your child's closest friends to your house for coffee, tea, and desserts and hold a discussion that one hopes will result in agreements about online activities for the group of friends. Here is a proposed agenda of issues to address:

- Sharing of email addresses of all of the parents
- Mutual strategies for limiting online activity during the period of time from when school ends to when parents are home
- The time at which Internet activity will cease at night
- The kinds of sites or activities that are approved for group participation
- Respect for other parents' desires related to their child's online activity when that child is at a friend's house
- Ideas about preventing children from multitasking while doing homework
- Regular review of the children's public online activities by all of the parents
- Parental agreement to report to other parents if the online activities of their children raise concerns
- Strategies to promote and facilitate non-Internet group activities
- Suggestions for highly creative or socially beneficial online or computer-based activities for group involvement

Some parents may seek to be even bolder in addressing these issues jointly with a larger group of parents. Parents could work with the school's parent organization to educate each other about Internet safety and responsible use concerns—and seek to create a set of recommended standards to be followed by all families in the school. There is, obviously, no way to require that all parents agree to enforce these standards, but if a large percentage of parents whose children attend a specific school make a commitment to abide by certain standards, it will certainly make it a lot easier for each parent to enforce those standards.

·8·

Red Flags!

WARNING SIGNS AND RESPONSES

"When should I start to worry about my child's Internet use?" is a common question. The key "red flags" that indicate potential concerns related to Internet use include the following:

- Internet addiction. Internet addiction is excessive use of the computer, especially late at night when parents may be less apt to monitor online activities. Internet addiction is a concern itself and is also frequently an indicator of other issues.

- Secretive behavior. If your child switches off the computer or rapidly changes screens when you approach the computer, this indicates an intent to prevent you from reviewing online activities. Recognize that in the teen years, some amount of privacy-protection behavior is to be expected and may not indicate a major concern. Use instances of secretive behavior to initiate a discussion of online activities. If your child engages in secretive behavior when you approach, ask your child why. Make your own assessment of the legitimacy of the response. Some responses may be very legitimate.

- Empty history file after Internet use. Finding the browser's history file empty on a regular basis, especially if combined with secretive behavior when you approach the computer, is a clear indication that your child does not want you to know what is happening online.

- Emotionally upset appearance during or after Internet use. Have your "emotional status detectors" engaged when your child is using the Internet. If your child appears to be emotionally distraught during or after Internet use, this may be an indicator that someone is victimizing your child online.

- Disturbed relationships with parents, family, and friends. Dangerous online strangers seek to disassociate their targeted victim from family and friends. Children and teens who are being bullied online may avoid friends and seek to avoid school. Any evidence of concerns with "real world" relationships should trigger questions about what might be happening online.

- Receipt of packages. Receipt of packages from companies or individuals when it is unclear how your child might have paid for such items should raise questions about what your child did to receive such material. Your child may be providing personal information to others in exchange for gifts, may be involved in inappropriate gaming activities, or may be engaged in a scam. Or your child may have developed a relationship with a sexual predator, child pornographer, or other dangerous online stranger who is using gifts as a seduction technique.

- Subtle comments. Subtle comments about the Internet indicate that your child may want to start a conversation but is concerned about how you will respond. Children and teens frequently are very fearful of parental overreaction if they raise concerns related to Internet use. If you overreact this could interfere with desired Internet activities. If your child's friends find out you were told what was going on online, he or she could face rejection. Your child may "test the waters" with a subtle comment before risking an open conversation about concerns.

Responding to Red Flags

Overreacting to any of the key red flag indicators or evidence of misuse is the absolute worst response you could make. Here are some response strategies:

- If your child has made a subtle comment about Internet use, responding effectively is critically important. Remain very low key and simply reflect back to your child a comment that is similar to what was just said. This can help to encourage your child to disclose more. It is critically important that you not immediately jump to conclusions. Also, avoid offering your own opinion. Do not say, "Here is what I think you should do." Rather, ask your child, "What do you think you should do?" Try to help your child sort out any situation that concerns him or her and come to a conclusion about appropriate steps to address the concern.

- Investigate further. If you sense some of these "red flag" indicators, the first step you should take is to conduct a more complete investigation of your child's online activities. If you have witnessed signs such as those already noted and your child has taken significant steps to hide online activities, this might be an occasion to install monitoring software without informing your child.

- Calm down before talking with your child. If you find any evidence that is disturbing, take the time to calm down before you confront your child. Consider discussing your concerns with a counselor or trusted adult friend prior to engaging in any interactions with your child. Addressing most Internet concerns now, and in the future, will require a parent-child partnership.

- Initiate your discussion carefully. "I know that going online is important to you. I also know that sometimes kids can get into tough places when they are online and may not know how to handle a situation. You have agreed to talk with me about Internet concerns and I have agreed to work with you and not to overreact. I am concerned . . ."

- Respond to evidence of unsafe or irresponsible Internet use with effective discipline. Instances of unsafe or irresponsible Internet use are the most important teachable moments for educating your child about making good choices. Discipline that imposes a logical consequence to inappropriate behavior can teach important values and provide the foundation for internalized control. Remember, your objective is not to punish your child or to ensure that your child remains under your control. Your ultimate objective is to ensure that your child makes safe and responsible choices when not under your control.

  - Focus your intervention on the reasons for your expectations or rules for safe and responsible Internet use. What harm or potential harm should be avoided?
  - Discuss how your child's violation of an expectation or rule was contrary to important values and demonstrated lack of respect for another, or was unsafe.
  - Engage in joint problem solving to develop skills to effectively address this or a similar situation that may occur in the future. Ask your child to sort out what went wrong and determine how a better choice can be made next time.
  - If any harm has been caused to another insist that your child develop and implement a plan of action to cure that harm.
  - Indicate that you will be engaging in more vigorous monitoring until your child has regained your trust. One effective logical consequence, especially if your child has sought

to limit your access to evidence of online wrongdoing, is the installation of monitoring software.

- Discuss the conditions that will be necessary for your child to regain your trust and Internet use privileges.

Important Caveat!

If you ever find indicators that your child is involved with a dangerous online stranger *do not confront* your child. Your child could erase evidence, warn the dangerous online stranger, or run away to be with this person. Contact your local police and ask to talk with their youth or computer crimes expert. Many countries also have national reporting services for online concerns. A listing of these reporting services can be found at http://cskcst.com [the Web site address for this book].

Troubling "What If's"

For some parents, the more challenging situations related to their child's online activities occur when their child's Internet use provides indications that the child is investigating values or information that challenges their own personal values. Remember that the teen years are a time for exploration of values and standards. Expect that there will be times when your child's online inquiries and activities will challenge your own beliefs and values.

- What if you find evidence that your child and a girlfriend or boyfriend are engaging in cybersex—online sexual fantasies?
- What if you find that your child is exploring spiritual or religious beliefs that are contrary to your own beliefs?
- What if you find that your child has questions about or is exploring different sexual orientations?

Think about these and other possible situations that could arise and consider how you might respond in a way that will preserve your good relationship with your child. Recognize the futility of trying to block access to material that is not in accord with your personal values and the risks of generating greater interest in "forbidden fruits."

·9·

Away from Home

USE OF THE INTERNET
AT OTHER PLACES

Children and teens may access the Internet from their school, the public library, or in a computer lab offered by an after-school club or organization. How can children be kept safe in these environments?

Schools

There are many excellent ways in which teachers can effectively use the Internet for high-quality, valuable educational activities. Effective professional and curriculum development is essential to ensure that computer technologies are used for the best educational purposes. Unfortunately, in some schools the installation of technology has outpaced efforts to provide professional and curriculum development. In such schools, the Internet may be used more for "Internet recess"—surfing, gabbing, and gaming. If this appears to be the case in your child's school, make your concerns known to the administration.

Many schools use Internet filtering software to seek to manage Internet use. Not only does filtering software not prevent student or staff access to pornographic materials, in many cases the filters are blocking access to perfectly appropriate materials that your child should have the right to access. These sites are blocked based on the biases of the filtering company or the selection of inappropriate blocking categories by the school technical personnel.

The explosion of interest in social networking has raised new concerns about the manner in which student Internet use is managed in schools. Social-networking-based activities should not be considered educational unless there is a specific instructional purpose, and some creative teachers are using social networking and blogging technologies in a very high-quality instructional manner. Concerns over the free-time activities of teens on social networking sites certainly should not prevent the educational use of these technologies. In fact, one of the best ways for schools to help students learn important values and standards for the material they post on these kinds of sites is to engage the students in specific learning activities. The key is whether the teacher has sufficient control over student postings to ensure use of the technology for high-quality instructional purposes.

The current standard response to these new concerns by many schools has been to block access to the commercial social networking sites using a filter. This is insufficient. Students know how to bypass most school filters using publicly available proxy servers or by setting up a proxy server on their home computer. Further, many students have some level of Internet access using personal digital devices or cell phones. In addition, student online interactions while off-campus are having a significant impact on the school climate and the well-being of individual students. If a major online controversy is brewing among students involved on a social networking site, this controversy surely will be distracting many students from their studies while in school.

It is imperative that schools reassess how they are managing student Internet use as well as the use of all other personal digital devices and cell phones on campus. An effective, comprehensive school-based approach to address these new issues requires the following:

- Well-written, comprehensive policies that are communicated to all users and their parents. The Internet use policy should specifically address unsafe or irresponsible use of the Internet, as well as standards for the online display of any personal information or work products of students. Policies addressing personal digital devices and cell phones should ensure limited use while on campus and no use in a classroom, unless for an instructional purpose. It must be clear that district policies of search and seizure, academic dishonesty, and bullying and harassment apply to all use of any personal digital device or cell phone while the student is on school property, including school buses.

- A strong focus on the effective use of the Internet for high-quality educational activities, with sufficient professional and curriculum development to support such use. It should be made very explicit to students that use of the Internet in school is for educational purposes only. The school's Internet system is not a public access system and should not be used for entertainment purposes. It is exceptionally important that students learn to govern their Internet activities. When students become employees, they similarly will not be allowed to use their employer's Internet system for surfing, gabbing, and gaming.

- The establishment of a school or district Web site that pro-vides safer places for primary or elementary students and directs all students to appropriate educational resources. There are commercial services available for schools that can help guide students to more appropriate research resources than they likely will find through any commercial search engine. Make sure you know how to access these research resources from home.

- Education of students about issues related to the safe and responsible use of the Internet. This education must be grounded in the knowledge, skills, and values necessary for students to learn to independently make safe and responsible choices online.

- Effective supervision and monitoring of student use of the Internet. Although filtering technologies have some significant limitations, technologies to enhance the ability of the school to monitor student and staff Internet use can be effectively implemented. Teachers cannot be expected to be able to visually monitor all computer screens at all times. No technological solution is perfect. But a monitoring system that has a high probability of detecting inappropriate use can be a very effective deterrent.

- Appropriate discipline. Disciplinary responses must focus on remedying any harm caused through inappropriate behavior and transmitting the knowledge, skills, and values necessary to avoid such inappropriate or harmful behavior in the future.

- Partnership with parents and the community. Schools must work closely with parents and others in the community, especially law enforcement and community mental health services, to ensure that the online activities of children and teens outside of school are not interfering with the school climate or the well-being of any student.

Public Libraries

Public librarians cannot be expected to be able to effectively "babysit" your child when he or she is using the Internet in the library. The children's section of a public library should establish safer places for young children's Internet use—easy access from the main screen to kid-friendly sites that have been reviewed for appropriateness. Institutions should not merely rely on fallible filtering software to protect younger children. But if your child is using the Internet in the library, you should be nearby to supervise.

It is more difficult for libraries to effectively monitor teen Internet use. Most libraries have placed the computer screens so that they are highly visible. This provides a significant disincentive for inappropriate online activities. Many libraries have installed filtering software, but, as already noted, it is exceptionally easy for any teen to bypass this blocking technology. Some librarians will use a "tap on the shoulder" approach if they see that a teen is wandering into questionable material online. But the librarian may be busy with other patrons, so you cannot count on effective supervision.

You should make your own assessment regarding whether or not you think your teen child has sufficient internalized standards to abide by your family's values when independently using the Internet in a library. Most libraries require the use of a library card for log-in and can establish "permissions" to ensure that your child's library card cannot access the Internet.

Libraries may also allow use of the Internet by adults in locations where children and teens are legitimately present. Libraries should have policies and procedures in place that seek to limit the possibility of display of adult material to children or teens who happen to glance at a computer screen while walking by. Although principles of free speech and access to information are indeed important, the intentional public display of adult material to minors is a violation of criminal laws in most jurisdictions.

Your child's right to be free from exposure to inappropriate sexual or violent material when simply walking through the public library should be considered to be of greater importance than the free speech rights of adults who might be interested in viewing such materials. Check policies and ask a librarian how they have addressed the concern of the possible exposure to adult materials in those areas of the library where children and teens have a right to be present.

After-School Clubs and Organizations

Children and teens may use computers and the Internet in after-school clubs or organizations. These clubs or organizations should have a comprehensive plan to manage Internet use that includes the same elements as the comprehensive approach used by schools, with one exception—that use for surfing, gabbing, and gaming is acceptable. Even so, the club or organization should have specific guidelines on the kinds of entertainment sites and activities that are considered to be unacceptable.

· 10 ·

Get It in Writing

PARENT-TEEN
INTERNET USE AGREEMENT

E very time your child registers on a new site, there is a step in the registration at which your child must click on a box: "❏ I agree to [name of site] Terms of Use." The vast majority of Internet users never read these terms of use documents. Even if the terms of use are read, they frequently are not internalized.

Sometimes the same approach can be recommended for children and teens. A prewritten agreement with safety "rules" is provided for the child or teen's signature. This approach is likely to result in a relatively rapid dismissal of the importance of abiding by such rules—especially when the rules are written in a simplistic and overbroad manner.

Appendix A sets forth a template for a "Parent-Teen Internet Use Agreement." You can also download this template from the *Cyber-Safe Kids, Cyber-Savvy Teens* Web site at http://cskcst.com.

As you will see, the agreement has a lot of blank spaces—well, it does include some key commitments for you. The reason the portion for your child is incomplete is that the objective of this activity is not to obtain your child's commitment to a list of prescribed "rules" that someone else created, but rather to help your child think about his or her own personal values and standards for Internet use.

The key to success in the use of this agreement is that your child is writing the agreement. This creates the conditions in the mind of your child that will significantly enhance the potential that he or she will act in accord with this agreement. This agreement elicits a commitment that can be very influential.

Is it necessary for you and your child to address all of the potential risks and concerns surrounding Internet use in an agreement? No. The agreement focuses on some key issues that underlie all of these risks and concerns. If you think that there are other specific issues that should be addressed, please include them.

There are different strategies that you could use to have your child complete this agreement. The easiest strategy will be if your child is just turning thirteen. At this time, your child is legitimately able to register on many new kinds of sites, including most social networking sites. Make the completion of this agreement a requirement prior to allowing your child to register on a social networking site.

It would be best for you and your child to complete the agreement together. Take your child out to a favorite eating place for a special treat. For each item in the agreement, explain your understanding of the risks, concerns, and protection strategies and ask your child about his or her understanding. Support your child in making the statements in his or her own words that reflect the understanding and values necessary to promote safe and responsible online behavior. To strengthen your child's statement, pose questions such as "Have you considered . . .?" "What do you think you should do if . . .?" "What if . . . happens?"

Prepare to be pleasantly surprised at your child's responses to these concerns. Teens pay attention to the news, and they have no doubt heard of concerns about teen online activity. Especially if your child has spent significant time online already, it is highly likely he or she already has excellent insight into online risks and will welcome the opportunity to share this insight with you.

View this document as a living document. If there are any teachable moments that arise from your child's actual interactions or activities online, or from information about situations that have occurred that involved some other teen, revisit the agreement to make sure the commitments are sufficient to address the risk or concern that was raised. Add new provisions if it seems necessary.

If your child acts in a manner that is not in accord with the commitments made in this document, it is best to start your conversation with your child with a statement such as "You made a commitment to me that you would . . ." Whenever you become aware of instances when your child is abiding by the commitments made in the agreement, be sure you indicate your recognition of his or her positive actions. This is especially important if your child comes to you for assistance in addressing a concern.

If your child first completes the agreement around age thirteen, then you likely will want to revisit the agreement several years later. Definitely revisit the agreement if your child is sixteen and you are going to allow him or her to have a computer in the bedroom.

If entering into a written agreement appears to be too formal, you also can use this agreement in an informal manner. Consider each of the issues addressed in this agreement as topics for discussion in the context of "teachable moments."

Part Two

•

FOUNDATIONAL ISSUES

· 11 ·

Me and My Friends

ONLINE SOCIAL NETWORKING

Amy is eleven years old. She has registered on a social networking site, indicating that she is eighteen. On her profile she has posted a provocative picture of herself. She has decorated her profile with Playboy bunnies. Amy has provided the name of her school and her favorite fast food joint. In her communications with "friends," she uses quite graphic language. Several of Amy's "friends" appear to be older men.

John is a high school student who has a critical illness and cannot leave his house. John is receiving constant messages of support and caring from his friends through his social networking site. Recent messages of care and support include "Just wanted to let U know I was thinking about U. Hope U are doing better today" and "Love U and miss U. Hugs!"

Several middle school students, using anonymous usernames, have created a profile denigrating Raymond. They have posted stories, jokes, and cartoons ridiculing Raymond's size and questioning his sexual orientation.

North High School students are communicating regularly with Gary, a recent graduate who is now stationed in Iraq. Gary posts frequent updates about his activities in Iraq, which is allowing the high school students to really understand the issues related to military action in the region. The students provide Gary with updates on school happenings, including sports scores, crazy events that have happened at school, and news of the local community.

The hottest new craze among teens and young adults on the Internet is social networking. Currently, social networking can be considered the quintessential foundational concern. The greatest concerns related to teen use of social networking sites include unsafe disclosure of personal information, addictive behavior, risky sexual behavior, cyberbullying, involvement with dangerous communities and groups, and posting real or not-real cyberthreats. There are also more generalized concerns related to teens engaged in online communities with many young adults, whose lifestyle choices may be developmentally inappropriate for teens.

Features of Social Networking Sites

On social networking sites, users create individual profiles that allow them to publicly share their identity and interests. These profiles are similar to Web pages on other sites, but the social networking sites have made it very easy to create these profiles without having to learn HTML, the Web site design language. To create their profiles, teens incorporate graphics, upload photos, provide information about their favorite musicians and other artists, and share, both in images and text, aspects of their personality. Teens can also create a blog, where they can post regular commentary and images.

The social networking environment allows members to link their profiles with the profiles of their friends. The linking feature reveals a web of social relationships and affiliations. Once linked as friends, members can post comments on each other's profiles, send messages, engage in IM, and respond to blog entries. For teens, social networking has become their favorite asynchronous communications tool, whereas most adults still use email.

Most social networking environments also contain public features, such as discussion groups that all registered users can participate in. The environments also allow members to establish their own discussion groups, which they can set up as public or private groups. Teens can form online groups to discuss issues that relate to their own particular community or school. These discussion groups provide the opportunity for members to meet other members who share their interests. Teens may meet someone in a discussion group and then invite that person to establish a friendship link.

What do teens do on social networking sites? Teens who are members of a social networking site frequently will go online to check the comments feature of their profile and their messages, to see if anyone has written to them. They will then either reply to any messages or perhaps send a few messages. They then might visit the sites of their best friends to see if anything new is "happening" on their friend's sites, such as new photos, blog postings, or comments posted by others. They are likely to leave a comment on friends' profiles as they cruise by. If they are active in any discussion groups, they also will check out any new postings in these groups. If they are feeling especially creative, they might add some new materials to their own profile or blog.

Recent news coverage has raised significant concerns about interactions with strangers, especially sexual predators, on these sites. Many teens spend little time, if any, interacting with online strangers. The vast majority of teens are using social networking sites to engage with known friends and acquaintances from within their school and community. For some, their friendship network may expand to include others they meet in discussion groups. These friends likely are ones with whom they share mutual interests.

Although the social networking sites seek to restrict youths under the age of thirteen from registering, social networking has become a highly popular activity for middle school students. Because young people turn thirteen during the time they are attending middle school, there is significant social pressure among all middle school students to establish a profile on the site that has attracted other students. As has already been mentioned, young people know how easy it is to lie about their age to register on sites.

Privacy Concerns

Many teens do not appear to fully comprehend the public nature of material posted on these sites. Even material shared "privately" with one or selected others can easily be made public by the recipient. This lack of sensitivity to the potentially damaging nature of such disclosures is extremely evident on social networking sites, where some teens are posting personal contact information, intimate information, and material that is highly damaging to their reputations and current and future opportunities.

Many social networking sites have established mechanisms that allow members to make their profiles and discussion groups private. Used properly, these features can enhance the safety of teens using the site. For early teens, parents of the group of friends can mutually ensure that all of the teens are using privacy features and all of the friendship links are to good friends. This can create a very safe environment.

Although teens appear to have limited sensitivity to privacy concerns with respect to public disclosure, many appear to be highly alert to what they consider to be parental intrusion into their online activities. Some teens use the privacy features of the social networking sites as a screen to limit parental review. This is not safe or acceptable. Further, some teens who are making use of the privacy protection features to prevent parental review may also think that because they are using these features, it is acceptable to post material on their profile that is unsafe or irresponsible.

Parents must know their child's username and password to be able to fully access their child's profile. The degree to which these sites make it easy to review a child's activities on the site differs from site to site. If your child is active on a social networking site and wants to restrict your access to review online activities, this may be relatively easy on some sites. One strategy to find out your child's password is to use the "forgot password" feature on the site. It is necessary to use the computer your child used to register on the site and have access to your child's email account, as the "forgot password" service will send information to this email address.

Terms of Use and Complaint Procedures

Most social networking sites, including all of the most popular sites, have "terms of use" agreements that disallow online activities that are injurious to others. These sites also have a formal complaint process that members can use to file a complaint against any other user whose actions are causing injury or are a violation of the terms of use agreement. There may be some renegade social networking sites without such protection processes, but they are unlikely to be attractive to most teens.

Many sites also have specific provisions and processes by which parents can intervene to address concerns about use of the site by their own children. Some sites allow parents to cancel their child's membership. But the degree to which this is possible on specific sites will vary.

Most sites have strategies to seek to identify and remove harmful material and terminate the accounts of users who are violating the terms of use agreement, but it is impossible for their personnel to review all postings. Many sites have millions of members. It generally is necessary for someone to file a complaint to seek enforcement of the terms of use agreement.

If your child has or wants to register on a social networking site, make sure you take the time to review the terms of use with him or her. Note to your child the not-so-amazing coincidence that the provisions of the terms of use agreement are quite similar to your own family's values and standards.

Social Networking and Social Status

Teens use the features of the social networking sites to establish and demonstrate their self-worth and social status. The degree to which they use social networking sites for this purpose appears to be related to their underlying inclination to seek external validation of their self-worth and status in the "real world."

Similar social status games are played out every day, in every hallway, in every school. Many of the difficulties educators must address pertaining to bullying and social relationships between students are grounded in the interactions involved in establishing social status within a community. For some students, being considered part of the "in-crowd" is exceptionally important. Some students are quite comfortable finding a group of friends with whom they associate and leave the social status game-playing to others. Unfortunately, some students get labeled as "losers" or "outcasts" and are treated as such by others.

Some teens are secure in their feelings of their own self-worth and do not require frequent external validation. Other teens have difficulties in perceiving their value as a unique individual and appear to need constant reinforcement from their peers. Still other teens have very low self-esteem. This can lead them to engage in interactions that may result in reinforcing their low opinion of themselves.

It appears that for many teen members of the social networking sites the number of friendship links and amount of communication activity are considered indicators of self-worth and social status. Teens who have an inherent need for external validation can become excessively involved in using social networking sites to achieve such validation. Teens who are not well-connected within their school communities or who are angry or depressed may seek out new connections. They may become attracted to online communities with other teens or young adults who also are angry or depressed.

Young Adult Lifestyle

Most social networking sites are attracting both teens and adults, primarily young adults. Many parents would consider some of the profiles and discussion groups that involve young adults to be premature, if not entirely unacceptable, for their teens. This specifically includes material that is sexually provocative in nature.

Although many sites seek to limit teen members' exposure to advertising that is more appropriate to adults, many teens lie about their age during registration. If a teen has provided an age over eighteen, adult-level advertising will be displayed on the site. Heavy advertisers on such sites include the online dating services, which frequently are overtly sexual and promote a sexual "swinging" lifestyle, as well as products for an adult lifestyle. Teens who register with an age of under eighteen and who limit their social networking activities to involvement with known friends and acquaintances likely will not have substantial exposure to the kind of material that would make many parents concerned.

Positive Online Interactions

Many teens are safely and responsibly engaged on social networking sites. They use their profiles to build and experiment with aspects of their own personal identities. They are making connections that are contributing to their social well-being and expanding their perspectives and understandings of themselves, their close friends, and other people from throughout the world. Many have developed personal standards and guidelines for safe and responsible behavior in these environments.

The social networking sites are actually much safer environments for meeting strangers than are chat rooms because members of these sites review the profiles and communications of any new contact. This can provide a savvy young person with a significant amount of evidence that, if viewed in depth and over time, should allow the young person to determine whether a new online contact has the values and standards that can support a continued friendship.

Adults should not underestimate the attractiveness of these online environments—or expect that the legitimate concerns associated with these environments and a "just say no" response will make the environments or the associated concerns magically disappear. These environments are a natural progression of Internet information and communications technologies. They are attractive to teens and they are here to stay. Parents simply must pay attention to the need to ensure that their children have the knowledge, skills, and values to make safe and responsible choices on these sites.

· 12 ·

Eyeballs and E-Wallets

E-COMMERCE AND
YOUR CHILD

MarketResearch.com helps you discover effective marketing strategies for the children's demographic with a collection of market research reports, providing insight into product and market trends, children's time spent online and watching television, pocket money, analyses of child eating behaviors and other projections, sales, and marketing strategies for this growing consumer group.

MarketResearch.com[1]

Brittany, age thirteen, recently registered on a games and activities site. During the registration process she was shown a blinking banner ad that stated, "Keep our site free. Support our sponsors." There was a prechecked button that said, "Free Offer. Certain sponsors want to mail you teen-related offers and samples. Leave this box checked and you will receive an email message with easy to follow sign-up instructions. Fill in your mailing address, hit submit, and you will be given 300 points!! Sign up now!!" Brittany left the box checked and received an email message that requested her full name and address, which she provided.

Brad, age nine, loves the Neopets site. He spends hours online playing games on the site, earning "Neopoints" on the site, and spending those Neopoints to support his Neopet. Some of the most recent games he played were "Cinnamon Toast Crunch Umpire Strikes Out" and "Hot Wheels World Race." Brad also earns Neopoints by answering market surveys and watching commercials and movie trailers. Frequently he purchases food at McDonalds for his Neopet.

Kayla, age sixteen, is a "Girls Intelligence Agency Secret Agent." As a GIA Secret Agent she regularly provides insight about products designed for the teen girl market by responding to market surveys. GIA regularly sends Kayla discount coupons and product samples. Kayla received a special GIA "Slumber Party" kit that included products and promotions, together with recommendations on how to host a GIA Slumber Party for her friends.

The Internet may look like a wonderful playground for your child. For major commercial companies, the Internet provides the vehicle to capture the "eyeballs" and "e-wallets" of your child for commercial purposes. Children and teens are a highly targeted online demographic. Companies know that the younger generation controls or influences billions of dollars worth of family purchasing decisions. They are the future of online commerce.

Commercial Web sites for children and teens are gigantic market research and advertising environments. These sites are free for their young users. They receive income from market research and advertising activities. This is a bargain our society has struck—free or inexpensive information or entertainment, supported by advertising. But, unfortunately, the negative impact of this bargain on our children is not well understood. If you want to get a sense of what the issues are when it comes to commercial marketing to your children online, search for "marketing, online, kids, tweens, teens."

When your children spend time on commercial Web sites, they are the target of many companies. Not only do children spend lots of money on their own, they have a tremendous influence on what you purchase for the family—from fast food to entertainment to cars. Young people play a very active role in influencing parental purchases. The "nag factor" refers to the inclination to nag parents to purchase items they may not otherwise buy. Advertisers know that it is possible to influence children and teens to make persistent pleas for items or make arguments to justify purchases. During the teen years, brand loyalty—a preference for a specific brand of product or service—is established. So not only do marketers seek to influence children's current spending and children's influence on parental spending, they also want to influence future spending when the children become adults.

The Risks of Advertising

The risks of advertising to young people are clear:

- The messages our children and teens are being bombarded with are having an impact on their social, emotional, and physical well-being. Advertisers work closely with child psychologists who have in-depth information about child development, including emotional and social development and needs.

- Advertisers capitalize on the insecurities of children and teens by promoting the "cool" factor. This can have a very damaging impact on self-esteem. Anyone who does not fit the advertiser's image of what is "cool" or who does not have the products or use the services that are necessary to be considered "cool" is then defined as a "loser." Children and teens judge themselves and others based on these advertising messages.

- There is a significant relationship between advertising and obesity in children. Products most frequently advertised to children are fast foods, soft drinks, candy, and presweetened cereal—junk food.

- Advertisers frequently promote rebellion against adults. They convey the message to young people that they, not adults, should decide what is right for them—but, of course, the young person should decide that the product or service offered by the company is "right." This advertising strategy can interfere with the ability of parents to impart healthy attitudes and behaviors to young people.

- Advertisers promote highly sexualized images of teens. The underlying message is that being skinny and sexy and having these "cool" products is necessary for popularity and happiness. This marketing can fuel inappropriate sexual behavior and low self-esteem, as well as eating disorders.

Advertisers and the Internet

All of the most popular commercial sites for children have advertisements. The advertisements may be in the form of banner ads. The sites may also have advertisements embedded into the Web site activities. Sometimes the site carries no advertisement, but is itself an advertisement—a site with fun games related to a product or service. This is not to say that all commercial sites that have advertising directed at children are bad sites. Most parents would consider a Web site that promotes creative play with certain kinds of toys as beneficial, despite the fact that the site is promoting the sale of more toys. But a Web site that promotes addictive access and nagging for junk food might not be considered so beneficial. The reasons that advertisers really like the Internet include the following:

- Young people frequently use the Internet while alone. This allows for a much more direct relationship between advertisers and young people than through more traditional methods, such as television.

- Television advertising to children is regulated in most countries. Advertising on the Internet is largely unregulated and international, so laws affecting advertising to children in one country do not apply to sites located in other countries.

- Companies can easily collect information from young people for marketing research and to target individual children with personalized advertising based on their interests.

- Web sites can use many techniques to enhance their "stickiness." "Stickiness," a measurement of how frequently users visit the site and how long they stay, is considered by Web sites to be a desirable trait. Creative techniques are used to encourage this level of interaction. Web site "stickiness" is a contributing factor to Internet addiction.

- Some companies want to market adult products to teens, including entertainment products such as video games, movies, and music, as well as alcohol and tobacco. These companies know that teens routinely lie about their age to register on sites for adults. The sites can represent that they seek to limit advertising for adult products to people who are over the age of eighteen, knowing that many users of their site are teens.

Internet Market Profiling

The mantra of direct marketers is "People want companies to know all about them, so that companies can send them information about products and services that will be of interest to them." You may not agree with this statement. But direct marketers are actively seeking to influence the younger generation to think that sharing personal and interest information is expected, appropriate, and beneficial.

All commercial Web sites for children and teens engage in significant market profiling. Profiling means the development of an extensive database of demographic information about and interests of a specific individual or an overall user base. Profiles may include information provided online at various sites and may be combined with information revealed on product registration forms or other surveys. Companies also are able to track Internet users as they visit different sites on the Internet and combine information about Internet use with the other database information. Market profiles are used to deliver advertisements for products or services that are most likely to be of interest to individual users.

Many young people simply will not recognize when advertisers are collecting product-interest information from them. Here are a couple of the strategies marketers use to get personal contact and interest information from children and teens:

- Registration forms or profiles that suggest that members provide information about their personal interests to be able to meet other young people with similar interests. Sometimes these registration forms include a checklist of interests, with an indication that if the child completes this checklist, the site will send information about products or services that might be of interest. This will merely result in more advertising email in your child's inbox.

- Online contests, tests, quizzes, and "tell us what you think" surveys or other marketing surveys. Frequently, the site offers some kind of reward for completing these surveys, including bonus points, discount coupons, or a possibility of a reward. Young people are really excited to think that someone wants their opinion or they have a chance to win something— however remote the chance. So they "tell all."

In addition to the obvious ways that sites collect information, registration on the site is accomplished by placing a "cookie" on your child's computer. A "cookie" is a small piece of information that a Web site places on your computer hard drive. The main uses of a cookie are to identify a specific user and to customize the material presented to that user. This cookie is necessary to reenter the site because it provides user registration information. But the cookie also can be used to track and transmit a significant amount of information about your computer, sites visited, links accessed, and the like. Young people may also accidentally download "spyware" on their computer. Spyware is software that tracks all Internet use and allows for a highly refined assessment of interest—and results in more advertising, especially banner ads.

Privacy Policies

Commercial Web sites for children and teens post a privacy policy that outlines the kinds of information that the site will collect and how that information will be used. Frequently, these policies start with a bold statement of a commitment to protecting privacy. But if you continue to read the legalistic fine print, you will find all of the ways the site intends to gather information from your child, use this information for marketing purposes on the site, and possibly even provide your child's personal information to other companies.

The Children's Online Privacy Protection Act (COPPA) is a U.S. law that applies to U.S. commercial Web sites for children under the age of 13.[2] COPPA places restrictions on information these sites can request, including limits on requests for personal contact information. COPPA requires that the site have a privacy policy that addresses the types of personal information collected, how the site will use information, whether personal information is provided to third parties, parents' rights to review and remove information, and the site contact. COPPA provides that parental consent, usually solicited via email, is required for registration.

When you are helping your child register on a new site, make it a routine practice to read the privacy policy for that site and interpret what that policy says in light of the market-profiling and advertising objectives of the site. Help your child learn to recognize how the information provided online will affect the amount and type of advertising received. Here is what to look for:

- What information is collected? Assess what information is absolutely necessary for your child to register and participate on the site and note the additional information the site indicates it might collect. Generally, seek to limit the information provided to username, email address, gender, and accurate age.

- How is that information used? Most sites will indicate that the information is used to deliver advertising, but they will make this sound very helpful, with words such as "offer information on products or services that might be of interest to our members." Explain to your child that what the Web site will do is use the registration information and any other information your child provides, as well as information about your child's activities on this and other sites, to determine what your child is interested in. Then the site will show your child advertisements for products and services that the site thinks will be of greatest interest.

- Will the site provide your child's information to others, generally referred to as "third-party sites and sponsors"? Make sure that your child knows that the term *sponsors* means advertisers. Most sites will not provide your child's information to other sites, unless your child takes an action that will result in such disclosure. How might this occur? There are several ways:

  - Advertisers on the site may offer users the opportunity to enter a contest. To enter a contest, it is necessary to provide personal information.
  - The site may offer a reward to your child, such as bonus points or an opportunity to win a prize, to complete a market survey that will result in your child's personal contact and interest information being shared with the market-profiling company, as well as all of the other sites that use the services of the market-profiling company.
  - Your child might be encouraged by the site to "opt in" to receive advertising from site sponsors. For example, a site might indicate to teens that the site's sponsors will mail

them offers, samples, and discount coupons if they will provide the site with their names and addresses and information about their personal interests, which will then be provided to all advertisers on the site.

Internet Advertising and Marketing Practices

There are several specific Internet advertising and marketing practices that your child should be able to recognize. Help your child understand how these advertising practices might be used to influence purchasing.

Permission Marketing

The opening step in permission marketing is an opportunity offered to your child to "opt in" to receive advertising. Permission marketing is based on the theory that if a company asks permission to send advertising information to a person, and that person agrees, this provides the opportunity for the company to form a closer relationship with the person and to build brand loyalty.

Your child needs to understand how this advertising method works and how to "opt out" of receiving these kinds of commercial messages—especially from sites that have many advertisers. If your child has a special interest in a product or service from an individual company, you and your child may decide that it is appropriate to approve the receipt of advertisements from this company. For example, if your child really likes a specific line of toy products, you may allow him or her to provide personal contact information to this company, knowing that this will result in the receipt of advertising, such as a newsletter with discount coupons.

Permission marketing clearly has some advantages over the annoying pop-up banner ads. Do you think that it is appropriate for your child to agree to receive advertising from companies whose products and services are of interest? Do you think it is appropriate for your child to give blanket permission to a Web site to allow all of the Web site sponsors to directly contact your child?

Advergaming

"Advergaming" is the integration of advertising messages into online games and activities. It's all the rage in the Internet advertising community. Playing games is a very popular online activity for children and teens. Instead of a thirty-second TV advertisement or a banner ad on a Web site, which most children ignore, advertisers can create conditions for children to immerse themselves for extended periods of time interacting with advertising material in a gaming and activities environment.

Targeting this type of advertising to children is of particular concern. It is known that younger children are not good at distinguishing between advertising and content on television. They are even less likely to recognize advergaming as an effort to influence their purchasing.

One of the Web sites that has been most successful in using the advergaming approach is Neopets. Neopets calls its advertising approach "immersive advertising." The objective is to immerse your child in advertising throughout all of the activities on the site. Greater insight into the company's advertising approach can be gained through a review of the "Press Kit" located on the Neopets site at http://info.neopets.com/presskit/index.html.

As with permission marketing, parents may decide that the benefits to their child of participating on a site outweigh the risks of highly influential advertising. But be wary—the combination of addictive use of the Internet and strong promotion of junk foods can have a significantly damaging effect on your child's social, emotional, and physical well-being.

Viral Marketing

Viral marketing is essentially "word of mouth" marketing online. Web sites use a variety of strategies to enlist children and teens to send advertisements to their friends. One simple and effective strategy to initiate viral marketing is to encourage your child to send an email greeting from the site to friends. The email will reference your child as the source, will contain an invitation to the friends to come and participate on the site, and likely will also contain advertisements.

More sophisticated advertisers will seek to identify active and connected teens who appear to like specific products or services. These teens are considered to be "influencers." By identifying these teens and their specific interests, advertisers can then offer free products and discounts in exchange for, or in the hope that, the teens will tell their friends about this "cool" product or service. Within their online communities, other teens likely already admire these "influencers" and are therefore very inclined to follow their lead regarding which products or services are "cool."

This technique can be implemented in a manner that is very subtle and not even mention the company's desire that teens communicate about the product to their friends. Teens are simply provided with free or discounted products with the well-founded expectation that their response will be to tell all of their friends. In other situations, influential teens are specifically recruited or offered the opportunity to align themselves with the company.

Check out the Web site of the Girls Intelligence Agency at www.girlsintelligenceagency.com for an example of how this approach works. Note under "Market Research" the following: "40,000 GIA Secret Agents are on call nationwide, ready to invite you into their bedrooms, to hang out with their closest friends, and give you candid feedback on your concept, product, and brand." Now go to this site: www.giaheadquarters.com. This is the site used to attract girls to become GIA Secret Agents.

Parents will need to consider the degree to which they want their children to be the unpaid "promoters" for specific products and services. Make sure your child understands this advertising approach.

Social Network Advertising

Social networking sites obviously are where the current "action" is for companies seeking to target teens. Many social networking sites have banner ads, which are recognized to be the least effective advertising approach. The emerging advertising approach on social networking sites is a merger of the three approaches previously discussed.

Advertisers on social networking sites are creating attractive profiles with a fictitious corporate character or cartoon as a spokesperson. The advertiser profile is highly engaging, offering the opportunity for an entertaining visit, thus incorporating advergaming aspects. Members of the social networking site choose to establish friendship links with this advertising profile, thus incorporating permission marketing aspects and allowing the company spokesperson to send what essentially are advertisements to "friends." Once linked, members are encouraged to invite their friends to link to the profile, thus incorporating viral marketing techniques.

Strategies to Address Internet Profiling and Advertising

Our society appears to have accepted the idea of the provision of free or low-cost information or entertainment supported by advertising. If not for online advertising, the vast majority of commercial Web sites for children and teens simply would not exist or would require payment of a subscription fee. It is simply not possible to say "no" to online advertising directed to any child who is engaged on the Internet in any substantive way. Determine what your values are regarding the issue of advertising to your child.

Your approach to addressing Internet advertising will likely have to start in the "real world." Here are some strategies to raise your child's awareness of advertising issues:

- Talk with your child about the strategies advertisers use to make their product or service appear very appealing. Discuss the fact that advertising can be helpful in making us aware of certain products and services. But emphasize that it is always important to look carefully at the product or service and determine whether or not it is really desirable and necessary— and not simply respond to the advertiser's techniques.

- Pay attention to the "nag" factor. If your child starts nagging you for a certain product or service, ask where this product or service was advertised and what was said in the advertisement that made this product or service attractive. Indicate that you will make an independent decision about whether purchasing this product or service is a good idea and not simply purchase something because an advertiser has promoted it.

- When you see or hear an advertisement that illustrates one of the principles covered in this chapter, such as promotion of "cool," rebellion, needing to have something in order to fit in, or relating a product to sexuality, discuss with your child how advertisers seek to use these techniques to influence their choices. Specifically discuss how these techniques could end up making children or teens feel bad or judge others based on the images contained in the advertisements—and that this is wrong.

- Teens naturally tend to be rebellious and do not like to be manipulated. Use these natural traits against the advertisers. Raise your child to be an advertisement "rebel." "Just because they are trying to tell me 'it's cool,' doesn't mean I think it's cool." "I'll make up my own mind about whether or not to purchase something, based on whether or not I really want and need it."

This insight can then be transferred to the online environment:

- Pay close attention to the advertising elements of the sites you select as appropriate for your younger child. When looking at the site together, point out the banner ads and the games that include advertising. One of the primary reasons for the guidance to create your own set of bookmarked sites for your child is to reduce your child's exposure to advertising environments that you consider unacceptable. Find good-quality educational sites offered by nonprofit organizations that do not have advertising.

- When you review your child's Web sites, be sure to point out the market-profiling techniques and advertising approaches used by these sites. Make sure your child has specific knowledge of the Internet advertising techniques of permission marketing, advergaming, and viral marketing. This will allow you and your child to make a knowledgeable choice about whether or not to engage in any of these advertising environments.

- Discourage your child from completing any of the registration forms, surveys, and the like that will result in granting permission for him or her to receive advertising emails. Make sure your child understands the relationship between provision of information and receipt of advertising.

·13·

None of Your Business

PRIVACY PROTECTION STRATEGIES

Will hosted a great party at his house when his parents were not home—with drinking, drugs, and wild dancing. He took digital photos during the party and then posted them to his social networking profile.

Jessica is an eighth-grade student with a profile on a popular social networking site. She is planning a party at her house. She has invited her online friends, including new friends she has not met in person. She has posted her address online so they will know how to find the party.

Nick and his online buddies regularly use a social networking site to disparage other students at school. Someone alerted Nick's parents to the fact that Nick's online activities were getting out of hand. So they checked. When they confronted Nick, his angry response was, "Why have you invaded my privacy?"

Gregory's friend sent him information about a contest to win a gaming console. Gregory went to the site and entered the contest—providing his name, address, phone number, and email address.

Sara was very angry with Sue. She wrote a long message to her friend Brooke, telling her all of the nasty things she wanted to do to Sue. Brooke forwarded the message to several other friends. Now the message is in many in-boxes of the students at Sue's school, as well as in the school principal's in-box.

Sam, a middle school student, is trying to sort out his sexual orientation. He has been discussing his thoughts and feelings about this in his online blog. He spent some time "experimenting" with an older homosexual student, which he also described in his blog.

Help your child learn how to protect privacy and personal information online and why it is important to do so. Children and teens may disclose personal contact or other personal information through Web site registrations, on profiles they establish on social networking and other sites, on personal Web pages, in blogs, in instant messaging directories, and through all forms of electronic communication. Privacy protection is related to many Internet safety concerns, including predator or recruiter situations, online relationships, cyberbullying, and commercial relationships.

The biggest message that must be imparted to children and teens with respect to the privacy and the Internet is: *it's not private*!!! Anything and everything that is put into electronic form and sent or posted online is public or could easily be made public. Think before you post.

The Problem in a Nutshell

Young people, especially teens, post amazingly intimate and sometimes very damaging material in public places online. They share such information privately with no apparent understanding of the degree to which such disclosures can easily become very public. Many appear to have little to no sensitivity to the concerns of public disclosure of information that should remain private or the possible harmful consequences of such disclosure. There appears to be only one aspect related to online privacy that teens are extremely attentive to: parental review of their online activities.

The only way to address this is to have frequent discussions with your child about privacy to ensure that your child has a clear understanding of the issues and to engage in appropriate monitoring until you are assured that your child has learned these lessons well.

The Push to "Tell All"

To effectively address online privacy issues, it is necessary to understand the factors that underlie children's lack of attention to privacy. Young people are less sensitive to the possible consequences of certain actions—especially when consequences are not tangible. While it might seem absolutely logical to an adult that public disclosure of intimate sexual activity or images of a teen drug party could lead to an undesirable consequence, this appears to be something that many teens have difficulty comprehending. Younger children have even less sensitivity to privacy concerns.

Children and teens really need to have the risks of online disclosure spelled out to them very clearly. Simply telling them "do not disclose personal information online" is entirely insufficient. This often-imparted safety rule does not provide an adequate definition of personal information, address the risks, or provide sufficient insight into how to participate safely in desired online activities without dangerous disclosure.

There are several other reasons that underlie the failure of children and teens to pay appropriate attention to privacy concerns:

- Commercial Web sites actively encourage children and teens to "tell all" to support market profiling and advertising.

- Young people interact online with many other young people, all of whom have a very difficult time perceiving the potential harmful consequences of the disclosure of personal information. This has resulted in an online climate in which vast personal disclosure is considered to be the norm.

- Disclosure of personal information is often tied to social status issues, especially on social networking sites. Some teens perceive that their online social worth is directly tied to the number of friends who are listed on their social networking site and the level of communication activity. The more outrageous the material posted, the juicier the gossip shared, the more others will be attracted and, therefore, the higher these teens' social status will be.

Age-Based Guidelines

Children and tweens do not have sufficient cognitive development to fully comprehend privacy implications. Be fully in charge of managing or overseeing your younger child's online actions that could result in disclosure of personal information. Children and tweens should never register on a Web site without checking with a parent first. This will provide you with ample opportunities to discuss privacy concerns.

In the early teen years, start to shift responsibility for maintaining privacy online to your child. Review the privacy issues outlined in this chapter, discuss the risks, make agreements, monitor activities, and indicate your approval of your child's appropriate attention to privacy concerns. Older teens should know how to register on sites without unsafe disclosure of personal information, when it is acceptable to disclose personal contact information and financial identity information, and how to safely disclose other kinds of personal information under various circumstances online.

Different Types of Personal Information

It is difficult to participate in the online world without making some personal disclosures. If children and teens learn to exercise care, they can participate in select online communities by making limited disclosures in a way that will help to protect their safety and allow them to have healthy online interactions. The foundation for effective privacy protection requires recognizing the different kinds of personal information and then knowing how to effectively handle the different kinds of information online. There are five basic kinds of personal information, plus an additional category related to personal information about someone else.

Personal Contact and Financial Identity Information

Personal contact information is any information that others could use to locate your child in person. Financial identity information is information others could use to steal your child's identity for the purpose of fraudulent financial activities. Type up the following material and put it by your child's computer:

Personal Contact and Financial Identity Information
That Should *Never* Be Disclosed Online
Without My Advance Clearance
[signed Mom or Dad]

Full Name

Address

Phone number

Social Security number

Driver's license number

Student ID number

Bank account number

Debit or credit card number

Mother's maiden name (often used for identification purposes)

Password or personal identification number associated
with a bank account

Password for an online account requested at any other time
than the initial log-in on a site

Older teens should know how to safely disclose this kind of information for specific purposes involving approved financial transactions. Make sure that this is an issue you address specifically so that your older teen leaves home knowing how to conduct financial transactions safely online.

Some of the information listed earlier can be shared on secure sites for the purpose of conducting a financial transaction. If your child wants to make a purchase with a debit card and have that product shipped to your house, there is no other way to accomplish this transaction than to share some of the listed information. There is a high degree of privacy protection in legitimate sites through which users conduct financial transactions. Information entered on a secure Web site, identified by a URL that begins with "https://," is well-protected—unless the Web site is a fraudulent Web site set up for phishing.

Intimate Personal Information

Intimate personal information is private and personal information that generally should remain confidential or shared only with very trustworthy people. Sometimes this is information about problems young people are having with others or struggles they might be having in life. It is incredibly important that your child understands that sharing this kind of information online, especially in public places or with people they do not fully trust, is extremely dangerous. Others can use this information to hurt and exploit them.

But there may be circumstances in which disclosure of intimate personal information is perfectly appropriate. For example, there may be effective professional services available online to support young people who are trying to sort out challenging issues. Disclosure of intimate personal information is necessary to obtain such support. Young people must be advised of the importance of checking out the qualifications of a support site and not disclosing personal contact information unless absolutely necessary to receive assistance.

It also is likely that teens will ignore guidance to never discuss intimate personal information online. It is necessary to help them to determine the best strategy to do so. This is actually an important life lesson—knowing how and with whom we ought to share and discuss the intimate details of our lives. In general, intimate information should be shared only with very trustworthy friends using private forms of electronic communication—recognizing that there is always the risk that a trustworthy friend might turn out not to be so trustworthy and may forward intimate personal information to others.

Reputation-Damaging Material

It seems illogical that there is a need to remind teens that it is not smart to post material that is highly likely to damage their reputation. Remind your child to consider how school officials, coaches, college admission officers, scholarship program officials, police officers, and prospective employers, not to mention you, might view the material posted on public sites. A review of the postings on social networking sites leads to the conclusion that many teens need this reminder. Some teens are discussing sexual exploits, denigrating others, and using lots of trash talk or posting pictures of themselves in sexually provocative poses, drinking alcohol, or doing drugs.

Sometimes your child may not be the one who has posted the reputation-damaging material. Make sure your child knows to tell you if someone has posted images or information that could damage his or her reputation. Your child should contact the child who has posted such material and demand that the material be removed. If the material is not promptly removed, you should contact the parents and file a complaint with the site asking for the material to be removed.

Personal Interest Information

Personal interest information is more general information about personal interests and activities. In most online locations, it generally is safe for teens to share this kind of information. This is the kind of information teens can post in profiles, on Web pages or in blogs, and the like.

The disclosure of personal interest information will allow your child to make contacts with other teens, and possibly adults, who share similar interests. Teens must understand that there is a risk that a dangerous adult could learn about their interests through the personal interest information provided and could use this information in an attempt to form a relationship based on "shared interests." Also be aware that Web sites use personal interest information for market profiling.

Personal Information About Others

Young people also disclose information about others online. They might disclose information about you. This disclosure could be embarrassing or could cause significant harm. Sometimes the personal information or images young people transmit about others is in the form of vicious rumors or highly damaging material.

Make sure that your child knows that the personal information of other people is their business and simply should not be shared publicly online—especially if the information includes personal contact information, intimate details, or reputation-damaging material, or if the reason your child is disclosing this information is to harm the other person.

Pictures and Video Images

Children simply should not post pictures or video images of themselves online. For teens, the risks involved when posting pictures or video images of themselves or others include the following:

- The combination of the picture or image with other identification information could allow a stranger to find the teen in person.

- A dangerous stranger could gain some additional insight from the picture or image that the stranger might use in seeking to seduce the teen. "I saw your picture. You are so pretty. You could be a model. Do you have any pictures of yourself in a bathing suit?"

- There may be danger involved in obtaining the picture or image, or from the inappropriateness of some pictures or images. Some teens are posting sexually provocative images or images of themselves engaging in inappropriate activities, such as drinking or drug use. The posting of these kinds of images could lead to contact from predators or could damage the child's reputation. Some teens are taking great joy in capturing embarrassing images of others, including teens being beaten up in a fight or a teen changing in a school locker room. It seems that anywhere teens go these days, someone has a digital camera and may be prepared to record images of incriminating material and post them online. Some teens compete in the degree of outrageousness that they can capture, of both their own behavior and that of others, and they may seek to obtain an image of themselves engaged in highly risky activities, which could result in their suffering significant harm as a consequence.

- There is the potential that someone else could digitally alter a picture in a harmful manner and disseminate the new image. This might occur in a cyberbullying situation. For example, a teen's face could be superimposed onto a picture of a pig or a nude model.

These risks need to be balanced against a teen's strong desire to establish an online identity, which necessarily includes "this is what I look like and these are my friends." As long as you are paying close attention to the pictures and images your child posts online—and your child knows you are paying attention—posting appropriate, nonprovocative pictures or images online is not likely to be any more dangerous than any other aspect of online activity.

Privacy Protection Strategies

Everyone who uses the Internet must cultivate practices to protect their privacy as best as possible, while still allowing engagement in desired online activities. The following are general privacy protection strategies.

Gender-Neutral Username

Help your younger child create a gender-neutral username for all computer activities, including computer games on your home computer. Make sure your teen knows the importance of using a nonprovocative, gender-neutral username for all public communications and registrations. Make sure that your child's username or email address does not inadvertently provide a full name. A child who uses a username or email address name of <jsmith> combined with her use of a first name, "Jessica," has just revealed her full name.

Throw-Away Account

Consider helping your child establish a "throw-away" email account to use for all registrations and public communications. This account can be terminated or deserted if the spam (unsolicited email advertising) level gets too high or to get out of dangerous situations. Your child should limit distribution of the more permanent, personal email address to good friends. An alias account through your Internet service provider is safer than a Web-based account such as through Yahoo or Hotmail, because as the adult account holder you have the right to access all individual accounts.

Online Registrations

Teach your child to carefully consider all requests for personal contact information and respond in the best way to protect personal information. Frequently the information requested through registration is only a username, email address, age, and location (country and city or postal code). There is not much risk in disclosing this kind of information. Advise your child to look for and disable all "permissions" that enable the site to share registration information with "partners."

Social Networking Sites, Personal Web Pages, Blogs, and Profiles

With social networking sites, personal Web pages, blogs, and profiles it is necessary to balance the benefits of allowing your child to engage in creative self-expression and make new friends against the possible risks of disclosure or misuse of the information shared by your child. Carefully research the online environment that your child wants to participate in and consider whether you are comfortable with the prevailing social norms for public disclosure that are evident on the site. If you are not comfortable with social norms, consider whether you can trust your child and friends to maintain their own safe information disclosure standards despite such norms.

Teens should never disclose personal contact information other than an email address, which is necessary for registration. If you allow a younger child to create an online presence, make sure that your email address or a family email address is the only address that is associated with the registration.

Limited, nonprovocative personal interest information generally can be safely shared on these sites. Sometimes the standard information requested for profiles is inappropriate; for example, asking teens to disclose their sexual orientation. Make sure that your child knows that it is not necessary to provide information just because a form on the site asks for it.

Review any material posted by your teen prior to posting. Periodically review the material posted by your teen to make sure you think the information shared is appropriate and safe.

Product Interest Surveys or Questionnaires

Teach your child to recognize that these surveys and questionnaires are merely market-profiling tools. No one at the site is really interested in them or their opinions other than as a prospective purchaser. The sites just want the information so that they can send advertisements.

Privacy Protection Technologies

Privacy protection technologies can restrict disclosure of information that parents require be kept private. Technically sophisticated teens likely can circumvent these technologies. Education and supervision are more effective strategies because they will prepare your child to make good choices regardless of the presence of any "techie tool."

·14·

Wired 24/7

INTERNET ADDICTIVE BEHAVIOR
AND MULTITASKING

When Dawn gets home from school, she goes quickly to the computer to check on the comments posted on her social networking site and to read her mail. As she is doing this, she is also IMing with the friends she just left at school. Dawn takes a short break from the computer to eat some dinner. Then she gets to her homework—while continuing her IMing and frequently checking her email. The computer Dawn uses is a laptop. It generally is located in the family room, but many nights, after her parents have gone to bed, Dawn sneaks out to get the computer and bring it to her bedroom. She can access the computer through the wireless connection. She puts a towel along the bottom of the door so her parents can't tell she is up. Frequently, she is online until 2:00 A.M. She depends on caffeinated drinks to be able to stay up late at night and then in the morning to wake up. Her grades are dropping.

The Internet offers a time-warped place where children and teens can get away from their "real world" concerns—they can be free, independent, and uninhibited, and can find acceptance. The Internet is always "on," 24/7. The game is always going on. Friends are always available. Life online constantly beckons. Regardless of what your child is doing online—surfing, gabbing, or gaming—if these activities are taking too much time and the place of other activities that contribute to a happy, productive life, then your child is in trouble. If your child is trying to do homework along with surfing, gabbing, and gaming, his or her work and school performance will suffer.

Internet Addictive Behavior

Internet addictive behavior is when one spends an excessive amount of time using the Internet, resulting in a lack of healthy engagement in other areas of life.[1] When your child's use of the Internet is interfering with those activities that make life rewarding, fulfilling, and successful, your child may have Internet addictive behavior. Internet addictive behavior is itself a concern, but also is an indicator of other problems. Excessive amounts of time spent on the Internet may become a slippery slope leading children and teens into the darker sides of Internet activities. Internet addictive behavior is a behavioral addiction. Individuals who are under stress or suffer low self-esteem appear to be most "at risk."

Many teens appear to have a hard time unplugging from social networking sites for any period of time. This addictive access appears to be tied to social anxiety. Researchers who studied teens and cell phone use discovered that the teens who were most active in use of their cell phones scored highest on assessments of depression and anxiety.[2] Many teens are highly concerned about their social status. If teens measure their social worth based on the level of electronic communication activity with friends, this can fuel addiction.

Internet gaming environments are also highly addicting, especially the role-playing simulation games. The game is always ongoing in these environments, and after a player leaves, something really exciting might happen. Many game features encourage addictive behavior.

Internet Addictive Behavior Indicators

Internet addictive behavior indicators include the following:

- Excessive fatigue associated with consistent late-night Internet use. Teens will wait until after their parents have gone to bed to get back on to the computer to gab with friends or participate in gaming. Frequently, late-night use is associated with drinking heavily caffeinated drinks.

- Preoccupation with the Internet. Your child is online much of the time and when not online appears to be preoccupied with thoughts about being online.

- Decline in grades. The decline in grades is a natural result of fatigue and preoccupation with the Internet. Decline in grades can also be related to multitasking—your child is trying to do homework along with surfing, gabbing, or gaming online.

- Decline in interest and involvement in other life activities, including reading, hobbies, sports, and other similar activities. Your child's sole interests are now related to online activities.

- A decline in quality and quantity of connections and activities with family members.

- Use of deceit and lies to cover up time spent online. Waiting until you have gone to bed so they can get back online is a frequent method of deceit.

- Efforts to restrict Internet access being met with intense anger, denial of any concerns, and efforts to get around any restrictions.

Although this book is focused on children and teens, you should be aware that Internet addictive behavior is a significant concern for young people in college. If your child is not performing as well as should be expected, discuss this concern—especially if you are the one footing the bill for college tuition.

Strategies to Address Internet Addictive Behavior

Preventing Internet addictive behavior requires focusing on the quality of your child's relationships with family and friends, practicing effective stress management, and helping your child to keep life in balance—spending an appropriate amount of time engaged in important life activities. These include school and homework, chores and work activities, time with family and friends, organized activities and personal interest time, physical activities, "screen time," and sleep. Behavioral addictions generally are associated with underlying emotional concerns—frequently involving relationship issues. Relationships with other teens are very important in the teen years. Pay close attention to the manner in which your child is relating to other teens.

The best way to address Internet addictive behavior is to not let it become an established pattern. This requires paying close attention to your child's activities and ensuring that those activities are well-balanced. Some strategies to accomplish this include the following:

- Focus on the quality of your child's "real world" relationships and activities. Children who engage in healthy activities with friends and family generally are far less prone to spending too much time online.

- Seek to focus your child's attention on some important life goals and future directions. This can help to focus your child's energies in positive directions.

- Set limits or develop joint agreements about the total amount of "screen time." This includes television, video, or computer games, and text messaging. Require use of a timer when your child is online or install time-monitoring software to reinforce these limits.

- Consider your own behavior. Do not foster your child's use of the Internet as a "baby-sitter."

- Require that certain activities, such as homework, reading, and chores, be completed prior to any "screen time."
- Arrange for participation in sports and other group activities. Facilitate in-person get-togethers with friends. Support the pursuit of hobbies and reading.
- Look at the Web sites that your child likes to visit and discuss with your child the "sticky" features of these sites.
- Collaborate with the parents of your child's friends to set time standards for the group of friends.

If your child has slipped into an addictive pattern of Internet use, recognize that any intervention actions will be met with a denial of addiction or of the harmful consequences of that addictive behavior. To address the denial, keep a log of the amount of time you see that your child is online for a week. If your child disputes your record keeping, require that he or she keep a time log. Continue to keep your log so you can compare. Also pay attention to instances when Internet-addictive behavior has led to a loss—such as a decline in grades or loss of a friend. This loss can provide direct and tangible evidence to your child that life is out of balance.

It is best to arrange for some period of time when your child is away from any technology to have a discussion about your concerns. Take your child to a coffee shop or go for a drive in the car. Confiscate your child's cell phone or require that it be turned off. If your child is heavily addicted to the receipt of text messages, simply placing the cell phone off-limits for the duration of your discussion likely will provide evidence of the degree to which your child is unable to effectively disengage from the technology.

Make it clear to your child that you are significantly concerned that an excessive amount of time spent online is hurting other important activities and that the situation must change. Give your child the opportunity to think about the situation and develop a plan of action to gain effective time management over Internet use.

Make it clear to your child that if a workable plan of action is not developed, you will develop a plan for him or her.

Work with your child to achieve time-management goals. This almost certainly will require much more time and involvement on your part to ensure that your child has something to do other than spend time online. Be prepared to support get-togethers with friends and other activities, especially enrichment classes, sports, martial arts, and the like. Be sure to reward successful steps to achieving balance. If your child is more resistant, taking control of the computer may be necessary. You can remove the keyboard and mouse, or even the computer itself, if it is a laptop, when the computer should not be used. Or you can install time-limiting software.

It is probable that much of your child's activity online is spent surfing, gabbing, and gaming with friends. If this is the case, another approach to addressing the concern is to do so in conjunction with the parents of your child's friends. If your child's online activities primarily involve interacting with strangers, this is a clear indication that your child is having problems with friendships. To effectively address Internet addictive behavior will require attention to the quality of your child's friendships.

If your child's Internet use is out of control and your efforts to gain control have not worked, it may be necessary to consult with a professional who understands behavioral addiction issues.

Multitasking

It likely will not concern you to find that your child is simultaneously watching TV and playing a video game, as well as IMing or talking on the phone. It is fine to multitask, if none of the things you are doing are really important. But what if your child is talking on the phone, IMing, watching TV, listening to music, or surfing the Web when doing homework?

A recent *Time* magazine article addressed this concern.[3] In this article, the chief of the cognitive neuroscience section at the National Institute of Neurological Disorders and Strokes was quoted as saying, "Kids that are instant messaging while doing homework, playing games online and watching TV, I predict, aren't going to do well in the long run."

Other researchers quoted in the article echoed this concern. The ability of the brain to multitask has clear limits. Human brains are designed to focus on one task at a time. Our brains cannot simultaneously do two different tasks. What appears to be multitasking is rapid switching from one task to another—task-shifting. Task-shifting takes time. Every time attention is shifted from one task to another, the brain has to shift gears and refocus. If the tasks are unfamiliar or complex, even more time is necessary to shift from one task to another. The time it takes to do two tasks in task-shifting mode is longer than it would take to do either task independently, and errors increase significantly.

But this is the younger generation. They have grown up with this explosion of media input. Aren't they better able to multitask? No, in fact they are even less able to multitask. The reason for this is that the part of the brain that controls task-switching is the frontal lobe—which is the part of the brain that is developing during the teen years.[4] During the time that a young person is in school—up to and including college—the capacity to effectively task-shift has not yet even fully developed.

Homework generally involves tasks that represent new learning. Completing homework successfully requires focus and ideally will lead to an in-depth understanding of the topic being studied, rather than surface awareness. It is simply not possible for children and teens to maintain an adequate focus on learning if they are media multitasking while doing homework.

It is important to recognize the role of other teens in fostering such media multitasking. The "totally connected teen" is most likely strongly influenced by friends to be available electronically at all times. Teens addicted to this level of media involvement who are required to "unplug" to do homework may demonstrate anxiety symptoms. They may also receive negative feedback from their friends about their electronic unavailability. The inability to "unplug" from the Internet for the period of time necessary to do a good job on a homework assignment provides clear evidence of Internet addictive behavior.

Strategies to Address Multitasking Concerns

If your child is media multitasking while doing homework, it is time for a serious talk about priorities and responsibilities. Encourage your child to read the *Time* article for insight into the issue. This will assist your child in understanding that mom or dad is not simply overreacting, there are solid research findings that back up your concerns. Other strategies to address concerns of media multitasking while doing homework include the following:

- Encourage your child to keep a log of multitasking activities during a week. It is quite possible that your child is not even fully aware of the degree to which this is occurring.

- Discuss specific strategies for eliminating media distractions while doing homework, including turning off the cell phone, unplugging the landline phone that is in the location where homework is being completed, setting IM on "do not disturb" if it is necessary to use the computer or the Internet for the homework assignment, and making a commitment not to go online to check out the happenings on the social networking site.

- Encourage your child to set accomplishment goals, with "reconnecting" for a period of time as the reward. For example, "I will complete this math assignment in full or work on this project for thirty minutes, and then check my messages." This is a strategy that is used by many successful adults in today's multitasking environment.

- Encourage your child to be a leader within a group of friends to reinforce the importance of "unplugging" to complete homework. If your child can convince friends that it is necessary for their success in the future to "unplug" while studying, the influence of your child's more peripheral online connections will be diminished. You may find that one or two of your child's friends may be the source of the majority of the distractions. Encourage your child to be direct with these individuals and indicate that focusing attention on homework is important.

If your child is unsuccessful in discussions with friends, a parent-to-parent discussion may be necessary. A group commitment of parents that all friends will "unplug" during homework can be very helpful.

· 15 ·

Read with Your Eyes Open

THE IMPORTANCE OF INFORMATION LITERACY

Kenneth just received a message indicating that if he would go to a profile on a social networking site and enter a contest, he could win a video game device. The message encourages him to respond rapidly, or he will lose this opportunity.

Connie is concerned about her appearance and wants to find a way to lose weight. She starts looking online for some information. She has found a number of sites that sell weight loss supplements that they "promise" are safe and effective.

Jordan is writing a research paper on the subject of harvesting timber after a forest fire. In conducting his research, he has found a variety of studies that offer extremely diverse opinions on the subject. While he was conducting his research he discovered some interesting information. A graduate student's research paper that pointed out significant damage caused by logging activities had been published in a prestigious scientific journal. But faculty members in the Department of Forestry who were financially supported by the timber industry tried to block the publication of the

paper. Contrary opinions that had been offered by these faculty members were being used to back up legislation to support logging. Unable to decide which information was
accurate, Jordan decided to outline the various perspectives.

Disinformation abounds on the Internet. Information literacy is
an essential skill for success in the Information Age. Recognize
that there are no "cyberspace truth monitors." There is no person,
company, or government agency making sure that what people tell
you or the information found on a Web site is accurate and unbiased.
Even if there were, they likely would have unacceptable bias. Consider the times in history when what was considered the "truth" was
challenged by those who had other thoughts. Is the world really flat?

Eventually your child must be able to independently assess the
accuracy of information found online. This is not an easy task when
anybody can be a publisher of information. Sometimes effective
information literacy skills can be extremely important—such as
looking for health information online that will be used to make a
decision about health matters. At other times, the need for accuracy is less important. Information literacy is also an important
foundational skill for avoiding scams.

Web Site Credibility

Determining the credibility of online information is complicated by
the fact that everyone—from credible, nonbiased information
providers to "snake oil salesmen"—is using the same techniques to
create Web sites that appear to be highly credible.

Consumer Reports has launched a "Credibility Campaign" to
improve the trustworthiness of all Web sites.[1] As part of this campaign, it established credibility guidelines that call for easy-to-find
disclosures of site identity; ownership; and policies on advertising,
sponsorships, customer service, and privacy; and for making a commitment to quickly and prominently correct wrong information.
But when it did a study of how people assess credibility, it found

that people did not look at these features to assess credibility. In fact, the study provided indications that are of significant concern:[2]

> *The data showed that the average consumer paid far more attention to the superficial aspects of a site, such as visual cues, than to its content. . . . Participants seemed to make their credibility-based decisions about the people or organization behind the site based upon the site's overall visual appeal. We had hoped to see people use more rigorous evaluation strategies while assessing sites.*

Another recent study assessed the ability of subjects to determine the credibility of Web sites in the context of concerns related to phishing—online schemes designed to trick people into providing financial information for the purpose of identity theft.[3] The participants in the study were shown twenty Web sites, only seven of which were legitimate, and asked to determine which were the legitimate sites. The participants knew that some of the sites that were presented to them were fake sites. The researchers found that almost all of the participants were easily fooled.

There was, however, one participant in this study who was highly successful in determining which sites were the legitimate sites. His strategy was not based on an analysis of what was on the site, but rather how he got to the site. This is a very important finding. It is easy for someone to produce a site that is credible in appearance. But it is much harder for someone to create a site that professionals and search engines will link to. In the information literacy guidelines that follow, there will be a strong focus on effective strategies to get to credible sites.

Information Literacy Strategies

- Consider how important it is that the information or site be credible.
  - Information searches vary in importance, and thus the need to pay attention to credibility varies. Consider the

importance of determining the credibility of a site that provides health information as compared with one that supplies information about a new movie.

- Assess how controversial the issue is.
  - The degree of controversy over a subject is related to the likelihood of finding sites about that subject with potential bias. Compare the potential for bias between online information about the features of cars and online information about the biological basis of homosexuality.

- Reflect on how you got to any Web site or how the information came to you.
  - If you get to a Web site following a link from a Web site that already has credibility, such as a list of good research sites for students provided by an education group, it is likely that the Web site is equally credible. Web sites found through a search engine will vary in quality and credibility. Information provided in a message from a stranger or information on a site accessed through such a message is highly likely not to be credible.

- Evaluate the source of the information.
  - Has a university, a government agency, or a well-respected organization or individual with expertise provided the information? But note that even institutions, agencies, organizations, or individuals have potential bias. The material on a university site may be from a researcher who has been funded by a company that has direct financial interest in the results of the research. Government agencies may provide information to support the policies of the political party currently in power.
  - Is there independent evidence of the expertise and credi - bility of the source? Type the site name in quotes in a search engine, without using "http://," and you can determine who links to the site. Assess the possible motivations

and biases of the people or organizations behind the sites that link to this information.

- Look for evidence of bias.
  - Does the material appear to be presented for the purpose of providing information or is the site an advocacy site designed to persuade people to agree with a certain position? Does the entity presenting the information have anything to gain by convincing people to agree with the facts or opinions set forth? The material presented by an advocacy site is likely to be more biased. This does not mean the information is inaccurate, but you need to be more careful in an evaluation.
  - Is there any evidence of self-interest, such as a source of funding, seeking participants in advocating for a cause, or selling of products or services?

- Determine whether the information is fact-based or opinion-based.
  - Fact-based information is likely to be more credible than opinion-based information. But you should still investigate the source of the facts.

- Determine whether the information is consistent with information found through other sources.
  - Is the same or similar information present at several locations? Or is the information conflicting? If information is conflicting, evaluate the source of such conflict.

- Ask for the opinions of others, especially a parent, teacher, or librarian.
  - What do they think of the information and source?

- Evaluate the information itself.
  - Is it logical? Is it consistent with what you already know is true? Does it "feel" right?

· 16 ·

Don't Take Candy from Strangers

ONLINE STRANGER LITERACY

Stephanie has an account on a popular social networking site. One day she got a message from someone she did not know. This message said, "Jeff would like to be added to your friends list. By accepting Jeff as your friend, you will be able to send Jeff personal messages, view Jeff's photos and journals, and interact with each other's friends and network! Click the following link to view Jeff's profile and accept or reject this user as your friend." Happy to have a new friend, Stephanie immediately accepted this friendship link. Now her picture appears on Jeff's profile and Jeff's picture appears on her profile. They are able to communicate privately and post comments on each other's profile pages.

Dustin and Lisa are high school students who met each other online in a discussion group for their favorite regional band. They live in nearby cities. Dustin and Lisa are linked as friends on their social networking profiles. They have exchanged many messages over the last six months. Their favorite band is going to be playing in an open-air arts festival in Lisa's town. Dustin has decided to come to listen to the band. They are both excited, because this is the first time they will be able to meet in person.

With the expanded ability to meet and interact with new people online comes the need for a new skill—online stranger literacy. Online stranger literacy is the ability to determine the trustworthiness and safety of individuals who are unknown in person, with whom one is communicating online. It is the "people" equivalent of information literacy. Online stranger literacy requires a set of skills that are specifically related to the fact that people can create extensive false "personas" online that enable them to present a personal image that is not accurate. When a young person meets a stranger online, it can be difficult to ascertain whether this person is trustworthy and safe.

Many people your child will meet online will be perfectly wonderful young people who present no danger to your child whatsoever. Young people can use the Internet to form friendships with others who live in very different communities or countries. These young people can help your child gain an expanded awareness of social cultures throughout the world. Your child may also meet perfectly nice adults who share your child's interests.

But there is always the possibility of running into a dangerous stranger online. Most discussions about online strangers found in Internet safety literature focus on "stranger danger" with respect to sexual predators. A frequently expressed concern is the significant danger that a child might go and meet an "online stranger." With respect to sexual predators, focusing on "stranger danger" concepts is problematical. By the time a young person goes to meet a sexual predator, this person is no longer thought of as a "stranger." To the young person, this predator has become a "special friend."

The greatest danger from online strangers may not even be related to an in-person meeting or sexual predation. An online support group of friends who encourage each other to commit suicide, engage in cutting, or commit hate crimes may never meet in person—and these are very dangerous online strangers.

Some Internet safety surveys have asked questions such as "Have you ever communicated with a stranger online?" or "Have you ever gone to meet someone who you first met online?" The sense conveyed by these survey questions is that any young person who communicates with or goes to meet an online stranger has taken a very dangerous action. But a secondary or high school student who has been introduced to and formed a friendship online with a student from a nearby school might agree to meet with this person under safe conditions in a local coffee shop. The student would answer "yes" to these questions, when the encounter raised no danger concerns whatsoever.

Rather than trying to convey an irrational fear that every stranger a child meets online is a dangerous person intent on harming that child, it is essential to provide young people with the knowledge and skills necessary to determine the trustworthiness and safety of people they meet online and how to safely meet in person, if a meeting is desired.

Interactions with strangers on social networking sites are generally safer than those with strangers in chat rooms when it comes to effective online stranger literacy. Everyone whom your child meets in a social networking community has a profile with personal information, links to other friends, and a history of communications. While creating and maintaining a totally false "persona" could be done, it certainly is harder—especially over a longer period of time. The social networking profile can provide very useful evidence about another person's values and interests, this person's friends and their values and interests, and the manner in which this person treats other people through ongoing communications. This is very valuable information for assessing the trustworthiness and probable safety of this online stranger.

Types of People

It will be helpful for your child to distinguish among three types of people: good friends, acquaintances, and strangers.

Good Friends

Good friends are people whom your child knows in person and trusts. If your child generally has strong friendships with other young people whom you consider to have appropriate values and standards, then there is likely no danger associated with this group of people online. Sadly, sometimes the people you think are friends do not turn out to be good friends. Assuming that your child's closest friends are very trustworthy, it likely is safe for your child to disclose intimate information with these friends through private electronic communications.

Acquaintances

Acquaintances are people your child knows, but not very well, and certainly not as well as their good friends. Acquaintances might include people your child knows from school or other in-person gatherings, such as summer camp, school-sponsored events, and the like. This group may also include people whom your child does not know personally, but who are friends of your child's good friends.

The key feature of an acquaintance is that if your child ever has any questions about the trustworthiness or safety of this person, there are others whom your child knows in person who can be consulted for additional input. Acquaintances likely are able to find your child's personal contact information through some other source. Your child should not consider it safe to share any intimate information with an acquaintance, because of the lack of closeness in the relationship. Over time, acquaintances may become friends.

Online Strangers

Online strangers are "everyone else." This category includes anyone who does not fit into the two preceding categories. Everyone in the online stranger category should be considered potentially dangerous until proven otherwise. Unfortunately, there is no easy way to independently verify the trustworthiness and safety of these strangers. Your child should know to never, ever, share personal contact or intimate personal information or images with an online stranger.

However, it is actually possible that someone who starts out as an online stranger might over time become a good friend. Your child might end up marrying someone who initially was an online stranger!

Online Stranger Literacy Guidelines

The following are some online stranger literacy guidelines that your child can use to determine the trustworthiness and safety of an online acquaintance or stranger:

- Know yourself. Your child should have a clear sense of personal values and use these values to guide an assessment of strangers online. This does not mean that your child should immediately reject a relationship with someone who has a different perspective on life. Your child always can learn from such encounters. But it is also important for your child to assess others based on family and personal values.

- Check the person's online presence. If someone wants to establish a relationship with your child online, such as a friendship link in a social networking environment, your child should carefully check this person out. Evaluate the material in the profile. Check out the person's friendship links and evaluate the material in profiles of these "friends." Evaluate how this person interacts with others. The old line "you shall be known by the company you keep" is highly relevant to this assessment.

- Advise your child to take some time to get to know people online. People have difficulty keeping up a façade for a long time. If someone is seeking to maintain a false "persona," sooner or later inconsistencies will emerge.

- Your child should pay attention to details of communications and check for inconsistencies. Be very sensitive to comments made that are inconsistent with information presented in a profile or comments made at a prior date. It may be appropriate to ask about any inconsistencies. "Didn't you tell me before that . . .?" Carefully consider the legitimacy of the answer to this question.

- Your child should be warned to watch out for "sweet talk" and other signs that the person may be overly interested in establishing a close relationship. Your child should be very leery of anyone who appears to be interested in establishing a "special" relationship. This includes anyone who offers gifts or uses excessive statements of praise.

- If your child knows someone who knows the person, more information about this person can be requested. If your child is communicating with someone who is not known to any of your child's friends, he or she might want to ask some friends to review the person's profile and some of the communications to get their opinion of the person.

- Your child should *never* agree to meet with an acquaintance or stranger without your approval! Frequent guidance provided to teens is that they should make sure their parent accompanies them to this meeting. Quite frankly, there are very few teens who are going to be entirely comfortable bringing "mommy" or "daddy" along to a meeting with someone they have met online. It is better to give your child some options that are more likely to be followed and will keep your child safe. Your child should

  - Provide you with complete contact information for this person, just in case there is an immediate need for this information.
  - Arrange to meet this person during the day at a public place, like a busy coffee shop or an eating section at a mall.

- Make sure that either you or trusted, level-headed friends are present in this public place. Tell your child that you can simply pretend to be a disinterested stranger enjoying a cup of coffee or a burger. If your child is an older teen who generally makes safe choices and has friends whom you trust, ensuring that these friends are present in the public place is likely safe. However, you may still want to be close by. Also, make sure the parents of your child's friends know about this plan and have approved.

- Make sure your child has a cell phone and have a pre-arranged agreement that you are going to call about five minutes into the planned meeting. Have agreed-upon code language that your child can use to indicate to you that the meeting needs to end or other assistance is required.

- Your child should know how important it is to never leave the public place with the online stranger. If it looks like this is a person who could be a nice new friend, your child should make arrangements to meet in a public place another time. Your child should take the time after a meeting to think about the interaction and consider the opinions of others.

Teachable Moments

The way to ensure that your child is thinking about these issues is to spend lots of time reviewing them—every time that you mutually review your child's online activities, especially activities in a social networking community and list of IM contacts. Use these times to review the status of all of your child's contacts.

- Ask your child to distinguish between good friends, acquaintances, and strangers among the people that your child is linking to as "friends." You should discourage or prohibit your child from adding anyone from the stranger category to an IM contacts list unless it is possible to review this person's profile on another site.

- It may be appropriate for your child to include people in the stranger category as "friends" in a social networking community on a temporary basis until it is possible to check these people out following the stranger literacy guidelines discussed earlier. This can present an excellent learning opportunity for your child to practice the strategies to assess the trustworthiness and safety of an acquaintance or stranger. You and your child can mutually review the profile, friend's links, and communications of this person. Discourage your child from simply collecting friendship links with anyone who asks to be their friend.

- Whenever your child initiates a conversation about an online contact, pay close attention—but in a subtle manner. Your child may have some concerns, but not know what to do. Let your child take the lead in developing the conversation. Reflect back to your child what you hear your child saying. Be careful not to criticize this person. Ask questions that will assist your child in making an effective evaluation of this person. Ask if your child's good friends have any connections with this person and what they think. If it seems appropriate, suggest that you both look over this person's profile. Be sure to note the name or username of the person and other details. You likely will want to do some investigations on your own— just to be sure.

Turning Down Friendship Links

One of the hardest things for someone to do on a social networking site is to turn down a request for a friendship link. If someone has offered your child the "gift of friendship," your child will feel incredibly bad turning this gift down. The person who is seeking the friendship link could be a dangerous stranger, another teen who is simply "collecting" friendship links as a way of establishing social status, or a really nice person who shares your child's interests and could become a good friend or adult mentor.

Discuss this issue thoroughly with your child. Given that some people use the process of establishing friendship links for unacceptable purposes, it is perfectly appropriate for your child to turn down an offer of friendship if the other person does not appear to be a safe or welcome friend. If your child ever tells you about turning down a friendship, be sure to ask some subtle questions about the interaction—and to praise your child for having the independence to make a safe choice.

Part Three

•

INFLUENCES ON ONLINE DECISION MAKING

· 17 ·

Working on the "Hard-Wiring"

BRAIN DEVELOPMENT AND ONLINE DECISION MAKING

Just as we do not expect an infant to walk, or a toddler to read, we should not expect a young teen to be capable of consistently making the right choices online. It takes at least twenty years for a child's brain to become fully mature and capable of consistent well-reasoned and ethical decision making. Along the way, there are certain stages of development.

During the first ten years of life, development occurs in the back portion of the brain—the sensory lobes. During these early years, children master verbal and written language, and gain a basic understanding of mathematical concepts, time and space, and natural concepts, as well as social and cultural information. Children expect adults to make decisions for them and tend to be inclined to follow adult-delivered rules and guidelines for behavior.

Young children also readily believe in such magical creatures as the "tooth fairy." If children still believe in the tooth fairy, how can they begin to understand the Internet or be trusted to make safe and responsible decisions? They can't. To them, the computer is a "magic box." Internet parenting strategies for children must be guided by this understanding. Children need parents to establish safe online places and provide simple safety rules that do not require extensive thinking on their part.

In the second decade, brain-development activity shifts to the frontal lobes. The frontal lobes are responsible for reasoned decision making, assessing right and wrong, and recognizing cause-and-effect relationships—actions and their consequences. Studies have shown that development of the frontal lobe area of the brain continues into the early twenties. The teen brain is in the process of developing and formalizing neural connections, called synapses. The synapses allow effective neural processing to occur. This neural processing is the foundation for reasoned decision making.

It has also been demonstrated through brain research that when teens are asked to perform tasks that involve the processing of emotions, the area of the brain that is most active is the amygdala. The amygdala is the area of the brain that is associated with more primitive "fight or flight" responses. When adults process emotions, they use their frontal lobes. This means that when teens are trying to make a decision and there are emotions involved, they are even less likely to be thinking clearly—because the area of the brain that is responsible for thinking clearly is simply not fully developed or engaged.

Practicing Responsible Decision Making

As much as parents want to protect their teens from making bad decisions, the answer is not for adults to make all of the decisions. Learning to engage in effective problem solving requires practice. This practice must include making decisions and paying attention to the consequences.

Think back to when your child was a toddler. Toddlers learning to walk have to practice walking in all sorts of different environments. They will strenuously resist being carried. They want and need to practice walking because this is absolutely essential for their development. Sometimes, they will trip and need rescuing and reassurance. Parents must pay close attention around stairs and streets, because toddlers do not appreciate the dangers of height and cars. Eventually, through practice, young children are able to walk and run safely.

A similar phenomenon occurs during the teen years. Teens must practice solving problems and making decisions. Teens will resist authoritarian adult decision making on their behalf because it is essential for their brain development that they practice making decisions on their own. The power struggles that emerge in teen-parent relationships are grounded in this dynamic—with some "raging hormones" thrown in just to spice things up.

To learn how to make responsible decisions requires recognizing whether the consequence of a decision was good or bad. Teens must make the association between cause and harmful effect. Unfortunately, learning to make good choices on the Internet is more difficult because use of the technology interferes with the ability to understand or recognize the consequences of certain actions. There is a "disconnect" between cause and effect.

Another reason that it is difficult for teens to make good decisions online is that most teens are interacting online with other teens, all of whom have immature frontal lobes. This increases the potential that teens will jointly make and support each other in making unsafe or irresponsible decisions.

Because understanding the potential consequences is so important to making good decisions, Internet safety instruction provided to teens must be grounded in an understanding of how certain actions might lead to potential harmful consequences. Offering teens simplistic rules, such as "Do not provide personal information online," will be entirely ineffective because no information is given about why providing personal information online might lead to an undesirable consequence. Further, rather than simply following "rules," teens need guidance in how to make safe and responsible decisions under different circumstances.

Teens sometimes resent parental intrusion into their decision making. Explain the issue in terms of biological development. This can help your child to understand the underlying reasons why you need to stay involved in assisting him or her in making good decisions, especially online. Here is a way you might express this to your child:

> One of the difficulties in being a teen is that your brain is really not yet fully developed. [Show your child the research.] This means that sometimes you might unintentionally make bad choices. This is why it is important that I continue to be involved in guiding and reviewing your decision making. When you are using the Internet it can be harder to make good decisions, because it is harder to figure out what might happen. And other teens may also be making bad choices.
>
> My job as a [mom or dad] is to make sure that you learn to make good decisions, including good decisions online. This requires that we talk about possible problems that might arise online and discuss how to make good choices. This also means that I will pay attention to the choices you are making online and, if you make a bad choice, I will intervene in a way that helps you learn not to make a bad choice in the future. As you demonstrate to me that you are making good choices online, I can allow you more freedom to make choices on your own.

·18·

You Can't See Me,
I Can't See You

HOW TECHNOLOGY CAN INTERFERE
WITH RESPONSIBLE DECISION MAKING

Moral development is a process that is tied closely to brain development. During the teen years, in addition to developing the capacity to engage in reasoned decision making, teens develop their own "moral identity"—their personal, internalized values about what is safe and unsafe, responsible and irresponsible, right and wrong.

Researchers who investigate online behavior have long recognized that people engage in activities online that they would not be as inclined to engage in if they were in the "real world."[1] Researchers use the term *disinhibition* to describe this phenomenon. It is necessary to understand how and why the use of technology might lead someone to make decisions that are unsafe, irresponsible, or wrong.

Let's consider this issue from the "real world" moral development perspective first. There are four external influences on the development of internalized values. These are

- *Values and Social Expectations.* Parents are the primary source for the transmission of values and social expectations to young people. Child-care facilities, such as schools, are another major source of values and expectations, especially through the establishment and enforcement of rules or policies. For many families, spiritual or religious beliefs provide a valuable source of values and expectations for behavior. An additional major source of values and expectations in the lives of our young people are the messages imparted by advertising agencies and entertainment media—which unfortunately can promote unhealthy values and expectations. As children become teens, peer norms become an important additional source of values and expectations.

- *Social Disapproval.* When a young person engages in inappropriate action and recognizes that others have become aware of and disapprove of this action, this can lead to "loss of face" and feelings of shame.

- *Punishment by Authority.* When a young person engages in an inappropriate action that is detected by a person with authority over the young person, such as a parent or a teacher, this can result in punishment. Punishment that focuses the attention of the young person on the reason the action was harmful can lead to a feeling of regret. A feeling of regret can influence a response to that harm or an intention not to cause similar harm in the future. Punishment that merely demonstrates an exertion of power will shift the young person's attention from the harm that was caused to anger at the authority and will not contribute to understanding or regret.

- *An Empathic Response.* Empathy is an innate response to the feelings of another. As children mature and gain the ability to take the perspective of others, the perception that someone has been harmed can lead to an empathic response. An empathic recognition that an action has caused harm can lead to remorse. A feeling of remorse can influence a response to that harm or an intention not to cause similar harm in the future.

Rationalizations

In addition to the four influences, another process is at work. When people perceive that they have done something wrong or want to do something they know is wrong, they likely will feel guilty—unless they can rationalize their actions in some manner.[2] All people are willing, under certain circumstances, to waiver from their personal values and standards. People appear to have an internalized limit about how far they are willing to waiver and under what conditions they will waiver.

But when people make a decision to engage in an action that is contrary to their personal values and standards, this leads to "cognitive dissonance"—a contradiction between what they think is right and what they plan to do. To alleviate the anxiety caused by this cognitive dissonance, they tend to create excuses or rationalizations for why what they want to do is okay. Some common rationalizations are

- "I won't get caught." There is an extremely limited chance or no chance of detection and punishment.
- "It didn't really hurt anyone." The action will not cause any perceptible harm to anyone else.
- "Look at what I got." The harm may be perceptible, but is small in comparison with the personal benefit.
- "It is not a real person." The harm is to a large entity, such as a corporation, and no specific or known person will suffer any loss or harm.
- "Everyone does it." Many people engage in such behavior, even though some may consider the behavior to be illegal or unethical.
- "They deserve it." The entity or individual that is or could be harmed by the action has engaged in unfair or unjust actions.[3]

Impact of Information and Communication Technologies

The Internet, and other information and communication technologies, can have a profound impact on the external influences of behavior and rationalizations.

You Can't See Me

When people use the Internet they have the perception that they are invisible. In fact, people are not totally invisible when they use the Internet. In most cases, they leave "cyberfootprints" wherever they go. But despite this reality, the perception of invisibility persists. Some actions using technology are relatively invisible, such as borrowing a friend's software program and installing it on your own computer. It is also possible to increase the level of invisibility with the use of technology tools that can mask your identity or simply by using an anonymous username. Establishing an account with an anonymous username enhances invisibility. The fact that many people may be engaged in a similar activity also leads to a perception of invisibility, because individual actions are such a "drop in the pond" they likely will not be detected.

When people perceive they are invisible online, this takes away their concerns about detection, which could result in disapproval or punishment. If detection and punishment are unlikely, then threats of punishment will not have much impact on online behavior. The perception of invisibility online also makes it far easier to rationalize inappropriate behavior. As noted earlier, one of the ways people rationalize doing something they know is wrong is by thinking, "I won't get caught." The misperception of invisibility is implicated whenever teens post material that could damage their reputation online—they may think no one knows who they are even if it is really quite obvious.

The concern of the impact of invisibility on human behavior is not new. Quite a few years ago, and well before the Internet, Plato raised this very same concern in a story called "The Ring of Gyges." In this story, a shepherd found a magical ring. When the stone was turned to the inside, the shepherd became invisible. Thus the question was raised: How will you choose to behave if you are invisible?

The invisibility factor presents a dilemma for parents. There are very good reasons for young people to be anonymous on the Internet. Children and teens should always use anonymous usernames in all public Internet environments. This is an important self-protection strategy. Because of this, parents have to address a direct conflict: actions that are deemed necessary for personal safety reasons could enhance the perception of invisibility and thus the perception of the freedom to engage in irresponsible behavior.

An essential Internet parenting strategy is to remove your child's misperception of invisibility with respect to your oversight of online activities. Make sure that your child knows that you will be paying close attention to online activity and that there is a high probability that you will detect any inappropriate online actions. But most important, encourage your child to make good choices based on personal values regardless of the potential for detection, disapproval, or punishment. Here is what you can say to your child:

> You are never truly invisible online. If you do something really wrong, there are ways that the people who have been harmed can find out who you are. The actions you take online can have very damaging consequences. You should know that I intend to pay attention to what you are doing online, because that is my responsibility as your parent. But, most important, you should think about what your online actions say about the kind of person you are.

I Can't See You

When people use technology, there is a lack of tangible feedback about the consequences of their actions on others. This lack of tangible feedback undermines an empathic response and feelings of remorse. It also makes it easier to rationalize an inappropriate action. If there is no tangible feedback that an action has caused harm, then it is easier to rationalize that no harm has actually been caused. The lack of tangible feedback of harm also interferes with the recognition of possible self-harm. This is another factor that is implicated in incidents in which teens post material on social networking community sites that is clearly damaging to their reputation or self-interest.

If your child has done something online that has or could have caused harm to another, the consequence you impose should be designed to focus your child's attention on the harm caused or the potential for harm caused by his or her action. Requiring your child to remedy any harm caused to another can be an effective disciplinary consequence.

> Your actions online could cause harm to others. But since you cannot see or hear other people when you are online, you might not be able to tell that you have hurt someone. Or you might not pay attention to how your actions might be harmful to you. It is always very important to think about the possible consequences of your actions on others and yourself while you are online.

It Wasn't Me

During adolescence, teens are inclined to play out different roles and identities.[4] This facilitates their development of a core sense of their own identity. Internet technologies significantly enhance the ability to create and experiment with multiple identities. Many teens create different "personas" that allow them to assume different personalities and even different genders. There is nothing wrong with creating an online "persona" to explore different aspects of personality. Character creation is a standard practice in online role-playing gaming environments. Teens may also create different "personas" on social networking sites or in chat rooms.

The ability and inclination of teens to maintain multiple identities on the Internet provides the basis for a new rationalization to support irresponsible or harmful online behavior that should be added to the earlier list of common rationalizations:

- "It wasn't me, it was my online character. I can deny responsibility for actions taken by one of my online characters."

Here is how to discuss this with your child:

> When you are online, you might want to pretend to be someone else. Regardless of who you are pretending to be, make sure that your online actions are not causing real harm to real people.

It's Just a Game

Within many online games, the objective is to harm others. Of course, it is one thing to harm another person's character within a game and quite another to engage in an activity, such as cyberbullying, that might harm a real person. Activity in online gaming communities may provide the basis for yet another rationalization:

- "Life online is just a game. I haven't really hurt anyone, because it is all just a game and they are just game characters."

To address this with your child, use the following explanation:

> It is okay to create a character for a role-playing game and for that character to engage in hostile activities, if this is part of the game. But make sure you recognize the difference between online games and other online activities that involve real people. It is not okay to cause real harm to real people you are interacting with online.

Everybody Does It

People tend to gravitate to certain online group environments. The social norms of these groups may vary widely. Although the influence of in-person social cues might be diminished, it appears that most online groups create their own social norms for behavior within the online community. In some online environments, the social norms support irresponsible online behavior. This supports the "everyone does it" rationalization. Discuss this with your child as follows:

> Sometimes other young people and adults engage in unsafe or irresponsible behavior online. You might think it is okay for you to do the same thing, because they are. You need to make decisions about online actions based on our family's values and the standards we have discussed for your online behavior.

·19·

Why We Believe What "They" Say

SOCIAL INFLUENCE TECHNIQUES ONLINE

One important foundation for making safe and responsible choices online is ensuring that you are, indeed, the one who is making the choice and that someone else has not influenced you inappropriately. Our society is awash with individuals and organizations that seek to influence our attitudes and behavior.

It is helpful for parents to have a better understanding of the ways in which others can influence the attitudes and behavior of their children and even themselves.[1] Sometimes influence can have a very beneficial impact—for example, influences that have encouraged recycling, energy conservation, racial tolerance, and the like. The positive parenting strategies presented in this book can be considered social influence techniques. But sometimes these powerful influence techniques can be used unethically to manipulate your child.

All of the Internet risks and concerns are grounded in the negative impact of social influence. Dangerous online strangers frequently use these techniques. They have their own online discussion groups in which they provide each other with suggestions on seduction techniques. Internet commercial advertisers work closely with child psychologists in the development of effective strategies to influence children and teens to purchase products or services and to stay on sites for a long period of time. Young people often use social influence techniques with each other.

Empower your child with the knowledge of how social influence works, skills to resist such influence, and a fierce commitment to act in accord with family and personal values—and to not be swayed by those seeking to influence attitudes and behaviors in the wrong direction. Be highly alert to incidents that occur in everyday life that demonstrate social influence techniques and discuss these incidents focusing on the types of strategies and techniques that can be used to resist each strategy. This is not a one-time lesson. Repeated focus is necessary. The payoff of this will affect your child's choices not only online but also in "real life." So many of the concerns about the behavior of teens—drinking, sex, drugs, reckless driving—all involve the negative impact of social influence.

The following are highly effective social influence techniques that have been identified through extensive social science research.

Rule of Reciprocity

The rule goes like this: if someone gives you something—a gift, a favor, or a concession—you have an obligation to give something back to that person. The rule of reciprocity triggers the feeling of indebtedness, which requires a return. This rule is an extremely strong norm in human culture. In fact, the "golden rule," which is a component of every major religion, is grounded in the principle of reciprocity.

Obviously, there are many socially beneficial impacts of this rule. But because this rule is so strong, people seeking to intentionally influence others in a direction that is not safe or responsible have a powerful tool to use. The rule of reciprocity works even if the person receiving something did not expect or ask for the gift or favor. Have you received a solicitation for a donation that included a "gift" of address labels? Organizations soliciting donations know that there is a significantly higher rate of return if they include such a gift. Sometimes the rule stimulates a return that is greater than the value of the original gift or favor. When people feel obligated to return a gift or favor, this creates an uncomfortable feeling of indebtedness to another. The person who has given the gift or favor may ask for something in return that is of greater value than what was given.

The rule of reciprocity functions at a very subconscious level. Your child should be able to recognize when this rule is at work, especially when someone is seeking to use this technique to influence attitudes or behavior in a wrong direction. To defend against the unethical use of this technique, it is necessary to be consciously aware of gifts, favors, or concessions that are made. Many times there is no malicious intent to influence. Such gifts or favors can be accepted in good faith, and a return may be made in good faith. But if it appears that the person who is offering the gift, favor, or concession is doing so in an unethical attempt to influence behavior or to take advantage, the knowledge of the intention behind the gift can be used to cancel the feeling of obligation or indebtedness.

This principle is clearly at work on social networking sites when friendship links are established. Users will receive a message from someone that states something like, "[Person's username] wants to be your friend. Do you accept or reject?" Having been offered a "gift of friendship," any teen who has received such a message will likely feel very bad if he or she rejects the request for friendship. But your child must always be aware that this gift of friendship might be from someone whose values and standards are simply not acceptable or safe. It is not wrong to deny a friendship link to, or later remove a friendship link from, someone who might not be safe or might have unacceptable values. Sexual predators or hate group recruiters frequently use this principle by sending a gift that will influence a child to feel that something must be provided in return.

To discuss this with your child, explain as follows:

> Sometimes people who are trying to manipulate you may
> give you something, like a gift. Or that person may do a
> favor for you. If someone gives you something, you naturally
> feel like you should give something back. But if the gift was
> given in an attempt to manipulate you into making a bad
> choice, this cancels any obligation you might feel.

Commitment and Consistency

People have a strong desire to act and think in ways that are consistent. Consistency is valued because it leads to trustworthiness—a person who is consistent can be trusted to act in certain ways under certain conditions. Being consistent is also convenient. If we always respond in a certain way to a certain situation, then there is no need to take the time to figure out how to respond.

People are strongly influenced to be consistent with a commitment they have made. If a person makes a commitment, takes a stand, or expresses a position, then that person is extremely likely to act in accord with that expressed commitment, stand, or position. This is true even if the circumstances that led to the original commitment have changed.

The commitment and consistency technique provides the foundation for the positive impact of a parent-teen Internet use agreement. Having your child make a commitment, especially a commitment expressed in personal words, to engage in safe and responsible behavior online can be very effective in encouraging behavior consistent with that commitment. Reminding your child of this commitment on a regular basis will reinforce the power of this influence technique.

If your child engages in an action that is contrary to any commitment that was made in the agreement, you can use the commitment in a very influential manner: "You made a commitment to me that you would always treat other people online with respect. But this posting demonstrates that you have not treated [name] with respect. I expect that you will abide by the commitments you have made with respect to Internet use. Now, how are you going to fix this situation?"

To resist unethical manipulation grounded in commitment and consistency requires paying attention to the clues our body will give us that something is not right—a "gut reaction" that someone is trying to influence us in a direction in which we really do not want to go.

Seeking commitment is a manipulation technique that sexual predators use very frequently. Early in the relationship, the predator will encourage the victim to make a commitment of trust. He will ask, "You trust me, don't you?" A child is very unlikely to respond to this question by saying, "No, I do not trust you." This would be rude. Once the predator has solicited from the child a commitment of trust, the predator will later use this commitment as a vehicle for manipulation. If the predator seeks to push the child out of a comfort zone and the child is resistant, the predator will remind the child of the prior stated commitment, "But you said that you trusted me." When reminded of this prior commitment, the child is likely to feel a strong obligation to be consistent to this prior commitment.

Another extremely dangerous way in which commitment and consistency can influence harmful behavior is in the context of unsafe communities—groups of young people who are promoting suicide, self-harm, hate, gang activity, violence, or any other dangerous or illegal activity. A commitment to the social norms of the group can influence behaviors in accord with those norms—including self-harm, suicide, violence, and murder.

Here is how to explain this to your child:

> Sometimes people will try to get you to commit or agree to something and then later use your commitment or agreement to manipulate you into doing something that is unsafe or irresponsible. Someone might ask you, "Do you trust

me?" Then later this person will ask you to do something that does not feel right and remind you of your commitment of trust. This will make you will feel like you have to demonstrate that trust. Other times you might be in an online group and express agreement with what others think. Later, you might feel that you have to go along with activities that the group thinks appropriate because you made a commitment to this group.

The way you can tell that it is wrong to act in accord with a commitment you have made is to pay close attention to how you feel inside. If you have a "gut reaction" that something is wrong, be sure to pay attention. Your decision about whether an action is a good choice or a bad choice should be based on what you think now—not on a commitment or agreement you made in the past.

Social Proof

People are influenced by what other people think and do. This principle demonstrates the influence of social norms. Social proof—or going along with "group think"—works best when there is some level of uncertainty or ambiguity in the situation. People are also much more inclined to go along with others whom they perceive as being similar. To reduce susceptibility to "group think" requires independence of mind and the willingness to make decisions based on an honest appraisal of the situation—not on what others think.

Social proof influence factors are alive and well online. Teens post sexually provocative images, because this is what others are doing. Teens collaborate with each other to engage in cyberbullying, because it is okay to say whatever you want online. Teens stay up well past midnight surfing, gabbing, and gaming online, because that is what all of their friends are doing. All of the unsafe online communities function in harmful ways, because of the contagion of "group think." Commercial advertisers use the social proof technique for online marketing, especially "viral marketing."

Here is a way to address this issue:

> Sometimes groups of people, especially teens, can make bad choices. If you are in a group that has made a bad choice, you likely will feel that you should go along with the group. If you are in a group that wants to go in one direction and your "gut" is telling you that this is a bad choice, listen to your "gut" and take a close look at the situation. You might need to get away from others to think about this on your own to make the right choice. Don't do what others are doing just because they are doing it. Make your own choices based on our family values.

Liking

People are more influenced by others whom they like. There are many factors that go into a consideration of whether or not a person is likable. We like people who are physically attractive, those we perceive are like us and share our interests, and those we have known for a long time under favorable circumstances. We also like people who give us praise, make us feel good about ourselves, and make us think that they care about our interests. If we like someone, we are far more inclined to comply with a request from that person. This is fine, if the person deserves our good opinion and is making an appropriate request.

Predators make significant use of this principle of influence. They have an in-depth understanding of youth culture, research an intended victim's profile, and, not so surprisingly, indicate that they share many of the same interests as the victim. They also seduce victims through frequent use of praise: "You are so wonderful. I am so happy I met you."

The Internet provides the ability to "image manage"—to create an online image that is very attractive. This can create the presumption of trustworthiness. Individuals, as well as many companies marketing products and services online, can use these principles to establish an online image that is "likable"—and thus influential. Many people rely on the visual appearance of Web sites as the primary determinant of credibility—if the Web site is attractive, then the information must be credible. This is a technique that can result in deception. Share the following thoughts with your child:

> You have to be careful about appearances online. If you are communicating with someone who seems to share lots of your interests and says lots of nice things to you, be careful. This person may be trying to seduce or manipulate you. Also, watch out for appearances when you consider the accuracy of information on a Web site. Judge the accuracy based on the quality of the information, not simply on appearances.

Authority

People are very likely to comply with requests or demands from a person in a position of authority. Our society would not operate effectively if some level of deference to authority were not one of the prevailing norms. Unfortunately, sometimes deference to authority can lead us in a very bad direction. There are two key questions that one can ask to assess the appropriateness of deference to someone asserting authority to seek compliance, to appear credible, or to influence attitudes or behavior:

- Is this authority truly an expert? Is there independent evidence of this person's expertise and credibility?
- How truthful can we expect this expert to be? What does this person have to gain by our compliance or approval? Is there any evidence of self-interest?

Indicators of authority are an exceptionally important aspect in assessing the credibility of information presented on Web sites. Predators and hate group recruiters often assume a position of authority to aid in their grooming or recruitment of a young person.

You can discuss this with your child as follows:

> It is important to be respectful of all people online. But it is also important to pay close attention if someone appears to be an expert or an "important person" who is trying to convince you to do something. Always take the time to investigate and make your own decision about someone's authority and credibility. Is this person trying to convince you that something is right, or good, when your "gut reaction" is that something may not be right?

Scarcity

People think something is more valuable if it is less available or if restrictions may be imposed. The "something" could be a product or any type of opportunity. The scarcity principle is grounded in two factors. When something is more difficult to attain, it typically is perceived to be more valuable. Also if something is less available, the freedom to have it may be lost. Advertisers make full use of this principle to promote sales: "Only a limited number." "Offer ends soon." "Get it now, before it is too late." "Offer good for today only."

The scarcity principle has an interesting impact in the teen years. For many teens, if restrictions are placed on engaging in a certain action, engaging in the action frequently becomes much more desirable. Efforts to manage teens' access of pornography through the use of filtering software frequently backfires by creating an increased inclination to seek the "forbidden material." Parents should remain mindful of the scarcity principle in seeking to guide their child's Internet use. Ensure that your child understands the reasons for any restrictions and, when appropriate, how to earn the right to have certain restrictions lifted.

Scam artists use a version of the scarcity principle in an effort to get people to provide personal financial information through identity theft schemes. Many identity theft email messages threaten some kind of a loss: "We have been reviewing our accounts and think that there has been an unauthorized attempt to access your records. We will be forced to limit your access to your account unless you update your records here: <link>." This kind of "you will lose" message is known to be effective in influencing people who do not even have an account with the particular institution to provide personal financial information.

Web sites strive to ensure that they are "sticky," that children and teens will stay for a long time and return often. Many of the strategies Web sites use involve variations of the "scarcity" principle. Users perceive that they will lose something—game points, status, opportunity to participate—if they are not frequently present on the site.

The scarcity principle is also very present in online role-playing gaming environments. Because the game is ongoing, if the user leaves the game to attend to other life matters, something will be lost. It will be "too late" to participate in whatever event occurred in the game while the user was gone. Also, often in the playing of an online game a series of actions are necessary to achieve a higher level. If a player plays for a period of time and then quits before reaching a new level, then all of the effort made during that playing session is lost. The scarcity factor fuels gaming addiction.

Online scams also often employ the scarcity principle. "Act now, and you might win this [name of offered prize]." One of the key warning signs of a probable scam is the implementation of the scarcity principle threat of loss of an opportunity to encourage action without thinking.

It is hard to defend against the scarcity principle. If we think we are going to lose something, we get upset. When we are upset, our brain does not think as clearly. One protection technique is to pay attention to when something is making us feel like we are going to lose out and take another look at the situation.

Explain this as follows:

> If you feel like you are going to lose something, it frequently makes that something seem even more important than it

really is. Sometimes when you are online it will seem really hard to leave because you think you are going to lose something—like an opportunity to communicate with a friend or participate in a game move. This can make you feel as though it is really important that you stay online. Whenever you feel like you are going to lose something and this makes you feel like you have to take some action to make sure that you do not lose, take a good look at the situation. Are you really going to lose something? Is what you are going to lose all that important?

· 20 ·

Looking for Love in All the Wrong Places

YOUNG PEOPLE WHO ARE AT GREATER RISK ONLINE

For many different reasons, some children have a harder time growing up than others. Differences in brain chemistry, learning challenges, developmental concerns, past and present family conflict, and other biological, family, and external influences can all have an impact on a child's path to adulthood. For some, this leads to a situation in which a child is considered "at risk." At *risk* is a term social service workers and educators apply to children who for one reason or another are struggling with challenges to their wellbeing and appear to be likely to have even greater difficulties in the future.

A young person may be consistently at a high level of risk. Or a young person may not generally be "at risk," but may be temporarily going through a period of heightened "teen angst" because of a significant event, such as the breakup of a relationship, parent divorce, and the like.

It is critically important to understand that if your child is facing significant challenges, on either a continuing basis or temporarily, then he or she is at even greater risk online. All humans crave companionship and acceptance. Children who, for whatever reason, do not have healthy relationships and do not feel accepted in the "real world" will be inclined to seek out online connections and communities in which they will feel accepted. And this can lead to greater danger online.

In addition, young people who are "at risk" are almost always dealing with some emotional trauma. When young people process emotions, they do so using the "fight or flight" part of their brain—which makes it impossible for them to engage in rational decision making. An "at risk" child's online decision making is likely to be very impaired. "At risk" young people

- Are more vulnerable to those who might seek to manipulate or seduce them. This includes sexual predators and recruiters for hate groups or gangs.

- Are more vulnerable to attack by cyberbullies and less resilient in responding to such attacks.

- May become connected with other "at risk" young people, and become part of an unsafe online community. Within a community of "at risk" young people, there is sharing of dangerous or unhealthy attitudes and support for unsafe or irresponsible behavior.

- Are more likely to become addicted to Internet pornography, gaming, and gambling.

An assessment of the degree to which your child might be "at risk" will help to guide your approach to Internet parenting. This requires an assessment of four aspects of your child's life:

Internal Personality Traits or Life Experiences. Reflect on your child's personality traits and life experiences. Is your child happy, emotionally secure, and well-adjusted? If so, your child is likely at a lower risk online.

Alternatively, is your child dealing with any kinds of emotional, behavioral, or learning difficulties? Does your child seem depressed or withdrawn? Is your child frequently angry? Is your child ever violent? Is your child deceitful or manipulative? Does your child appear to lack motivation? Does your child show signs of being sexually promiscuous? Does your child show signs of using drugs or alcohol? Does your child's appearance or dress reflect emotional challenges? Has your child ever expressed thoughts of suicide or self-harm? Does your child appear to have a low perception of self-worth? Is your child addressing questions regarding sexual orientation? Has your child been diagnosed as having attention deficit disorder, autism traits, bipolar disorder, depression, anxiety, or any other similar disorder? If you answered "yes" to many of these questions, then your child is likely at higher risk online.

Family Relationships. Reflect on the quality of your child's relationships with you, any other parent or adult in the household, and any siblings. Is the quality of these relationships secure and supportive? Young people with secure family relationships are likely at lower risk online.

Alternatively, are there any concerns present? Does your child have difficulty meeting your expectations regarding rules and behavior? Do you frequently have arguments with your child? Is your child verbally abusive toward you or any other family members? Do you have difficulty getting your child to perform expected household chores? Does your child engage in activities you do not approve of? Have there been any recent major upsets or challenges within the family environment, especially any losses such as a divorce or death in the family? Young people who are facing challenges within the family environment are likely at higher risk online.

School Performance and Relationships. Reflect on your child's school performance and relationships with school staff. Is your child performing well in school? Does your child feel supported and welcomed by the teachers and within the school community? If your child has any learning challenges, is the school proactively addressing these challenges and is your child comfortable with the progress? Young people who are successful in school are likely at lower risk online.

Alternatively, is your child struggling and frustrated? Are your child's grades of concern? Does your child frequently have disciplinary problems at school? Does your child perceive the school to be a hostile and unwelcoming environment? If your child is struggling with school performance and relationships, this presents a situation in which he or she might be at higher risk online.

Friendships and Other Relationships. Reflect on your child's friendships. Does your child have good friends from families whose values are in accord with your own? Are your child's friends emotionally stable, and do they appear to be making good choices? Does your child regularly get together with friends to engage in healthy activities? Young people with healthy friendships with other young people who are also emotionally stable and make good choices are at lower risk online.

Alternatively, is your child a loner without any close friends? Is your child frequently being bullied by other students at school? Are any of your child's close friends "at risk" due to internal personality factors, home relationships, or school difficulties? Do you have concerns about the emotional well-being of your child's friends or about their choices? What is the possibility that your child's friends might be inclined to engage in inappropriate online activities—and possibly pull your child along? If you have concerns about the quality of your child's friendships or the emotional stability and values of your child's friends, then your child is likely at greater risk online.

Life is a process. Unfortunately, uncontrollable things might have happened along the way that may have created a situation in which your child is more "at risk." If your assessment is that your child currently is in a state that would be considered "at risk," then when it comes to Internet use, it is essential that you recognize the high potential for concerns and remain vigilant. This includes placing strict time limits on use, placing limits on approved activities, and engaging in highly consistent monitoring of online activities.

There is one "silver lining" to this situation. If your child is having difficulties with friendships or is struggling with some personal issues, there are online support services offered by professional social service organizations that might be able to provide assistance. These online services may offer professionally moderated discussion groups, an opportunity for teens to join a supportive community. Teens who have difficulties fitting in with other teens can experience excellent support in these online support groups. Through such online experiences, your child can gain insight and strength to address issues in the "real world." Or your child might simply find some new friends online who are truly safe and supportive. Be sensitive to the fact that this might occur. You might even search for a service such as this and try to guide your child into participation. If your child has become associated with a positive support group, carefully gauge your monitoring of online participation to ensure that you are not being overly intrusive.

Obviously, addressing the underlying factors that are placing your child "at risk" is also very important. Ask your school counselor or a community resource center for assistance.

If your child is emotionally secure, has strong family relationships, is doing well in school, and has good friends, then he or she is at a much lower risk online. Your child is also in a situation in which he or she could provide tremendous help to other young people. Teens participate with each other in online environments. They are far more likely than adults to witness situations in which other teens make unsafe or irresponsible choices. Teens are much more inclined to consult with, and listen to, other teens in all areas of decision making, especially when addressing any decisions about Internet use.

Encourage your child to recognize situations in which another teen might be making a bad choice online. Your child could seek to communicate with this person and try to explain the risks to him or her. Advise your child that if this intervention is unsuccessful or if your child does not have a relationship that would support such a communication, it is extremely important to report such concerns to you or to another responsible adult. Downloading any evidence of risky or irresponsible online behavior would be very helpful.

Responsible teens have prevented other teens from becoming entangled with online sexual predators, provided assistance to teens who have been targeted by cyberbullies, prevented possible suicide, and prevented violent attacks at school by disclosing the online evidence of these situations to responsible adults.

·21·

On the Net, What You Do Reflects on You

CORE VALUES AND STANDARDS ONLINE

The previous four chapters discussed key issues that affect the ability of children and teens to make safe and responsible choices online. As has already been discussed, parents should not expect younger children to independently make safe and responsible choices and must "hold their hand" by using controlled access and communications to ensure that their Internet use is safer. This chapter provides guidance on specific strategies that parents can use while their children are younger, and especially as their children move into the teen years, to encourage the values and standards necessary to support safe and responsible online choices.

The Challenge

Young people do not have sufficient brain development to independently and consistently make safe and responsible choices—but it is essential that they practice making these choices to develop the capacity to do so. When young people use the Internet, the lack of tangible feedback can interfere with their ability to understand the consequences of their online actions, and the perception of invisibility and online social norms may create an environment in which they are less attentive to risks, values, or the potential of detection. Further, there are powerful social influence factors in operation online that could be used to inappropriately influence young people to make unsafe or irresponsible choices. And children who are already more "at risk" are more vulnerable online.

Laying the groundwork for your child to independently engage in safe and responsible online behavior starts in the "real world" with a strong focus on imparting values and standards, and decision-making strategies that are likely to reinforce those values and standards.

- Focus your child's attention on the reasons for the values and standards you have established. Actions that violate the values or standards can cause harm to yourself or others. The primary focus must be on the benefits that following those values and standards will achieve or the potential harm those values and standards seek to avoid. These can be expressed both in the positive and the negative. "Treat others with respect because they will be more inclined to treat you with respect." "Don't [describe action] because you could harm someone by [describe the possible harmful impact]." By focusing on the reasons for the values and standards, you can help your child better internalize those values and standards.

- Help your child learn to do what is right in accord with his or her own personal values and standards and your family's values and standards—regardless of the potential for detection and punishment. Shift your focus away from rules and threats of punishments to an emphasis on values and standards, the reasons for those values and standards, and the importance of acting in accord with values and standards at all times. The message "Don't do this because it is against the rule" has limited impact when children perceive they are invisible and their actions will not be detected or punished.

- Help your child understand how actions can cause harm to people they cannot see by helping him or her learn to gain the perspective of unseen others. Whenever you are discussing situations involving other people, especially those who are not present, ask your child, "How do you think that person might feel?" This will help your child gain greater skills in predicting probable consequences and feelings of others.

- Help your child learn to use ethical decision-making guidelines when faced with a situation that calls for a decision to be made about responsible online actions. Questions that encourage a focus on ethical values and standards include

  - Is this kind and respectful to others?
  - How would I feel if someone did the same thing to me, or to my best friend?
  - What would my mom, dad, or other trusted adult think or do?
  - Would I violate any agreements, rules, or laws?
  - How would I feel if my actions were reported on the front page of a newspaper?
  - What would happen if everybody did this?
  - Would it be okay if I did this in person, or in the "real world?"
  - How would this action reflect on me?

- Help your child learn to identify rationalizations as excuses for irresponsible behavior. Listen carefully for these common rationalizations when your child attempts to explain or excuse unsafe or irresponsible behavior. Identify the rationalizations for what they are.

- Make sure that your child knows the challenges of making a safe or responsible decision when emotionally upset. Explain this in terms of brain processing. A decision made when angry or emotionally upset is highly likely to be the wrong decision.

A helpful guideline is "If you are mad or sad, keep your fingers off the keyboard."

- Challenge the unhealthy values and standards that are raised as you go about your life in the "real world." Our children and teens are constantly being bombarded with extremely harmful messages—frequently through advertising and entertainment media. Parents must constantly be aware of and challenge these unhealthy values and standards. The fact that advertisers and the entertainment industry are trying to convince your child that the only acceptable standard for girls is to be skinny, cute, and sexually attractive to boys and the only acceptable standard for boys is to be strong, virile, and sexually attractive to girls does not mean that these are the values that your child must accept.

If I Can Do It Online, It Must Be Okay

Some young people view the Internet as a vehicle that supports anarchy—"If I can do it online, it must be okay." There are some important external sources of limits on online behavior that should be emphasized to your child. These include family values, religious or spiritual values, school rules, terms of use agreements, civil law standards, and criminal laws. All of these external sources of limits are quite consistent in regards to what is considered responsible and irresponsible behavior.

Ultimately, the most important limit is your child's internalized personal values. The teen years are the time when your child is developing internalized personal values that he or she will use to guide decision making throughout the rest of life. Paying attention to your child's internalization of values is probably your most important job during his or her teen years.

The "Parent-Teen Internet Use Agreement" in Appendix A is based on values and standards. The approach seeks to emphasize to your child that these are not simply "Internet safety rules" that they are supposed to follow. This agreement is all about honoring one's personal values and standards.

Family Values

What are your family's values? Make a commitment to live in accord with these values and teach these values to your child. Emphasize to your child repeatedly that your family's values should guide all online activity. The following are some possible family values that relate to Internet risks and concerns. They are presented in terms of both the value and the contrary online social norm.

- Personal privacy—when others seek to know all or encourage you to tell all
- Respect—when others condone or encourage disrespect of others
- Modesty and restraint—when others flaunt promiscuous sexuality
- Responsible consumption—when others promote excessive consumption and the need to have it all
- Peaceful resolution of conflict—when others glorify, promote, or resort to violence
- Hard work—when others promise a "free lunch"
- Self-protection—when others encourage taking risks
- Care and concern—when others glorify "me first"
- Search for truth—when others seek to mislead and coerce
- Balance—when others promote excess
- Responsible behavior—when it might appear that cheaters win

Religious or Spiritual Values

Religious and spiritual teachings can be used as a basis for judging whether or not an action is considered to be appropriate. The world's primary religions or spiritual traditions all endorse a version of the "Golden Rule"—treat others as you want to be treated.

If your family is strongly religious or spiritual, an extension of the work done to complete the "Parent-Teen Internet Use Agreement" would be to discuss the specific religious or spiritual standards that apply to the Internet risks and concerns. This is also an exercise that could be done within a religious or spiritual youth group meeting. This would combine the power of reliance on religious or spiritual teachings with peer pressure—a potent social influence strategy that combines the influences of authority, social proof, and commitment and consistency.

School Rules

When students use the Internet at school or through the school district Internet system, even if accessed from home, they have an obligation to follow the rules set forth by the school in the school's Internet use agreement. School policies are set forth as "rules." Remember, an important component of your strategy is to ensure that your child understands the reasons for the rules. Take the time to review the Internet use agreement for your child's school, and for each rule, ask your child to describe the reason for that rule.

Terms of Use Agreements

Internet service providers, Web sites, and cell phone companies place controls on the material and communications transmitted through their technologies or posted on their sites. The sites all have a document that is referred to as "Terms and Conditions," "Terms of Use," or simply "Terms" that outlines the agreement between the site and users. Generally, terms of use agreements prohibit harmful speech, other actions that do or could harm others, copyright infringement, violating someone's privacy, and the like.

When your child registers on a new site, take the time to download the terms of use agreement and review its provisions with him or her. This is a good way to reinforce that your family's values and your expectations for your child's online behavior are similar to the rules that have also been established by the site. Take the time to discuss the reasons for the provisions in the terms of use agreements and note how similar these provisions are to your family's values.

Civil Law Standards

There are several civil law standards related to some types of irresponsible online behavior that are important for you and your child to be aware of. Your child should understand that parents can be sued if their children engage in truly harmful online activities, including copyright infringement, cyberbullying, and computer security violations. This knowledge should guide your child's online decision making. It is also important for you to understand that if someone truly harms your child online, litigation to recover financial damages and to stop the harmful actions is possible.

Parents can be held liable for the harm caused by their minor child under the theory of negligent supervision. In some jurisdictions, specific laws provide that parents are legally responsible for acts of intentional harm caused by their minor child. The fact that parents can be held liable for harmful actions of their children is one reason why parents should make it their business to know what their child is doing online. The civil law standards outline an important "line in the sand" for what our society considers highly inappropriate.

The legal standards that apply to harmful online speech include

- Defamation—publishing a false statement that damages someone's reputation
- Invasion of privacy—publicly disclosing information about another person's private life or affairs, when the effect would be highly offensive to a reasonable person
- Intentional infliction of emotional distress—intentionally or recklessly engaging in actions that are outrageous and intolerable and have caused extreme distress

- Copyright infringement—downloading copyrighted material, generally entertainment media
- Computer security violations—causing damage, generally financial, by engaging in a security intrusion of a computer system (also a violation of criminal law)

Criminal Laws

Other countries and jurisdictions have laws that could be applied to cases involving online harmful actions. Common criminal laws that could involve online actions include the following:

- Making threats of violence to people or their property
- Engaging in extortion or coercion—trying to force someone to do something they don't want to do
- Making obscene or harassing telephone calls, which also includes text messaging
- Harassment or stalking
- Hate or bias-based crimes
- Gang-related activity
- Creating or disseminating material considered "harmful to minors" or child pornography
- Sexual exploitation
- Taking a photo image of someone in a place where privacy is expected
- Sale of an illegal item or substance
- Computer security violations

Teachable Moments

A "teachable moment" is any situation that provides you with an opportunity to impart information to your child related to values, standards, and decision-making strategies. A teachable moment is a door that opens, sometimes very briefly, that can allow you to more casually influence the development of ethical values and effective problem-solving skills. Be continuously on the lookout for these moments to discuss issues related to online risks and concerns.

A teachable moment may emerge when your child engages in a new online activity. For example, if your child wants to find some information or a new site online and you are conducting a search, the process of analyzing the search returns provides a teachable moment to discuss safe searching strategies. The process of reviewing the site to determine whether or not it meets your family's standards can provide a teachable moment to discuss a wide range of issues, including the appropriateness of certain online activities and the kinds of advertising and other commercial-related activities evident on the site. Registering on a new site provides a teachable moment to discuss privacy protection in the context of site registrations, to discuss making smart choices with respect to agreeing to receive commercial advertisements, and to review the "Terms of Use" agreement.

A teachable moment may also arise when you have to make a difficult decision in the "real world"—especially one involving an ethical dilemma. It can be very helpful for a child to witness your thinking and your actions when presented with a situation in which you have to choose between right and wrong. Talk about these situations with your child, explore your own thought processes regarding ethical decision making, and ask his or her opinion.

Often teachable moments related to Internet risks and concerns will emerge in the context of some form of news or entertainment media. Pay close attention to any news stories about issues related to Internet risks and concerns. It is strongly recommended that you subscribe to *NetFamilyNews*, a weekly email newsletter that provides insight into current events related to children, families, and the Internet, at http://netfamilynews.org. This newsletter will significantly increase your awareness of news stories that can serve as teachable moments. You can say to your child, "I saw an article today that addressed concerns of [describe story]. What do you think? How would you handle this kind of a situation?"

Be especially attuned to any comments that your child might make about what has happened online. Your child may want to discuss an online event with you, but may not be sure how you are going to respond. In general, many young people are very afraid of an adult overreaction to any discussion about online activities, particularly a discussion related to online activities of potential parental concern. The response to any subtle comment about a witnessed online event should be equivalently subtle, but seek to continue the dialogue so that you can learn more about the situation and turn your discussion into a teachable moment.

Very significant teachable moments are any time that your child has had a bad experience online or if you feel it necessary to place restrictions on Internet use due to inappropriate behavior. A bad experience or the need to remedy the harm caused by a bad choice provides an opportunity for your child to learn why what happened was not appropriate and to use this knowledge to avoid making the same mistake in the future. This is precisely the way that we grow and learn. But this kind of teachable moment can only be effective if your child thoroughly understands what was wrong, why it was wrong, and how to make better choices in the future.

Teachable moments provide the opportunity to practice effective value-based problem-solving techniques. Here are some problem-solving questions:

- What is the situation? What issues does this situation raise? What are the risks and concerns? What values are implicated? Who is involved and what are their personal interests? Does anyone involved in the situation appear to be inappropriately trying to influence someone else? What are the possible actions and the possible outcomes for each of these actions? If there is a conflict between good choices or if there are only difficult choices, which choice has the greatest possibility in leading to the best possible outcome for all concerned?

- If discussing a situation that has occurred, what choices were made, by whom, and why? What was the outcome and was this outcome good or bad? What other choices were possible and what were the possible outcomes of those choices? Why might one of those other choices have been better or worse?

Part Four

•

SPECIFIC RISKS
AND CONCERNS

·22·

Sex and the Internet

RISKY SEXUAL ONLINE ACTIVITIES

Jake's buddies like to hang out at his house on Friday night, eating pizza and playing video games. Jake's mom had to run some errands and so left Jake and his friends alone. Andy, Jake's friend, had been doing some explorations of his own online. As soon as Jake's mom left, he encouraged the others to see what he had found. The young men spent the next hours looking at some of the pornography sites Andy had discovered.

Cheryl, age thirteen, a demure cheerleader at a religious school, had established a Web site titled "Sexy Me for You to See" on which she had posted many sexually provocative images of herself, hinting that other images were available. Under the username "2hot2handle" she frequently visited chat rooms in which she interacted with men who were interested in getting together with her. Cheryl frequently would arrange to meet with a man on a Friday night. She would meet these men at the mall. Her aunt, with whom she was living, took her to the mall thinking that she was hanging out with friends. On one Friday, the man she was having sex with accidentally killed her. Her friends knew about her site and activities.[1]

Ebony, age eight, is doing a school report on what she wants to be when she grows up. Ebony currently wants to be a cheerleader. She has written a nice paper and now wants to add some pictures of cheerleaders. She goes to Google Image and types in "cheerleader."

Anna has a major crush on Ben, a fellow student at her high school. Using her Web cam, she created a sexually suggestive video of herself, which she sent to Ben. Ben promptly showed the video to his friends and is sharing it through peer-to-peer networking.

Teens who are actively communicating on the Internet must be prepared to effectively handle the risky sexual issues that will arise. It is impossible to ensure that online environments that allow for interactive communications with strangers will ever be entirely safe. Web sites can take actions to reduce the potential for harmful interactions, but there are millions of young people online. Parents should never expect that these Web sites can effectively baby-sit their children. Preventing your child from engaging in risky sexual behavior and becoming involved with an online sexual predator is your responsibility.

As will become evident throughout this chapter, when addressing online sexual issues, some of them are safety risks—situations in which a young person is at risk of being victimized by another. This includes adult predators, who may groom a young person to engage in sexual activities or to provide pornographic images; accidental access of pornography; and receipt of sexual harassment. But other examples involve responsible online activities—situations in which young people engage in behavior that is risky, irresponsible, harmful, or even illegal. These situations include intentional addictive access to pornography, seeking sexual "hook-ups" with adults or other teens, engaging in sexual harassment, posting or sending sexually provocative or explicit images, and publicly discussing or sharing images of sexual exploits.

Parents will bring different values to a consideration of these issues. For some, looking for safer sex information or exploring information about sexual identity may be considered unacceptable. Others may consider a limited amount of exploration of online pornography and engagement in cyberdating to be expected teen behavior that does not raise significant concerns. On the critically important issues—sexual predators, child pornography, and teen involvement in sexual "trolling"—there is likely to be much greater unanimity of opinion among parents.

It is important to have a clear understanding of your personal values, the reasons for your values, and a commitment to act in accord with your values. And it is very important to discuss your values with your child. Also, expect that your child will challenge your values from time to time—just like you probably did as a teen. Listen carefully to your child whenever you are dealing with a situation in which your values are in conflict. Keep in mind that all teens are exploring their emerging sexual identity—this is what teens do. It can be expected that some, perhaps much, of this exploration will occur online. If parents overreact to the discovery of casual exploration, this is likely to prevent effective use of such incidents as teachable moments to have a parent-child discussion about healthy sexual values.

Recognize that excessive teen involvement in risky sexual behavior online is generally a symptom of deeper problems. Teens (and adults) who have social or emotional difficulties that are impairing their ability to form emotionally secure relationships with significant other people are at high risk of becoming involved with online risky sexual activities. If "at risk" teens become involved in online risky sexual activities, this can have a spiral-of-decline effect, with the online risky sexual activities now also contributing to the underlying social or emotional difficulties.

Ensure that your child can resist the anticipated peer pressure to become engaged in online risky sexual activities. Pay attention to the values and emotional stability of your child's friends and the parents of those friends. If there are members of this group whom you think might be inclined to pull the group into more excessive online sexual involvement, this should raise concerns. How can you strengthen your child's resistance if someone else is pulling in a direction that is not a good direction? If your child is involved in an "at risk" group, are there ways that you can help him or her form new friendships?

If your child is not accepted within a healthy group of friends, this should be considered a key "red flag" that your child may seek acceptance from others online—and those others could very well be dangerous adults or dangerous other teens. Teens who do not have healthy friendships are easier to manipulate and seduce sexually. Helping your child become engaged with a stable group of friends from families who share your values should be a high priority.

Basic Parenting Strategies to Address Online Sexual Risk

With younger children, the focus must be on establishing safe on-line environments. This includes ensuring they can only access sites that have been previewed and their online communications are limited to known, trusted individuals. For teens, engaging in risky sexual activities is not likely to occur when there is a chance for adult detection. Therefore, effectively monitoring your child's online activities and ensuring that your child knows you are paying attention is the best deterrence.

If you do not think your child is developmentally ready for an in-depth discussion about the issues discussed in this chapter, then your child is not ready to participate in any public online communications forums. Most students are introduced to sex education around the age of eleven. Most young people will also want to engage in expanded online activities around this time. So this would seem to be an appropriate time to start discussions about online risky sexual behavior. You absolutely must review all of these risks and concerns in depth with your child prior to the age of thirteen.

Research Findings Related to Sexual Risk Online

An August 2006 survey by the Crimes Against Children Research Center of online youths ages ten to seventeen addressed issues of unwanted access to sexual materials and sexual solicitations.[2] This was a repeat of a study that was done in 2000.[3] The 2006 study revealed that one-third of the young people surveyed had been exposed to unwanted sexual material. This was an increase from the one-fourth of young people who reported they had been exposed to such unwanted sexual material in 2000. The increase in exposure occurred despite the fact that there was a significantly increased use of filtering software in the home—55 percent of home computers had filtering software as compared with 33 percent in 2000. The study attributed the increased level of exposure in part to aggressive tactics by pornography marketers and the increased speed and capacity of computers and Internet connections to transmit images. The researchers noted that the findings called for a closer analysis of strategies to address unwanted exposure, given that reliance on filtering has not achieved desired results.

It is important to note how this unwanted exposure reportedly occurred. When questioned, the young people reported making mistakes in clicking on links without a clear understanding of where the link would go, mistyping the URL for Web sites, opening suspicious email, and being "porn-napped"—a programming technique that takes viewers to a site containing pornography when what they wanted to do was to leave the site. All of these concerns can be addressed through increased education about strategies to avoid such unwanted access.

The study further found that a smaller proportion of young people who used the Internet had received online sexual solicitations, only one in seven in 2005 compared with one in five in 2000. Sexual solicitations were defined as requests by peers or adults to engage in sexual activities or sexual talk or to give out personal sexual information. More specifically, 70 percent of those reporting the sexual solicitation were girls and 30 percent were boys, 81 percent were older than fourteen, and only 3 percent of eleven-year-olds were solicited. Only 4 percent of the young people reported that the incidents had left them feeling very or extremely upset or afraid. In 43 percent of the cases, the sexual solicitor was another teen.

In more than half of the solicitations, a request was made for a photograph, and in 27 percent of the incidents, the request was for a "sexual" photograph. In 15 percent of the incidents in which the solicitor requested a sexual photo, a sexual image of the solicitor was sent to the young person.

Most young people, 66 percent, handled the situation by removing themselves from the situation, blocking the solicitor, or leaving the Web site. Other strategies included telling the person to stop or simply ignoring the person. In 56 percent of the cases, the young person did not tell anyone about the solicitation.

The report attributes the reduction in solicitations to more cautious behavior by young people. They found that fewer were going to chat rooms or interacted online with people they did not know. Interestingly, the reduction in sexual solicitations occurred despite the significantly increased amount of time that young people are spending online.

The facts that the rate of sexual solicitation appears to be going down, young people appear to be taking better steps to protect themselves, and many appear to have effective strategies to respond to such solicitation are good news. It is also very important to understand, though, what this survey does, and probably does not, inform us. As noted, the prior 2000 study revealed that one in five young people had received a sexual solicitation—defined by the researchers as essentially an unwanted sexual communication. Unfortunately, the results of this study have been widely disseminated throughout the media and in Internet safety materials. The statement commonly made is "One in five young people have been sexually solicited online." Most people upon hearing this statement assume that this means that one in five young people are approached by a adult sexual predator under circumstances that presented clear danger to the young person. This assumption is clearly not justified by an analysis of the data.

In both of these studies, the vast majority of the so-called "sexual solicitations" came from other teens. Were these studies measuring communications related to online sexual predation? Or did many or even most of the reported incidents involve sexually harassing behavior that is unfortunately common among teens and young adults?

The study also failed to provide any evidence of an established connection between an "unwanted sexual communication" and the phenomenon of online sexual predation. Do online sexual predators generally initiate their interactions with "unwanted sexual communications?" If a communication is by definition "unwanted," how could this communication lead to a dangerous situation? As will be addressed further on, predators who are seeking to groom vulnerable teens are far more likely to initiate the communications with overly friendly messages, rather than unwelcome messages. Clearly, more research insight is needed.

Online Pornography

There are several issues related to the risks of online pornography, including limiting accidental access, limiting intentional access, risks related to creation of pornography, and teen creation of pornography.

Limiting Accidental Access to Online Pornography

Effective strategies can be used to reduce the possibility of accidental exposure to such materials, including establishing safer places for younger children and teaching effective search, Web access, and email-handling techniques. Most important, children and teens should know how to rapidly respond to any accidental exposure to limit the potential damage of such exposure.

One important step to take is setting the search preferences in the browser you use to implement the "safe search" features. However, this feature will definitely not provide much, if any, protection against any intentional efforts to access pornography. When your child is not present, try a test using "hot, teen, sex" with the safe search feature selected. But on other searches that are more innocent, the safe search feature may provide some level of protection against accidental access.

Image searches are much more problematical. Try a search on a term that you can imagine a very innocent eight-year-old girl using: *cheerleader*. Try this with and without the safe search engine on. The advantages of the safe search feature become more apparent with this search. Still, images are very difficult to categorize. It is very likely that image searches will always present more difficulties. Fortunately, the images are small and a quick finger on the back-button can help to limit exposure. Over-the-shoulder monitoring of children who are conducting image searches, with your finger on the back button, would be a wise precaution.

Make sure you do not allow peer-to-peer networking software to be installed on your computer. Peer-to-peer software makes a portion of the computing capacity and the files stored on a computer available to other individuals throughout the world who are using the same peer-to-peer software. In 2004, the U.S. Congress, General Accounting Office, released a study on the presence of pornography distributed through peer-to-peer networking.[4] The GOA learned that

> Child pornography is easily found and downloaded from peer-to-peer networks. . . . Juvenile users of peer-to-peer networks are at significant risk of inadvertent exposure to pornography, including child pornography. Searches on innocuous keywords likely to be used by juveniles

(such as names of cartoon characters or celebrities) produced a high proportion of pornographic images: in our searches, the retrieved images included adult pornography (34 percent), cartoon pornography (14 percent), child erotica (7 percent), and child pornography (1 percent).

Installation of peer-to-peer networking also presented concerns related to copyright infringement and security. The combination of these three risks makes the presence of this technology on any family computer ill advised.

Follow the guidelines and rules for children in Chapter Three of this book to reduce the possibility of exposure to adult material and to ensure that if accidental access occurs, children know how to respond quickly to reduce harmful exposure. As tweens and teens expand their boundaries of use on the Internet, it is time to use teachable moments to help them develop safe search skills, so that they can learn to independently avoid inadvertent accessing of pornography. In the context of discussions of how to avoid inadvertently accessing such material, you can convey your values about intentional access. The following are guidelines to impart to your child:

> When you search for information using a perfectly appropriate term, the search results could lead to inappropriate sites. Carefully read the site description. Only click on a link if you are absolutely sure it will be okay to go to this site. If you can't tell for sure, either don't click or ask my guidance.

> Some people try to trick kids into accessing sites with inappropriate material by using URLs that are similar to the URLs of the sites you might want to access. To avoid mistakes, never type a URL. It is too easy to make mistakes. Go to a search engine and type in the name of the site. Then read the site description to make sure you have the right site. Bookmark the site if you want to return.

If you conduct an image search on a perfectly appropriate term, it could lead to inappropriate images. Make sure the safe search feature of the search engine has been activated. If you see anything inappropriate come up, quickly click on the back button.

Some sites with inappropriate material trap users with many pop-up windows or by disabling the back button. If you are trapped, force-quit the browser, restart the computer, or turn off the screen. Tell me, so that I know what happened and can check the computer also—and also I will then know that you did not try to access this site intentionally. [If this happens more than once, your computer may be infected. You should seek technical assistance.]

Some email messages may contain pornography or links to pornography. Look carefully at the sender and subject line before opening any email. Never click on a link in an email message even from a friend, unless you are absolutely sure it is safe. If you have any questions, let me review the message.

Limiting Intentional Access to Online Pornography

As noted earlier, all teens are exploring their emerging sexual identity, and it can be expected that some, perhaps much, of this exploration will occur online. In addition, this is an area in which parental values may vary. Some parents may perceive that some limited explorations are to be expected and, if kept to a minimum, acceptable—other parents may not agree. Limiting intentional access requires a strong focus on transmitting your healthy sexual values to your teen—as well as keeping the computer in a public area and making sure that your teen knows that you are regularly checking the history file.

Intentionally looking at online pornography may occur when your child is "hanging out" with friends. This may take place at your house or a friend's house. You might want to prohibit Internet use when your child's friends are over or make it clear to your child that you will always look at the history file of the computer after any time that he or she and friends have been online. Make sure you discuss such standards with the parents of your child's friends.

The greatest concern with respect to intentional access is when a teen crosses the line from normal curiosity to excessive access. An inclination to access such materials in an excessive manner indicates some significant emotional or personal difficulties. Professional intervention may be required.

Preventing Victimization by Child Pornographers

It is highly probable that children and teens who are being sexually abused by someone from within their social environment are now also being further abused by the creation and dissemination of images recording such abuse. It is imperative that all responsible adults who have any relation with a child or teen be sensitive to the possibility that the child or teen may be sexually exploited. Signs to watch out for include changes in emotional stability and behavior, sleep disturbances, acting out in inappropriate sexual ways, fear of people or activities, pain or injury to private areas, and subtle hints of concerns about certain people. Young people who are exploited in such a manner may be very reticent to talk because they have been warned that dire consequences will occur to them or to a loved one if they tell.

If you have access to the computer that a person suspected of sexually exploiting a child has used, conduct a search for image files—those with names ending in .jpg, .tif, or .gif. If you find any inappropriate images, immediately call your local police and do not let anyone else use the computer.

Teen-Produced Child Pornography

A disturbing concern related to online child pornography is the involvement of teens in producing and distributing pornographic images of themselves or their friends. Sometimes teens are seduced by adult child pornographers into providing such images. They may be enticed by suggestions that they are so "attractive" or "beautiful" that they could have a career in modeling or movies. Or they might be offered money or a gift in exchange for images. Very frequently, the pornographers will use a step-by-step grooming process that involves requesting gradually more revealing images, in exchange for increasingly more valuable "gifts." They are expert manipulators. They appear to be "equal opportunity" seducers—they are interested in images of girls or boys. Sexual seduction techniques will be discussed in depth in the next section.

Teens who post sexually provocative images of themselves on their social networking site profiles, use sexually provocative usernames, and openly discuss sexual interests and activities in their blogs or in discussion groups are "advertising" their potential availability and interest in such activities. But even teens who do not post such kinds of material could be contacted by a child pornographer and must know how to detect and respond to such contact. A message that expresses the opinion that your child is very beautiful or could become a model, and other statements focusing on physical beauty, could very likely be from a child pornographer. The key "red flags" are a request from someone for an image that is just slightly more revealing than the images the child has posted online or the offer of a gift in exchange for another image.

Some teens appear to be setting up a kind of business, in which they post erotic or explicit images or offer to appear on Web cams in exchange for "gifts" that admirers can purchase for them online. Conduct a search for "Web, cam, teens." Some teens were likely seduced into these activities by child pornographers, but others appear to see this simply as an opportunity to make money. One significant news story on this issue that you can use as a teachable moment is a disturbing article in the New York Times, titled "Through His Webcam, a Boy Joins a Sordid Online World."[5] The article is available through the New York Times archives and on other news Web sites that republish *New York Times* articles (search on the title). This article should be considered a "must read" for any teen prior to using any online communications environments in which contact with strangers is possible.

The production and dissemination of sexually explicit images may also occur in the context of cyberdating or sexual trolling, which are discussed later in this chapter. Teens do not appear to recognize that the sexy video they just sent to an online admirer can easily be uploaded to peer-to-peer networking or shared via email with child pornography collectors throughout the world. Teens who engage in cybersex using Web cams are also very vulnerable. Either party in the transaction could keep a permanent record of the images and share this with others.

It is likely that for some young people, continuous exposure to images of "hot stars," including the sexually provocative images on the covers of far too many magazines at the grocery store check-out lane, are influencing attitudes about the desirability of presenting oneself in this manner. If you look at the images that many teens, especially teen girls, post of themselves on social networking sites, they bear close resemblance to the photos on these covers. Given the fact that these images are so readily present on your trips to the grocery store, this should provide you with ample teachable moments to discuss issues related to such images. Also pay attention to the entertainment media you allow your child to watch or you find your child watching. Young people who watch sexually provocative media are more likely to perceive that these kinds of images or presentations are desirable and appropriate.

Prior to allowing your teen to register on any social networking site, look around the site with your child at the images and information other teens have posted. Evaluate the social norms that seem to be present on the site. Determine the degree to which your child might be able to use the site and be shielded from exposure to other teens or adults whose social norms are not compatible with yours. Ask your child to talk to you about his or her personal standards concerning the kinds of images and information that should be posted.

The general guidelines of keeping the computer in a public place in the house, limiting use when you are not present, conducting a regular search for graphics files, and monitoring the sites where your child goes online are important ways to help address these concerns.

Give your teen the following guidelines for sharing images and other information online:

- Never post any information or images or use a username that would lead someone to believe you would be willing to provide sexually provocative images.

- Remember that relationships break up. Take care in any personal relationship not to disclose any information or provide any images that would be embarrassing if disseminated to others.

- The production and dissemination of sexual images of yourself or your friends is a violation of laws against creation and dissemination of child pornography.

- Contact from a pornographer could be direct or very subtle. If any online stranger ever asks for a picture or offers you something for a picture, do not respond, or respond by stating, "Leave me alone."

Tell your child that it is exceptionally important to save all communications from any individual who asks for images or other inappropriate information *and* to inform you. You and your child should report this contact to the Web site and to law enforcement or the Internet reporting agency in your country. The fact that your child has recognized and avoided falling for the advances of a child pornographer should be heartily applauded. But it is also exceptionally important to take these abusers out of action so that they cannot harm other children.

Online Sexual Predators and Pornographers

The Internet has provided a vehicle for predators and pornographers to connect with each other in online "support communities"—providing support for the idea that sexual engagement between children and adults is desirable. Digital imaging technologies allow pornographers to easily create pornographic images, which they exchange within these communities. Predators and pornographers also have the opportunity to share their seduction techniques and brag about their conquests. High social status in these communities is measured by the size of a person's pornography collection, the number and degree of outrageousness of the images shared, and the number of sexual conquests reported.

Although there is no clear data on this, these kinds of online interactions may be leading to increased sexual abuse by abusers who have an already existing personal relationship with children or teens—father, uncle, mother's boyfriend, parent's friend, neighbor, teacher, coach, club leader, or religious leader. The related concern is the degree to which these predators and pornographers are seeking connections with young people, generally teens, online.

Types of Predators

Predators are almost always men. There appear to be two general types of online sexual predators: groomers and trollers. Predatory groomers proceed more slowly, seducing more naïve teens through a process of becoming online friends and ultimately leading to sexual seduction. Predatory trollers troll through sites, groups, and chat rooms seeking teens who already have provided signs that they might welcome sexual contact from an adult, such as sexually provocative images or usernames, or participation in chats or discussion groups related to sexual activities. These relationships tend to proceed rapidly. Rather than two separate types, this may actually be a range of behavior. Unfortunately, at this time, there is insufficient research to really understand how much of what kind of behavior is going on.

Addressing the issue of predatory groomers with teens who are not "at risk" requires making sure that teens have a good understanding of the standard grooming techniques and know how to respond and report such contact. "At risk" teens are far more vulnerable and also are much less likely to pay attention to this kind of safety information or to demonstrate effective safety skills. They may want to meet with adults for sex because they perceive this will address an important need. It is essential to address the underlying social and emotional difficulties that are placing that child "at risk" and to ensure that their Internet use is more effectively monitored.

A peer-intervention approach also could help to stop the victimization of more vulnerable teens. Teens are more aware than adults when these predation situations are occurring. Knowledgeable and competent teens who know that other teens are making bad choices could either try to address the issue with the other teen or report their concerns to an adult.

Insight into Predatory Relationships

Researchers at the National Center for Crimes Against Children conducted a study of Internet-related sex crimes against children.[6] This research was based on data obtained from law enforcement officials in 2001–2002. The researchers evaluated the facts about arrests of predators and reported the following:

- The victims were young teens, ages thirteen to fifteen. (The age of consent is sixteen. This does not mean that older teens are not being seduced. It is just not a crime. But note from the younger age that predators appear to be targeting teens, not children.)
- Seventy-five percent of victims were girls. Twenty-five percent of victims were boys.
- Ninety-nine percent of the offenders were male. The vast majority of offenders were much older than their victims.

- Most first encounters happen in chat rooms, including chat rooms on sites oriented to teens, focused on geographic locations, dating and romance sites, and sites for gays. Some offenders appeared to have conducted research on the victim by reviewing the victim's online profile. (This research is from prior to the explosive growth in activity on social networking sites.)

- Most offenders spent some time developing the relationship and used multiple forms of communication, including the telephone. Many offenders sent pictures or gifts to the victims. (Note: given the time it took for predators to form these relationships, these kinds of predators would fall into the category of predatory groomers.)

- Deception about sexual motivations was rare. Most offenders openly sexually solicited the victims. The victims knew they were interacting with men who were interested in them sexually.

- The victims went willingly with the offender and most met with the offender more than once. Violence or threats of violence were rare.

- After the arrest, half of the victims described themselves as being in love with or good friends with the offender. (This appears to indicate that the other half of the victims willingly went to have sex with men who they were not in love or good friends with.)

The researchers speculated that it was probable that some teens are more vulnerable to the manipulation of predators due to poor relationships with parents, loneliness, and depression. Unfortunately, the researchers did not seek insight into the initial behavior or intentions of teens when entering the chat environments or communications with these predators. How many of these teens went to these locations and intentionally initiated or responded to communications with the intention of engaging in sexually oriented discussions with adult men? Visits to some chat rooms yield strong evidence that such risky teen behavior is common.

A key concern noted by the study was that current Internet safety messages are not based on an accurate understanding of these online sex offenses and are widely ignored and seen as unrealistic by young people. The researchers also felt that it is highly probable that the vast majority of such incidents have not been reported.

Teens Attracting Predators

Predatory trolling involves interactions between predators and teens who are demonstrating by their own online actions that they are inclined to welcome such contact. Teens indicate their inclinations by posting provocative images or other information, using sexually suggestive usernames, and engaging in discussion groups or chat rooms in which people are generally engaged in making connections for sexual interactions. Any time spent looking at profiles on social networking sites will result in seeing many profiles of young people who appear to be advertising their sexual availability.

An illustrative story is an Associated Press news story from October 2005.[7] Under legal pressure, Yahoo agreed to remove approximately seventy thousand user-created chat rooms with names that promoted sex between young people and adults. Chat rooms included those with names such as "girls 13 & up for much older men," "8–12 yo girls for older men," and "teen girls for older fat men." Many of these chat rooms were located within the "Schools and Education" and "Teen" chat categories. An undercover investigator, posing as a fourteen-year-old while visiting one of those chat rooms, received thirty-five personal messages of a sexual nature over a single twenty-five-minute period.

It really does not require a high level of "smarts" on the part of a teen to figure out what the topic of discussion might be in chat rooms such as these. While it is necessary to increase detection and prosecution of predators, it is also absolutely critical to start holding teens accountable for their own actions—and for parents to pay attention to the places their children are visiting online.

Teen Willingness to Meet with Predators

Examples of predatory trolling in the United States that demonstrate the problem of teen willingness to meet with adults for sex have been shown on a series by the *Dateline* news show called "To Catch a Predator."[9] The *Dateline* show set up stings with men who thought they were making arrangements to meet a teen to engage in sex—only to find themselves being interviewed on camera and then arrested. More information and the videotaped interviews with the predators are available online.

It is very important to note that the arrangements for the sexual encounters were made within a very short period of time. The predators did not show any signs of suspicion when the teen was so readily willing to meet for sex. This suggests that this kind of online behavior of teens may be common. But there is insufficient data available to fully understand this issue.

There also is insufficient research to fully understand the motivations of teens who are responding in a positive manner to online predators. Clearly these teens are searching for a relationship connection that they perceive to be missing. For some, there may be social status issues involved—being perceived as sexually desirable by men may raise their social status within their own social group. Young men who are sorting out sexual orientation issues may think this is a way to do so. It is possible that some teens have a misperception that by engaging in this activity, they will meet an incredibly handsome man for a very romantic interlude.

Predatory Grooming or Trolling Techniques

All teens need to know how sexual predators seek to groom potential victims so that they can recognize the signs if they are contacted—or if a friend is being groomed. The following are the typical steps and stages in a predator grooming relationship.[10] Predators may take a longer time going through these steps, or may attempt to move more quickly, especially if the teen appears inclined to welcome such contact.

- *Initial Friendship Formation.* Predators "lurk" in public communication environments seeking to identify teens who meet their interests and who are communicating in a way that leads the predator to think that they can be seduced. Predators take the time to review material posted in profiles and in public conversations, so that they can seek to establish a "friendship" based on mutual interests. Signs of vulnerability a predator looks for include images posted by a teen that are sexually suggestive or other information that suggests a sexual interest. Predators also are likely to notice signs that a teen is currently experiencing some social or emotional difficulties, is having problems with family or friends, and the like. Discussing intimate information in public places is a "red flag" indicating vulnerability.

- *Risk Assessment.* Early on, a predator is likely to ask questions about where the teen's computer is located, who else uses the computer, and how closely parents supervise computer use. He is seeking to determine the risks that the relationship with the teen might be detected. If someone asks questions like this, the best response your teen can make is, "Our computer is in the family room, everyone uses the computer, my parents pay close attention to what I am doing online, and I like to introduce them to my online friends." If the person makes a quick exit, the person likely had dangerous intentions.

- *Trust and Secrecy.* Next, the predator will take steps to seek to become the teen's "secret online friend." He will seek to ensure that the communications are private. He will say things like, "You are so wonderful." "I am so lucky to have met you." "You can talk to me about anything." "I understand what you are going through." "I will always be your friend." The predator may provide gifts, to stimulate the feeling of obligation. The predator also will encourage the teen to commit to him a level of trust: "You trust me, don't you?" This is a very important step in the seduction process. Once the teen has articulated a level of trust, at any later time if the teen becomes hesitant, the predator will remind the teen of this prior commitment.

- *Sexual Grooming.* Once trust and secrecy have been established, the predator will start talking about sexual issues. His desire in these efforts is to encourage the teen to view him as a "sexual mentor."

  - He may seek to convince the teen to provide him with sexually provocative photos or video images. Frequently, this proceeds in careful stages, with requests for photos and images that are more and more revealing. He may offer to pay the teen or provide gifts in exchange for such photos and images. Or he may provide a gift and then indicate that the teen owes him something in return. These images are then often shared with other predators and child pornographers.

  - The predator may also send the teen sexual images of other teens engaged in sex with adults. The predator may then talk about self-touching and suggest certain techniques. He will talk about how wonderful he could make the teen feel if he were present in person. He will seek to engage the teen in discussions of fantasy sexual encounters. Sometimes, these discussions can go back and forth between seduction and threats, especially if the teen becomes reticent. "I love you"—"Keep this a secret or I will show others the pictures you sent me." The predator specifically will seek to make the teen feel guilty or fearful of reporting the relationship to someone or of discontinuing contact. Eventually the predator will seek to meet with the teen to engage in sex.

Prevention Strategies

Give your teen the following information to help him or her avoid sexual predators:

- Putting sexually suggestive photos or information in a profile or using a sexually suggestive username is an "advertisement" to predators.

- Joining chat rooms or groups in which sexual issues are being discussed and presenting yourself as a teen could lead to contact of a sexual nature by predators.

- Sharing intimate information and discussing social or emotional difficulties in public communication forums may attract the attention of a predator. This suggests to the predator that you are vulnerable and would therefore be more willing to accept him as an online "friend."

- Predators do not fall in love with victims—they use victims. They are not "mentors" or "romantic partners." They are abusers and *losers*.

- The predator is likely to be discussing his grooming activities with other predators. If a teen gets into an argument with one predator, it is possible that another predator, who has online contact with the first, may try to establish a relationship.

- Any sexually suggestive or explicit image or video provided to the predator most likely will be distributed to other predators and child pornographers throughout the world.

- Meeting with the predator may result in forced engagement in risky sexual activity. There is a very high danger of sexually transmitted diseases. There have been reported cases of abduction and murder.

If you are not comfortable fully discussing the facts about sexual predators with your child, then do not let him or her participate in public communication environments. Your child clearly could be contacted by a predator online in any public communication environment and must know how to recognize and respond to such a situation. If your prepared child is contacted, rather than feeling fear and distress, he or she most likely will feel pride at being able to recognize and respond safely and effectively. And because you have discussed these issues together, your child also will be more likely to report the contact to you, which will enable you to investigate further.

The online material provided by *Dateline* can provide a valuable teachable moment. Most teens have a strong desire to avoid any affiliations with people who are considered "losers." Look at the videos of these captured predators. The word *loser* is the most obvious word that comes to mind. In their online communications with teens, these men presented an image of strength and desirability— an image that clearly fell apart when they were on camera. A joint viewing of some of these videos could be highly influential. Be sure to use the word *loser* very frequently. Then go and visit some of the teen profiles on social networking sites that these "losers" are likely to find attractive.

If your child is showing signs of questioning his or her sexual orientation, find an organization that provides information and support for parents, such as Parents and Friends of Lesbians and Gays (www.pflag.org). Gay or questioning teens, especially boys, who feel they do not have or will not have parental support are likely at very high risk for predation. Assist your child in becoming involved in a high-quality online support site for lesbian, gay, bisexual, or transsexual teens offered by a professional organization.

Make it totally safe for your child to report any suspicious contacts to you. The most important step to accomplish this is for you to open the discussion about sexual predatory behavior well in advance of any time when your child might receive an inappropriate contact. Frequently, Internet safety instruction provided to teens omits any discussion of the sexual intentions of online sexual predators. This instruction uses statements such as "the predator will harm you" or the predator "wants to form a special relationship." Then the curriculum advises teens that if they "ever receive a communication that makes them uncomfortable, they should tell an adult." If adults are so uncomfortable having discussions with teens about sex and sexual predation, then how do they expect that teens will be comfortable reporting to an adult that someone online is sending them sexually inappropriate material? Adults must open the communication channel.

Your child's greatest fear will be that you will blame him or her, overreact, and insist that a desired online activity is "off limits." The farther your child has "walked down the path" with a possible predator, the more likely there will be hesitancy to let you know about this—especially if your child has engaged in any actions that you would consider inappropriate. Do some up-front prevention to address this concern. Indicate that these predators can be very tricky, and can use powerful influence techniques to encourage teens to do things that they would not otherwise do. Promise your child that you will never impose a punishment as a consequence of a report about a possible sexual predator—regardless of the behavior your child has engaged in. This is part of your commitment in the "Parent-Teen Internet Use Agreement."

Tell your child that if there are suspicions that someone may be a predator, it could be dangerous to raise any concerns in communications with that person. The predator could shift to more stringent self-protection techniques—including suggesting the possibility of harm to your child or family members if his actions are reported. A high priority should be placed on ensuring this person's arrest and prosecution. If the predator is not informed, a police officer can take over the communications, playing the role of your child, and gain better evidence to ensure imprisonment. This is the best approach to protect your child—and other possible victims.

Warning Signs

The following are warning signs that could indicate your child might be involved with an online sexual predator:

- Becoming distanced from members of the family, especially parents
- Receiving gifts from someone unknown to the family
- Receiving or making telephone calls to someone unknown to the family
- The presence of child pornography on the computer
- Sexualized behavior
- Dropping "subtle hints" of concern about new online friends
- Unexplained absences

Intervention

If you suspect or find evidence that your child is involved with a predator:

Do Not

- Confront or discuss this with your child. Predators work very hard to disrupt the relationship between their victims and their parents. Because your child might have developed a warm relationship with the predator, your child could warn the predator, take steps to remove implicating material from the computer, or run off with the predator.
- Confront or make any contacts with the possible predator. This will alert him to your concerns and allow him to take steps to vanish.
- Let anyone, other than a law enforcement officer, conduct further investigations on your computer.

Do

- Contact law enforcement and ask for the youth or computer crimes expert.

Teen Sexual Trolling

The promotion of promiscuous teen sexuality is rampant—through music, movies, television, magazines, clothing, advertisements, and the Internet. Even if you limit access to such media, the parents of your child's friends may not. The promotion of promiscuous sexual behavior is evident in many social networking and other teen sites. Part of the problem is that these sites are attracting tweens, who really should not be participating on such sites, as well as teens and young adults. For tweens and teens, there are strong influences to act older than they really are—and a major part of acting older is related to sexual behavior.

Some teens post provocative information about themselves in profiles, as well as provocative images. Online contests on some sites allow teens to judge others based on how "hot" they are. Some teens openly and explicitly discuss their sex lives in teen discussion groups. Some teens regularly use chat rooms, social networking sites, or online matching services to meet others who want to engage in cybersex. Some teens use the Internet to meet other teens who live within a reasonable commuting distance to arrange for "hook-ups"—commitment-less, in-person sex. In the context of forming such online and off-line relationships, teens use digital cameras, cell phone cameras, and Web cams to produce and send sexually suggestive or explicit pictures of themselves.

For some teens, their profiles on social networking sites are used for demonstrating their sexual attractiveness, and friendship linking is a mechanism for trolling. There appears to be a competitiveness component to these activities. Some teens seek to demonstrate their social worth by the number of links to other "hot" teens, young adults, or older adults. This can translate to competitiveness in numbers of sexual hook-ups.

Before you allow your child to participate in any environments in which this kind of behavior might be evident, visit some of these sites together. Discuss how the behavior demonstrated by some teens online is leading down a very unhealthy, unhappy path. Listen closely to your child's reactions and responses to the behavior of their friends and comment positively on all expressions of more healthy values. Work with the parents of your child's best friends, find teen and social networking sites where this kind of online behavior is not as prevalent, and encourage the group of friends to set up their "home base" on such sites.

Safer Cyberdating

As teens get older, they very likely will see the Internet as a way of meeting people with whom they might form a significant friendship or relationship. Online cyberdating has become part of the way our society functions. For an older teen with healthy sexual and relationship values who has demonstrated a history of safe and responsible online behavior, cyberdating should not present concerns. Cyberdating may not be appropriate for younger teens.

There is actually a key advantage to cyberdating—the initial stages of relationship formation involve significant communication, which is the foundation for a healthy relationship. When your child becomes a young adult and moves out of the house, he or she is very likely to engage in cyberdating, so allowing your older teen to do so while you are closer by provides you with the opportunity to impart good values and skills.

Strategies to assess the relative safety and trustworthiness of online strangers were discussed in Chapter Sixteen. These strategies are all highly relevant in the context of safe cyberdating, especially the guidelines for a safe first meeting.

Friends Don't Let Friends . . .

Teens can play an important role in addressing the dangers to all teens presented by pornographers and predators, as well as risky sexual behavior of other teens. Teens are more likely to be present in the online places where such dangers are possible than are responsible adults. Encourage your child not only to be responsible for his or her own safety and behavior online, but also to think about helping friends safely navigate cyberspace.

- Friends don't let friends get involved with online predators. Your child's friend may talk about an online relationship with someone whom your child may suspect is a predator. If your child has a good understanding of the predator danger detection skills and appropriate responses when dealing with a suspected predator, he or she can provide very helpful guidance to this other child. However, if the friend is continuing the relationship, your child should report concerns to you or to a counselor or school resource officer. If your child reports to you, report this problem to a counselor, to a school resource officer, or to law enforcement. If your child can identify the online sites in which these interactions are occurring, it will be very helpful to the authorities.

- Friends don't let friends post sexually provocative material online. Posting such material is asking for trouble. Talking with the child who has posted such material might be the first step. Otherwise, you or your child should download this material, noting the URL, and, depending on the circumstances, provide this material to a counselor, school resource officer, or the parents of the child who has posted the material. This material can be provided anonymously, if your child is afraid of possible negative consequences.

- Friends don't let friends take risks in meeting with an online stranger. If your child finds out that a friend is planning to meet with an online stranger, your child can review the steps for meeting with an online stranger described in this book with the friend. Your child might also be the trusted friend who is present for such a meeting. Make sure that your child knows that you must be informed in advance of any plans to be present when your child's friend meets with an online stranger. Make sure that you approve of all arrangements.

·23·

I Can Say
What I Want Online

CYBERBULLYING AND SOCIAL AGGRESSION

Matt reported to the principal that students were bullying another student. When Matt got home, he had thirty-five angry messages in his email box. The anonymous cruel messages kept coming—some from total strangers.

Laura watched closely as Emma logged on to her account and discovered Emma's password. Later, Laura logged on to Emma's account and sent a scathing message to Emma's boyfriend, Adam.

Greg, an obese high school student, was changing in the locker room after gym class. Matt took a covert picture of him with his cell phone camera. Within seconds, the picture was flying around the cell phones at school.

When Annie broke up with Garrett, he sent her many angry, threatening, pleading messages. He spread nasty rumors about her to her friends and posted in a sex-oriented discussion group a sexually suggestive picture she had given him, along with her email address and cell phone number.

Sue was really angry at Kelsey, who she thought stole her boyfriend. Sue convinced Marilyn to post anonymous comments on a discussion board slamming Kelsey. Marilyn was eager to win Sue's approval and fit into her group of friends, so she did as Sue requested.

A group of girls at his school had been taunting Alan through instant messaging, teasing him about his small size, daring him to do things he couldn't do, suggesting the world would be a better place if he committed suicide. One day, he shot himself. His last online message was, "Sometimes the only way to get the respect you deserve is to die."[1]

Unfortunately, there are increasing reports of teens using Internet technologies to post cruel text or images to bully others or engage in other cruel behavior. Cyberbullying is being cruel to others by sending or posting harmful material or engaging in other forms of social cruelty using the Internet or other digital technologies. Cyberbullying can take different forms, including the following:

- *Flaming.* Online "fights" using electronic messages with angry and vulgar language
- *Harassment.* Repeatedly sending offensive, rude, and insulting messages
- *Denigration.* "Dissing" someone online; sending or posting cruel gossip or rumors about a person to damage that person's reputation or friendships
- *Impersonation.* Breaking into someone's account, posing as that person and sending messages to make the person look bad, get that person in trouble or danger, or damage that person's reputation or friendships
- *Outing and Trickery.* Sharing someone's secrets or embarrassing information or images online; tricking someone into

revealing secrets or embarrassing information, which is then shared online

- *Exclusion*. Intentionally excluding someone from an online group, such as a "buddy list"
- *Cyberstalking*. Repeatedly sending messages that include threats of harm or are highly intimidating; engaging in other online activities that make a person afraid about personal safety

Research Findings About Cyberbullying

Two 2006 research studies revealed the extent to which young people are being cyberbullied:

- Fight Crime: Invest in Kids reported the results of a survey of a thousand youths in the United States.[2] Their key findings were that one third of all teens, ages twelve to seventeen, and one-sixth of all children, ages six to eleven, had mean, threatening, or embarrassing things said about them online. Ten percent of the teens and 4 percent of the children were threatened online with physical harm. About half of the children told their parents, but only 30 percent of teens told their parents. Forty-five percent of the children and 30 percent of the teens indicated that the cyberbullying occurred at school.
- The Crimes Against Children Research Center's 2006 survey of young people between the ages of ten and seventeen revealed that 9 percent of youths reported that they had been harassed online.[3] Fifty-eight percent of the targets were girls. Sixty-eight percent of the girls received "distressing harassment." Seventy-two percent of the harassment happened to teenagers. Half of the harassers were known to be male, 21 percent were known to be female. Forty-four percent of the harassers were off-line friends or acquaintances. Three percent of the incidents reportedly occurred at school.

Who, How, and Why

Cyberbullying text or images may be posted on personal Web sites or blogs or transmitted via email, discussion groups, message boards, chat rooms, IM, or cell phones. These days, cyberbullying frequently occurs on social networking sites. A cyberbully may be a person whom the target knows or an online stranger. Or the cyberbully may be anonymous so that it is not possible to tell. A cyberbully may solicit involvement of other people who do not know the target—cyberbullying-by-proxy.

Cyberbullying is frequently tied to social status issues—who is "better" than whom. It may also be related to in-school bullying. Sometimes the student who is victimized at school is also bullied online. But at other times, the person who is victimized at school becomes a cyberbully and retaliates online. Cyberbullying may involve relationships. If a relationship breaks up, one person may start to cyberbully the other person. At other times, teens may get into online fights about relationships. Cyberbullying may be based on hate or bias—bullying others because of race, religion, obesity, or sexual orientation. Teens may think that cyberbullying is entertaining—a game to hurt other people.

The Impact of Cyberbullying

It is widely known that face-to-face bullying can result in long-term psychological harm to targets. This harm includes low self-esteem, depression, anger, school failure, school avoidance, and, in some cases, school violence or suicide. It is possible that the harm caused by cyberbullying may be even greater than harm caused by traditional bullying. Online communications can be extremely vicious. There is no escape for those who are being cyberbullied—victimization is ongoing, 24/7. Cyberbullying material can be distributed worldwide and is often irretrievable. Cyberbullies can be anonymous and can solicit the involvement of unknown "friends." So the target of cyberbullying has no idea who can be trusted.

Teens may be reluctant to tell adults what is happening because they are emotionally traumatized, think it is their fault, fear greater retribution, or fear their online activities or cell phone use will be restricted.

Prevent Your Child from Being a Cyberbully

Talk with your child about the value of treating others with kindness and respect and your expectation that your child will act in accord with these values online. Make it clear that if your child engages in irresponsible online behavior, you will restrict access, install monitoring software, and review all online activity. Talk about the implications of cyberbullying that could lead to criminal arrest or civil litigation.

If your child is being bullied at school or has ongoing difficult relations with another student, warn against online retaliation. Retaliation allows bullies to justify their behavior because the target "lost it." Further, your child could be mistaken as the source of the problem. Ask the school counselor for resources to help your child gain the resilience to deal with bullies and assistance to stop any bullying that is occurring at school.

How to Respond If Your Child Is Cyberbullying

If you become aware through your own investigation or through a report from the school or a parent that your child is engaged in cyberbullying, it is essential that you respond in a firm and responsible manner. You should also be aware that if you know your child is cyberbullying and fail to stop your child from engaging in such harmful behavior and remove all material, there is a significantly increased potential that you can be held financially liable for the harm caused by your child.

- Establish very clear prohibitions about treating others badly online.

- Warn against taking any actions in retaliation or asking anyone else to engage in retaliation.
- Immediately install monitoring software. Tell your child that all Internet activities, public and private, will be closely monitored until trust has been reestablished.
- Ensure that your child cannot access the Internet elsewhere, such as through a friend's house or the public library.

Prevent Your Child from Becoming a Target

If your child is being bullied at school, there is a clear potential that the bullying will spread online. Start by seeking to "bully-proof" your child. Help your child build self-confidence and resilience. Pay special attention if your child has traits that can lead to victimization, including if your child is obese, perceived to be gay or lesbian, an alternative thinker, not willing to play social games, a "wanna-be," not fitting into the "in crowd," and the like. Pay close attention to what is happening online. Work with the school to stop the bullying.

Help your child develop personal guidelines for online involvement and to make a realistic evaluation of the quality of any online community. Your child should recognize when it is necessary to simply leave an online situation that has gotten out of control. When you visit your child's online environments together, pay attention to the manner in which your child's friends are communicating with each other.

Help your child cultivate the value of protecting privacy and personal information and recognize the dangers of excessive self-disclosure of information that could be used in a damaging manner. Discuss the risks involved in online relationship building, the need for self-protection in the disclosure of information or images, and how to end relationships gracefully so that both parties can move on without a desire for revenge.

Encourage your child to conduct a self-assessment of personal behavior or communications if others appear to be frequently attacking. Your child may be unintentionally communicating in a way that makes others feel bad. Look closely at how your child is communicating with others online and help your child see how these messages might lead to personal attacks.

Talk with your child about the need to avoid immediately responding if attacked online. What bullies want is to see their target "lose it." If your child responds when emotionally upset this will give the bully a "win." Anger shows weakness, which will encourage more bullying. In addition, others could interpret your child's retaliation or emotional response as evidence of his or her wrongdoing. For example, if your child is bullied in person or online and retaliates online by threatening to attack the bully, school officials and even law enforcement officials may think that your child is the one who needs to be punished.

Because Internet communications can be delayed, your child can take the time to calm down if attacked online. When calm, your child can better determine a path to resolve the problem.

Ask your child about cyberbullying. Indicate that if a situation ever emerges that causes concerns, you will be there to help. Make it clear that you will not respond by unilaterally restricting all Internet activities. Make sure you discuss with your child in advance when you think it is appropriate to seek assistance from an adult. Tell your child it is important to talk with you if

- The incident has been really upsetting.
- Efforts to get the cyberbullying to stop have not worked.
- The cyberbullying could be a crime.
- Any cyberbullying is, or might be, occurring through the district Internet system or via a cell phone at school, or the same person is causing problems in person at school.
- The cyberbully is anonymous.

- The cyberbully is also bullying other teens who may be more vulnerable and too afraid to get help.

Signs of Victimization

If you are concerned that your child may be a target, try to engage your child in a conversation about bullying and cyberbullying. Pay closer attention to what your child is doing online. The following are signs your child may be the target of cyberbullying:

- Signs of depression, sadness, anxiety, anger, or fear, especially if nothing apparent could be causing this upset or if your child seems especially upset after using the Internet or cell phone
- Avoidance of friends, school, and activities, or a decline in grades
- Subtle comments that reflect emotional distress or disturbed online or in-person relationships

Responding to Cyberbullying

The steps parents or targets can take to stop cyberbullying depend on the severity of the situation. Cyberbullying activities may range from rude, unkind comments to ongoing cruel harassment to lies and impersonation to physical threats. There are protective actions you and your child can take in any case.

Save the Evidence

The first step is extremely important: save all evidence of the cyberbullying—any email files, instant messaging or chat sessions, or blog or Web pages. It is necessary to take specific steps to save IMs and chats. Make sure your child knows how to do this—and that it is important to save this material if attacked.

Try to Identify the Cyberbully

Teens tend to be very bad in their attempts to establish anonymity. They generally make mistakes and leave clues that can allow for identification. Most likely the cyberbully is someone your child knows from school and most likely other students know what the bully is doing. If it appears the cyberbullying may be occurring through the school Internet system, the school can identify the cyberbully through a review of Internet use records. Even if the cyberbullying is off-campus, school officials may be willing to talk with students who might know the identity of the cyberbully to obtain a clear identification. If the bullying is severe enough to justify contacting the police or an attorney, leave the identification job to them.

Ignore the Cyberbully

In some cases, ignoring the cyberbully is the best option. Teens should know that if someone starts to flame or harass them in a communication environment, the best thing to do is simply leave or not respond. It is also possible to block all further communications. Use the block function for instant messaging and mobile phones (go to "Options" or "Preferences" and block the cyberbully's screen name). With email, set the email filter to direct all mail from the cyberbully into a specific folder. This way, it is saved as evidence if needed in the future but is not in your child's regular in-box.

Ignoring the cyberbully might not be as easy as it sounds. For teens, their online community is a big part of their social life.

Calmly and Strongly Tell the Cyberbully to Stop

In some cases, it may be appropriate for your child to seek to communicate with the cyberbully in an attempt to get the cyberbullying to stop. Your child should not communicate with the cyberbully when emotionally upset. But your child could take the time to write a strong message that simply demands that any harmful communications stop or any harmful posted material be taken down. The message could include a statement that indicates that if the communications do not stop or the harmful material is not removed, other steps will be taken to fix the problem. Depending on the character of the cyberbully and past interactions, this message could range from a stern warning to a more gentle approach.

Stop or Remove the Material

If the cyberbullying is persistent and ongoing, there are a variety of ways to stop the communications or get the offending material removed. Sending or posting inappropriate language is generally a violation of the terms of use agreement of most Web sites, Internet service providers, email services, and mobile phone providers. Most will (or should) respond to complaints. Make sure you retain copies of all correspondence. Here are some options:

- If the cyberbully is using email, contact the Internet service provider of the cyberbully. You can determine the ISP from the email address. Visit the Web site of the service provider and look for complaint procedures or a support services email address. Forward the messages that have been received, and request that the account be terminated.

- If the cyberbully's comments appear on a third-party Web site, such as a social networking site or Web host (for example, www.Webhostname.com/~kid'sname) go to the site's home page (for example, www.Webhostname.com) and find the terms of use agreement and the complaint procedure. Provide the troubling material or the URL for the material, indicate how it violates the site's terms, and request prompt removal and termination of the cyberbully's membership.

- If the comments are on a Web site with its own domain name (for example, www.xyzkid.com), you can usually find the owner of the site and the company that hosts the site by going to Whois (www.whois.net) and typing in the domain name. This usually will tell you the hosting company's Web site. Then go to the hosting company's site, find the terms of use agreement and complaint procedure, and file a complaint.

- If the cyberbully's comments are coming through text on a mobile phone, trace the number and contact the phone company.

Contact the Cyberbully's Parents

The cyberbully's parents may be totally unaware, concerned to find that their child has engaged in this kind of activity, and willing to respond very effectively. Or the parents could be very defensive. It is probably best to avoid direct confrontation. Send the bully's parents a letter, including copies of downloaded material, and request that the behavior cease. Indicate that other steps will be taken if the parents do not ensure that the harmful communications or postings stop. If you notify parents of the concern and they fail to take stringent corrective action, this can significantly increase the potential for liability, should you decide to sue them.

Contact Your School

If any cyberbullying between students is occurring through the district's Internet system or via cell phone while the students are on school grounds, school administrators or counselors must intervene. Insist that they do. You can demonstrate that the actions are occurring while students are at school by noting the time of the communications.

It is more difficult for public schools to impose formal discipline in cases of off-campus cyberbullying because of free speech protections. However, if the target and bully both attend the same school, there is a strong likelihood that cyberbullying is accompanied by face-to-face bullying or other disturbances at school. In these situations, school administrators have greater ability to respond with formal discipline. School administrators may also help resolve concerns, even if the cyberbullying is off-campus. For example, they could communicate with the cyberbully's parents or facilitate counseling or mediation among the students involved.

Contact an Attorney

In cases that have caused severe emotional harm, you may be able to sue the cyberbully's parents to recover damages and to get a court order for the cyberbullying to stop. Cyberbullying may meet the legal standards for a claim based on defamation, invasion of privacy, or intentional infliction of emotional distress. Some jurisdictions have parental liability laws that allow someone who is injured by the intentional tort (wrongdoing) committed by a minor to hold the parents financially responsible. Parents may also be sued for negligent supervision.

An attorney can send a letter to the bully's parents outlining the possible legal risks and requesting that the cyberbullying be stopped. Or if the damage has been severe and you are incurring expenses to fix the harm caused, such as costs of counseling, a claim for damages may be justified.

Contact the Police

Contact your local law enforcement if the cyberbullying involves any of the following:

- Death threats or threats of other forms of violence to a person or property
- Excessive harassment, intimidation, or extortion
- Threats or intimidation that involve any form of bias or discrimination based on race, religion, gender, sexual orientation, and others
- Any evidence of sexual exploitation

Friends Don't Let Friends . . .

Cyberbullying occurs in online environments in which responsible adults are generally not present. Usually the only people who know someone is being victimized are other teens. Increased teen intervention and reporting is essential! Your child may ask you, "If I am just watching and am not part of the activity, then how could I be doing something wrong?" Good question. Here is an answer: "Bullies crave an audience. By paying attention to their bullying, you are encouraging their behavior. You are part of the problem. I want my child to be part of the solution."

Help your child gain a sense of responsibility for the well-being of others and the willingness to make the effort to help another. Stress the importance of speaking out against bullies, or, if this is not safe, providing private help to the target or reporting bullying incidents to you or another responsible adult.

If your child knows someone who is being targeted by a cyberbully, he or she likely knows or could easily figure out where this child goes to school. If the target goes to the school your child goes to, download the material, provide instructions on how to locate the material online, and give this to the principal, counselor, or school resource officer. Your child can do this anonymously or make a request not to be identified as the source of the report. If the target of the cyberbullying goes to another school, it generally is possible to find the Web site for the school online and through this Web site find the email addresses for the principal, counselor, and school resource officer. Your child can send an email message to the school official indicating the concern and where to find the material online.

·24·

Questionable Support

SELF-HARM COMMUNITIES
AND "AT RISK" TEENS

Katie wears dark clothes with long sleeved shirts when she goes to school. Underneath the sleeves lies evidence of Katie's hidden habit—cutting. Katie started cutting several years ago, small, hidden cuts. Even though it hurt, it somehow made her feel better. She confided to another girl she met in a chat room that she was a cutter, and this girl invited her to visit a new site, where lots of teens and young adults who cut talk with each other every hour of every day. Sometimes Katie simply shares her woes, and she receives messages of support from others. At other times she finds helpful information on how to hide her habit from parents and teachers.

Young people are using the Internet to make connections with others with whom they share interests and attitudes. Socially adept teens use the Internet primarily to maintain their existing relationships with known friends, whereas socially isolated teens tend to use the Internet to create new relationships. If socially isolated teens become engaged in a healthy online group, this can provide a way for them to make supportive connections. For teens who are marginalized in any way in their own community—because of different sexual orientation, obesity, or chronic illness, for example—online support communities established by professional mental health organizations can provide excellent social and emotional support.

However, it appears that many distressed teens are forming online social communities that support and encourage self-destructive behavior—including self-injury, anorexia and bulimia, drug use, and suicide. Most of these communities express an approach to self-destructive behaviors that is grounded in personal choice. In this context, "personal choice" means whatever a person decides—to commit suicide or not, to cut or not—is perfectly justified and appropriate. These communities frequently involve teens and young adults, and can provide strong emotional support for their participants. But this support is provided through a community of like-minded, distressed teens and adults who have adopted destructive or injurious attitudes and behaviors as the means by which they are seeking to deal with their social and emotional difficulties.

The most attractive feature of these dangerous communities are the discussion groups, in which individuals support each other, exchange stories about events in their personal lives, and swap tips on techniques to engage in injurious behavior and hide the evidence of such engagement from others. One of the reasons that young people are inclined to share in such an environment is the disinhibition that occurs related to anonymity. This could be considered a positive aspect of disinhibition—that young people are willing to open up and share their hurts and pains. The problem is that such sharing is occurring in an environment with other distressed teens who are unlikely to provide effective guidance.

A teen's need to belong and to feel accepted combined with group norms for injurious behavior presents an extremely troubling situation. Teens without strong "real world" social connections will be strongly attached to online communities that provide them with feelings of acceptance and belonging. But being a participant in such communities leads to adoption or continuation of unhealthy thoughts and engagement in injurious behavior. Self-destructive behaviors are socially contagious. Exposure to information that others are engaging or have engaged in certain self-injurious activities can lead more individuals to engage in these behaviors or increase already existing behavior.

The use of digital imagery, including cameras and Web cams, in conjunction with participation in self-injurious behavior, is also increasing. Participants in discussion groups post images of themselves vomiting or graphic displays of cutting. Young people are no longer committing suicide alone. Some are broadcasting the images of their suicide via Web cam to their online "support" group.

News Stories

The following recent news stories can help to illustrate the kinds of situations that are occurring within these troubling online groups:

- CNN reported on the suicide of a young woman who became attached to a pro-choice suicide newsgroup.[1] The story reported, "Members of this news group trade advice on how to commit suicide, using code words like 'transitioning' and 'exiting' and 'catching the bus.'" The group maintains an archive called "The Methods File." This archive contains a list of recipes, recommendations, and tips on the best and worst ways to commit suicide. After this young woman's death, another member reportedly sent a message that stated, "Suzy had me proofread her notes and we went over all the details of her exit, just to be safe."

- The BBC reported on an incident in which a twenty-one-year-old man killed himself with a lethal dose of prescription drugs in January while chatting to online buddies.[2] A transcript of his final hours "shows that his online friends egged him on to take more and more drugs."

- A USA Today story describes sites that support individuals, again primarily teens and young adults, who are involved in anorexia and bulimia.[3] The introduction on a Web site was reported as saying, "I am very much for anorexia and this Web page is a reflection of that. If you are recovered or recovering from an eating disorder please, please, PLEASE do not visit my site. I can almost guarantee it will trigger you! But if you are like me and your eating disorder is your best friend and you aren't ready to give it up, please continue!"

Self-Injury Support Groups

It is estimated that there are over five hundred Internet discussion groups that bring together individuals who engage in self-injury—defined as inflicting harm to one's body without the obvious intent of committing suicide. A recent study of such sites and groups revealed that much of the dialogue was supportive in nature, but a significant portion of the dialogue reinforced the self-injury behaviors by providing information on techniques for cutting and concealment.[4] Although this study focused on self-injury, it is likely that the same activities are occurring in groups that are addressing other self-destructive behaviors.

Such environments also appear to attract predatory individuals who pose as participants or supporters for other reasons. They may attract individuals who gain some psychological, or even financial benefit, by promoting harmful or injurious behaviors. Self-injury discussion groups have connections with Web sites that sell self-injury products, such as bracelets and clothing. Communities that promote drug use are most certainly attracting drug dealers or have been organized by them. Sometimes individuals within the communities appear to distinguish themselves as "mentors," who are available to assist others in following through on certain harmful actions. Some of the communities appear to have been created by young adults who began engaging in self-injury as teens and who now apparently see their role as supporting other teens and young adults along the same path.

Suicide Support

Use of the Internet to support suicide is also a significant concern. Suicide support sites and groups provide guidance on the least painful and most effective ways to commit suicide and host discussion groups for people who are contemplating suicide.

The emergence of these sites and discussion groups appears to be leading to the creation of online suicide pacts. In the past, suicide pacts tended to involve older individuals who had long-standing relationships, such as older married couples who were facing declining health. The people who become involved in these activities now tend to be teens and young adults who did not know each other prior to their involvement in these communities. The majority of suicide pacts have been reported in Japan; however, the trend appears to be expanding to other countries.

Suicide Warning Signs

The following are warning signs for violence against self, provided by the U.S. National Suicide Prevention Lifeline.[5]

- Threatening to hurt or kill oneself or talking about wanting to hurt or kill oneself
- Looking for ways to kill oneself by seeking access to firearms, available pills, or other means
- Talking or writing about death, dying, or suicide when these actions are out of the ordinary for the person
- Feeling hopeless
- Feeling rage or uncontrolled anger or seeking revenge
- Acting reckless or engaging in reckless activities—seemingly without thinking
- Feeling trapped—like there is no way out
- Increasing alcohol or drug use

- Withdrawal from friends, family, and society
- Feeling anxious or agitated, being unable to sleep, or sleeping all the time
- Experiencing dramatic mood changes
- Seeing no reason for living or having no sense of purpose in life

For young people using the Internet, if some of these warning signs are present *and* occur in conjunction with increased time spent online and secretive behavior associated with Internet use, there are very substantial reasons for concern.

Addressing Unsafe Online Communities

Any child who is depressed, potentially suicidal, or known to be engaging in any self-destructive behaviors, and is participating online, is at high risk of becoming involved in these self-destructive behavior communities. It is also possible that a review of online activities may reveal that online harm directed at the child, such as cyberbullying, may be playing a role in causing the emotional disturbance that is leading to self-destructive behaviors. Your child's online activities should be closely monitored. This is one occasion when the installation of monitoring software, without providing notice to your child, may be very justified.

If your child has become psychologically attached to an online self-destructive support community, actions to terminate involvement in the community could lead to a dangerous situation. For depressed teens who perceive that they have finally found a place where people accept them for who they are, to be suddenly, summarily cut off from this community would be highly traumatic. Suicides frequently occur after a triggering event that involves a significant loss. The loss of connection to an online support community, however destructive that community may be, could trigger a suicide attempt.

These are issues that will have to be handled on a case-by-case basis. It is advisable to seek professional assistance. In some cases, placing a child in a protective environment might be a better choice. In other cases, a joint counselor-and-child evaluation of the communications within the self-harm community might help the child to see through the posted comments to the pain beneath those comments and, through this analysis, come to a better understanding of personal issues and then choose a different and better path. If it is possible to shift the child's activities to an online support group offered by a professional organization, this may also be an effective path.

Many times teens who are engaged in self-destructive behavior are also having significant difficulties in relations with friends at school. Many likely are subjected to denigration and bullying. Working with the school to ensure that this harmful behavior is stopped will be essential.

Your child might witness comments made by another young person online that indicates that this young person is engaging in self-harm activities or may be contemplating suicide. Make sure that your child knows that it is extremely important to report any of this kind of online material to you, as well as to a school counselor—especially if the young person is potentially suicidal.

·25·

"Us" Against "Them"

HATE GROUPS, GANGS, AND
OTHER TROUBLESOME GROUPS

John is a loner at school. Relatively large for his age, with clothing that does not fit, he is ostracized. John has created a profile online in which he expresses his hatred of life and of how he is treated by others. John has made some new friends through his profile. They have invited him to participate in the discussions on another site. This new site contains angry material detailing how certain groups of people are seeking to control society and how minorities are always seeking special favors and demanding special treatment. John's new friends have sent him music with lyrics that reinforce his hatred of others. John has downloaded graphics from the site, which now adorn the walls of his room.

Ryan, Don, and Gerald are considered "losers" at school. Other students regularly denigrate them. They all like to play a popular multiplayer role-playing game in which they frequently cooperate with each other, in their online characters, to complete violent missions. Tired of the constant bullying, they are now discussing how they could execute a similar violent attack at school.

This chapter may, at first glance, appear to be repeating the discussion of the previous chapter. Indeed, hate groups, gangs, and other troublesome groups are another form of a dangerous online community. The distinguishing feature between the dangerous communities discussed in the previous chapter and the ones discussed in this chapter are that the groups discussed in Chapter Twenty-Four are communities in which there is support for doing injury to oneself, whereas the groups discussed in this chapter provide support for violence and hatred against others.

Hate groups and gangs have common characteristics that are not shared with the other troublesome groups. Hate groups and gangs generally have a well-formed leadership structure and include both youth and adult members. They also have a tendency to use mechanisms such as a formal group name and symbols to identify members of the group and distinguish members of the group from others. Adult members of the hate group or gang may engage in recruiting behavior. Other troublesome groups are less formal and generally only include teens.

Hate Groups

Hate groups are groups that "advocate violence against, separation from, defamation of, deception about, or hostility towards *others* based on race, religion, ethnicity, gender, or sexual orientation."[1] Hate group members are generally from the race, religion, or ethnicity dominant to others within their social community and direct their hostility at members of one or more minority groups. Hate groups do not refer to themselves as "hate" groups, because they perceive that their beliefs of superiority and their justifications for the denigration of others are perfectly acceptable.

Hate group propaganda presented on Web sites generally places heavy reliance on conspiracy theories that describe ways in which other people or groups are intending to restrict or interfere with the rights of the majority group. Frequently there is reliance on spiritual scripture or pseudoscientific language to justify their belief in their own superiority. The sites often will present revised versions of history to justify members' disapproval of certain groups. Some may present their material in the context of patriotism or nationalism.

Teens are prime recruitment targets for hate groups, and the Internet has become a significant recruitment ground. Lonely and angry teens of the appropriate cultural group who do not have strong affiliations with their families and friends are the most frequent targets for recruitment.

Hate Web sites may be relatively up-front about their intentions and philosophy. Others may initially be more disguised in nature. The first impression is that they are presenting historically accurate information. Some sites may masquerade as fun sites for children—complete with activities like crossword puzzles, stories, and cartoon characters that communicate prejudicial thoughts.

Hate Web sites often offer free downloads of "white power" music—with highly racist and violent lyrics. Many also offer the ability to download hate-based games that allow the player to engage in violence to kill and maim members of minority groups, who are depicted as "sub-human." The most popular feature of such sites are the discussion boards or chat rooms. These discussion groups allow socially alienated and angry teens to vent and form strong, cohesive support environments on the basis of a mutual agreement to hate others.

Chat rooms and discussion boards also are locations for recruiters to identify and form relationships with likely recruits. Most community sites have strict policies against the posting of hate- or gang-related material and regularly remove such material if they find it or if they receive reports from other users. But it is more difficult for such sites to identify and remove recruiters who are simply communicating within the discussion groups. Teens who present themselves in these environments as lonely, angry, and searching for support are probable targets. Although not studied, recruitment techniques are likely very similar to the techniques used by online sexual predators—with the additional "value" of an emotionally supportive online group to welcome the new recruit.

Gangs

Gangs tend to be formed by members of minority groups within a society. It is not illegal to be a member of a gang. But unfortunately many gangs are involved in criminal activities, especially drug trafficking, money laundering, and human trafficking. Gangs are now moving into Internet piracy, computer security crime, and online identity theft.

Gangs are using the Internet and other technologies to communicate with each other, coordinate criminal activity, and avoid detection by legal authorities.[2] They can also use the Internet to track, identify, and target victims. Gangs create their own Web sites to facilitate recruitment and communication among members, brag about their accomplishments, or issue challenges to other gangs. They also use chat rooms and discussion boards for recruitment purposes, in a manner similar to the hate groups. Social networking sites and other teen sites generally have terms of use that prohibit display of gang symbols.

Teens who are having difficulties fitting into a healthy group of friends may seek involvement with a gang. Sometimes teens are "gang wannabes" and establish sites or engage in discussions that make it appear that they are gang members.

Informal Troublesome Groups

Sometimes teens form more informal troublesome groups. For example, a group of students who are being bullied and excluded at school may form an online group in which they support each other in expressing anger at other students. They may create their own Web sites where they denigrate the students who are bullying them and engage in continuous online dialogue expressing their anger. Activities such as this can become very dangerous.

Members of these troublesome groups may also actively engage in online violent gaming. In the online role-playing simulation environments, groups of online participants engage in planning and executing violent online strategies within the context of the gaming environment. The use of the Internet to plan violent attacks may seem to some members of a student "outcast" group to be a continuation of this common violence-planning behavior.

In the spring of 2006 came reports of a number of groups of five or six male students in the United States who were arrested for planning or threatening an attack at a school.[3] The plans were discovered because the students were communicating about the plans online. In the past, most school shootings have involved one or two shooters. The trend to larger groups of students planning school violence is of significant concern. It was reported that the students involved were bullied, were considered "outcasts" within the school community, and engaged in online gaming.

Detecting and Responding to Dangerous Group Involvement

A key indicator of hate, gang, or other troublesome group thinking is anger and the denigration of "others." If your child starts "distancing" him or herself from the family and making statements that are in significant discord with family values, consider the possibility that he or she is interacting with others online who are encouraging harmful values. If your child appears to be engaged in an "outcast" group with other students, consider the possibility of online hate, gang, or other troublesome group involvement.

Take the following actions if you are concerned about the possibility of hate, gang, or other troublesome group involvement:

- Pay close attention to Internet activities, especially checking the history file and then checking out the sites that your child is visiting
- Listen to the lyrics of the music your child is playing and watch the interactions on video games or online games
- Pay attention to your child's relationships with friends and other students

The "us against them" groups most frequently attract teens who have been bullied and tormented by other students in school. They are angry young people. Their anger may be justified due to the abuse they have received at the hands of others, but they are proceeding down a very dangerous path. If your child is being bullied, tormented, and treated as an "outcast" at school, insist that the school address these concerns. This will require a concerted effort that will include addressing the conditions that have led your child to not fit in, as well as ensuring that students who treat your child badly are dealt with appropriately. Unfortunately, in some schools, the students who bully and torment others are considered by the other students and staff to be the "popular" students. Students who are perceived as "outcasts" may also be mistreated or viewed suspiciously by staff.

It appears that one attraction of hate groups and gangs is older male members who assume a mentoring relationship with younger recruits. Establishing a mentoring relationship between a child who may be "at risk" of association with these groups and a strong, solid male who can impart positive values might be a very effective prevention technique.

If you suspect your child is involved with a hate, gang, or other troublesome group, seek professional guidance. Proceed exceptionally carefully. Your discovery of this information and attempts at intervention could provide incentive for your child to leave home to be with other members of the group or could even possibly spark retaliation by this group.

Bomb-Making Sites

Many teens who are involved in dangerous online groups are attracted to sites that provide information on the manufacture of bombs and other incendiary devices. Such information is available on many sites on the Internet.

If your child appears to be interested in weaponry or explosives, watch out for a combination of some of the following items in your house: buckets, soda, bleach, pipes, ammonia, glycerin, paraffin, containers, nails, screws, and opened shot-gun shells. The presence of these items raises concerns that your child might be involved in the manufacture of a bomb. If you find these items or anything that appears to possibly be a bomb, leave the area and call the police. This issue has gone beyond your parental control.

·26·

I'm Going to Get You

CYBERTHREATS AND
DISTRESSING MATERIAL

Andrew was involved in a private chat with Celia. As was reported in the newspaper, in the course of the chat, he said, "You bring a gun to school, you're on the front page of every newspaper. . . . I didn't choose this life but I damn well choose to exit it. I can't imagine going through life without killing a few people. God, that has to be so hard. Nothing wrong with killin'. All God's creatures do it in one form or another. . . ."

Jeff posted the following comments in a variety of places online: "I'm a retarded [expletive] for ever believing that things would change. I'm starting to regret sticking around, I should've taken the razor blade express last time around. Well, whatever, man. Maybe they've got another shuttle comin' around sometime soon." "I think most people who say this type of thing have never dealt with people who HAVE faced the kind of pain that makes you physically sick at times, makes you so depressed you can't function, makes you so sad and overwhelmed with grief that eating a bullet or sticking your head in a noose seems welcoming." "It takes courage to turn the gun on your ownself, takes courage to face death. Knowing you're going to die and actually following through takes heart, I don't care who you are."

Mike, a high school student, sent an anonymous IM to Amy, a friend, threatening to harm her and her friends the following day at school. Amy showed the IM to her parents. The parents called the school. The school went into "lock-down" the following day.

Charlie created an animated counter on his profile on a social networking site. Beneath the counter, which counts down days, hours, and minutes, were the words, "Until I kill Mr. Smith," his high school math teacher.

There are various forms of cyberthreats. Some cyberthreats are actual threats or provide clear evidence of plans to commit an act of violence against others or to commit suicide. These kinds of threats contain information about an actual event. Other cyberthreats may be in the form of material that provides strong clues that a young person is emotionally distressed and is in a state in which he or she may be on the verge of taking a drastic step to harm him or herself or others. This kind of online material bears close resemblance to what the U.S. Federal Bureau of Investigation (FBI) refers to in *The School Shooter* as "leakage."[1] Here is the FBI description of "leakage":

> *"Leakage" occurs when a [young person] intentionally or unintentionally reveals clues to feelings, thoughts, fantasies, attitudes, or intentions that may signal an impending violent act. These clues may take the form of subtle threats, boasts, innuendos, predictions, or ultimatums. They may be spoken or conveyed in stories, diary entries, essays, poems, letters, songs, drawings, doodles, tattoos, or videos. . . .*
>
> *Leakage can be a cry for help, a sign of inner conflict, or boasts that may look empty but actually express a serious threat. Leakage is*

considered to be one of the most important clues that may precede an adolescent's violent act.

An example of leakage could be a [young person] who shows a recurring preoccupation with themes of violence, hopelessness, despair, hatred, isolation, loneliness, nihilism, or an "end-of-the-world" philosophy. . . .

Another example of leakage could be recurring themes of destruction or violence appearing in a [young person's] writing or artwork. The themes may involve hatred, prejudice, death, dismemberment, mutilation of self or others, bleeding, use of excessively destructive weapons, homicide, or suicide. Many adolescents are fascinated with violence and the macabre, and writings and drawings on these themes can be a reflection of a harmless but rich and creative fantasy life. Some adolescents, however, seem so obsessed with these themes that they emerge no matter what the subject matter, the conversation, the assignment, or the joke.

Is It Real?

Sometimes what appears to be threatening material is not real. Children and teens make threats all the time—many times in jest, sometimes in anger without any real intention to follow through with the threatened action, and sometimes because they really mean it. An analysis of the circumstances under which the threats are made can help adults determine the legitimacy of the threat. Just because a threat is disseminated online does not make it "more real." What initially appears to be an online threat could be any of the following:

- A joke, parody, or game
- A rumor that got started and has grown and spread
- Material posted by a young person who is trying out a fictitious threatening online character
- The final salvos of a heated online argument, sometimes called a "flame war," that has gotten out of hand but is not likely to result in any real violence

- Material posted by someone impersonating someone else for the purpose of getting that person into trouble

- Distressing material posted by a depressed or angry young person that could indicate a violent or suicidal intention, but does not represent an imminent threat

- A legitimate imminent threat

The problem is that when school officials or law enforcement are first apprised of an online threat, it may be difficult to tell which of these possibilities might be involved. Obviously, the highest priority is doing what is necessary to protect against the possibility that whatever has been posted online is a legitimate threat. If a threat was not real, whatever happens as a consequence of responding to the threat can be remedied. But if the threat is real and whoever posted the threat follows through, this is a situation that may not be easily remedied.

The three previous chapters have presented information that is highly relevant to the material presented in this chapter. Sometimes cyberbullying reaches the level that would be considered a threat. Sometimes a target of cyberbullying will become highly depressed or suicidal, or may retaliate in a threatening manner. Teens who are involved in suicide or self-harm communities may post distressing material that provides clues that a more significant act of self-harm is imminent. Teens who are involved in any type of dangerous online group could make cyberthreats.

Examples of Cyberthreats

All of the examples at the beginning of the chapter are true incidents.

- Andrew Osantowski, then a high school student in Michigan, made those disturbing comments when engaged in a private chat with Celia, a student in Idaho.[2] Fortunately, Celia recognized the danger, saved the transcript, and reported it to her father, who was a college security officer. Her father reported the chat session to the police in Andrew's community. Upon investigation, it was found that Andrew was participating in a hate group and had many weapons, including an AK-47. He has been convicted and is now in prison.

- Jeff Weise was a student on the Red Lake Indian Reservation in Minnesota.[3] In 2005, Jeff killed nine people, wounded many others, and killed himself.
- Ben (not his real name) was arrested and charged with a felony for making a written threat to kill.[4]
- When Charlie (not his real name) was arrested, he said that he thought of the teacher as a friend and that posting the material was "just something to do."[5]

Talking with Your Child About Cyberthreats

There are two very important messages to communicate to your child about cyberthreats.

Always Report

It is extremely important to report online threats or distressing material to a responsible adult. Adults generally are not present in the online places where this kind of material is being posted. If the threatening or distressing material is not real, whatever happens as a result of the report can be fixed. But if the material does indeed provide indications of a real threat, and no one reports the material, very real harm could occur.

Your child should know the importance of saving any material that appears threatening or distressing and of reporting it to you or an appropriate adult. If the person posting the material is another teen who lives in your community, the first place to report such material is to the school that the student posting the material attends. Report to law enforcement if it is not immediately possible to report to the school or if there appears to be an imminent threat.

Your child might not know the location of someone posting a cyberthreat or may only know the general location, such as a city, state, region, or country. Try to figure out how you can file a report with law enforcement in the location.

Never Post

Never post material online that another person might perceive as a serious threat. The potential consequences of sending or posting threatening material include suspension, expulsion, arrest, and imprisonment.

Come and Play

ONLINE GAMING

Like most boys, Jacob likes video games. When he was younger he always had his hand-held gaming device in hand. Now, as a teen, Jacob has become a gamer on a multiplayer online game site. Jacob regularly spends hours every day engrossed in the game. He collaborates regularly with other players and never feels as if he can leave the game—because something might happen without him. Even when Jacob is not involved on the game site, he is thinking about game strategies. His school notebook is filled with scribbles of game characters and outlines of gaming strategies. Although he used to love soccer, Jacob has decided to drop out of the team to be able to spend more time with his gaming.

Young people, especially boys, are highly attracted to online gaming environments. There are different types of online games. Some games are played one person against a machine. Most games for younger children are this type. Other games may involve several players located anywhere in the world who play against each other to a specific end. The most sophisticated online games are rich simulated role-playing gaming communities that involve hundreds of thousands of players from throughout the world who participate in a constantly changing gaming environment. Popular multiplayer role-playing games are EverQuest, World of Warcraft, and Diablo.

The gaming environment is undergoing a merging of the more traditional video game format with Internet gaming. New video game devices can now be connected to the Internet, allowing interactive gaming. This type of merging of technologies can be expected to expand. The two primary concerns related to online gaming are addiction and fostering of violence.

Gaming Addiction

Gaming addiction is becoming recognized as a major concern.[1] Gaming addiction leads some young people and adults to essentially "check out" of the "real world" and live a significant portion of their lives online. Internet gaming addiction has been implicated in many instances of school failure and divorce. There are online support groups for spouses of gamers that operate in a manner similar to support groups for family members of alcoholic individuals. What about earning an income? No problem, gamers can find creative ways to earn money through their gaming activities.

The simulation games appear to be the most addictive. Within these simulation environments, the player creates a relatively long-standing game character. This character interacts with other game characters in endless simulated activities. Each player faces certain quests and challenges. Hundreds of thousands of players are involved in these gaming environments, and their actions have an impact on the unfolding of the game itself. There appear to be several reasons for the addictive nature of these online games:

- The game is always "happening" online—24/7. The storyline is constantly unfolding. Any player who leaves the game will feel "left out." Essentially, leaving a gaming environment such as this feels like you are leaving an ongoing party, when there is a possibility that something really exciting is going to happen just after you leave.

- The simulation gaming environments allow players to form groups or "guilds." These groups of players work together to accomplish certain goals. A feeling of belonging is generated. A player who is inactive with this group is likely to feel guilty if not present to assist in a key game strategy.

- The gaming environments also have extensive chat features that allow the players to interact with each other in their "personas." Many individuals with gaming addiction appear to have difficulties interacting with others in "real life." The online social acceptance for their online character can be very rewarding on a personal level.

- The games have a complex system of goals, levels, and marks of achievement. As players progress through the game, they achieve higher levels of power and status. The desire to achieve such power and status likely leads some players to addictive behavior.

- Within the game play, there are certain levels of accomplishment. If a player leaves the game before reaching a certain level, all of the work toward achieving that accomplishment is lost. This concept is referred to as "sunk cost." A player has "sunk" a level of time investment that will be lost if the gaming is not continued to a certain point of achievement.

- There is also a biological basis for gaming addiction. Involvement in gaming stimulates the release of a neurotransmitter called dopamine. Dopamine is associated with pleasure sensations—the more a player plays, the more pleasure the player feels.

- As with all addictive behavior, there frequently are also underlying social or emotional difficulties that contribute to the addictive behavior. Gamers participate in gaming because it provides an escape from their "real world" concerns.

Preventing Gaming Addiction

Gaming addiction is a concern that is simply better to address from a preventive approach. In this way you can hope to avoid a more stringent intervention. Here are some prevention strategies:

- Seek to find ways to engage your child in activities that foster challenge and competition that are not screen-based.
- Place specific limits on gaming activities, including time limits and limits against late-night gaming. Also restrict gaming while doing homework.
- Help your child maintain the perspective that a game is only a game. Specifically, discuss issues related to "sunk cost." The amount of time spent playing a game should be reward itself—not some fictitious achievement level established by the game company.

If your child is experiencing social or emotional difficulties, he or she is at much greater risk of becoming addicted to online games. It clearly is necessary to address the underlying social or emotional difficulties. Frequently, these difficulties relate to a lack of healthy involvement with friends. Involvement in online gaming becomes the substitute. At the same time, recognize that your child is "at risk" of online gaming addiction and take specific steps to limit the amount of time he or she can be involved in any video gaming, especially online gaming in simulation environments. This likely will require the use of time-monitoring software to enforce online time limits. If your child has become highly addicted to these online gaming activities and this is interfering with relationships and school performance, you likely will need professional assistance.

Violent Gaming

Involvement in violent gaming has raised concerns that young people will be more likely to engage in "real world" violence or become insensitive to such violence. The research in this area is highly con-clusive. A causal connection between media violence and aggres-sive behavior in some children has been clearly established.[2] Viewing or participating in entertainment violence can lead to increases in aggressive attitudes, values, and behavior, though some children are affected more than others. The effects of entertain-ment violence are measurable and long-lasting. These effects in-clude the following:

- Children who see a lot of violence are more likely to view violence as an effective way of settling conflicts.
- Children exposed to media violence are more likely to assume that acts of violence are acceptable behavior.
- Viewing violence can lead to emotional desensitization toward violence in real life. It can decrease the likelihood that one will take action on behalf of a victim when violence occurs.
- Entertainment violence feeds a perception that the world is a violent and mean place. Viewing violence increases fear of becoming a victim of violence, with a resultant increase in self-protective behaviors and a mistrust of others.
- Viewing violence may lead to real-life violence. Children exposed to violent programming at a young age have a higher tendency for violent and aggressive behavior later in life than do children who are not exposed to violent media.
- Violent interactive entertainment may have a significantly more severe impact than passive interactive entertainment.

In most countries, exceptionally violent games cannot be sold to children or teens. This has not prevented the companies mar-keting such products from finding creative ways to advertise and sell their products to young people. Through the Internet, the video game companies have direct market access to children and teens—access that may not be easily detected by parents. Violent gaming sites can present themselves to government regulators as being totally legitimate. They can have registration standards that, on their face, indicate that no children under the age of thirteen, or for some sites the age of eighteen, can register. Some sites may require parental approval or notice. But these sites, as well as most gamers over the age of ten, know that it is an exceptionally easy "game move" to fake both age and parental approval.

Simulation games frequently contain significant amounts of violence. Many teens will experiment with different personalities. The creation of multiple identities allows teens to disassociate themselves from the reality of the impact of their online activities. "I didn't hurt anyone. It was my online 'persona.'" Frequent involvement in gaming can create a perspective that online activity is not real and everyone online is just a player in a game— "Life online is all just a game." This disassociation can provide a rationalization for engaging in harmful online behavior in other environments.

Addressing Violent Gaming

To address violent gaming:

- Clarify your own values regarding media violence. Where does your family draw the line and why? Live, teach, and establish guidelines and joint agreements with your child in accord with these values.

- Foster your child's friendships with friends whose parents hold values similar to yours with respect to media violence. Peer influence is a significant factor in violent media involvement. Make sure your child has frequent opportunities to get together with friends for healthy activities.

- Pay close attention to all media involvement—especially if you have a child who would be considered "at risk" for negative impacts of media violence. This includes children with poor social problem-solving skills, poor emotional regulation, a history of aggression, a hostile personality, or attention deficit-hyperactivity disorder, and children who bully or are victims of bullying.

- Provide healthy alternative opportunities for competition and challenge.

- Set time and activity limits on Internet and other media activities. Especially limit late-night use. Use time-limiting software to enforce these limits, if necessary.

- Check history files to see what sites your child is going to on a regular basis. If your child is frequently visiting gaming sites, make your own assessment of the appropriateness of the games on these sites. If your child is involved in a simulated role-playing game, ask your child to show you around and introduce you to how the game is played.

· 28 ·

You Bet, I Win,
You Lose

ONLINE GAMBLING

Jerry's parents occasionally like to spend an evening at a nearby casino. Jerry, age nine, has heard them talk about the gambling games they like to play. Now Jerry has found that he can play these same games on his favorite children's site. Members on this site earn and spend points as they play games and engage in other activities. Just like mom and dad, Jerry can "wager" his points in gambling-like games in an attempt to win more points.

There are three concerns related to young people and online gambling:

- Some popular sites for children and teens feature "risk-free" gambling as a game activity.
- There is a morphing of the distinctions between online gaming and gambling.
- Some teens are becoming involved in adult online gambling sites.

Many adults enjoy gambling and engage in gambling very responsibly. But some adults become addicted to gambling, and this addiction can have very negative consequences. As with all addictive behavior, gambling addiction appears to be related to underlying concerns regarding personal emotional stability and healthy relationships. Further, there is a spiral-of-decline effect with respect to problem gambling in which the underlying social or emotional difficulties lead to involvement in addictive behavior, which leads to greater social or emotional difficulties.

The terms *gaming* and *gambling* are quite similar and many times are used interchangeably. The distinction maintained in this book is that *gaming* is an activity that requires skill, whereas *gambling* is an activity that involves risk and results in a financial reward or loss.

Researchers have found a clear connection between teen involvement in gambling and adult gambling addiction.[1] Teen involvement in gambling has also been linked with increased criminal behavior, poor family and peer relationships, and school failure. It appears that winning money is not the primary reason that teens gamble excessively. Winning money helps them to continue gambling for greater periods of time. Some teens appear to engage in excessive gambling for reasons that appear to be similar to engagement in excessive gaming—it is an activity that creates excitement and takes them away from their "real world" concerns.

Given the insight into the concerns of underage gambling provided by the research, it would be prudent to seek to reduce the exposure of children and teens to gambling activities online. From the perspective of some Web sites, however, there are good reasons to ignore this argument. Gambling is known to be an addictive activity, and commercial Web sites are highly dedicated to ensuring that their sites are "sticky." There are also business relationships to consider. Gaming sites may support themselves with advertisements from gambling sites. The gaming sites may limit this advertising to users who have registered as over the age of eighteen, but it is well-known that many teens register as adults. It goes without saying that gaming sites are interested in attracting their future customers, as well as any teens who can figure out how to participate even though they are still minors.

Many game sites and community sites that are attractive to children and teens allow users to engage in "risk-free" gambling-like games as a fun activity. These activities could more appropriately be considered "Gambling 101," because they introduce children to the ways in which online gambling works. These kinds of grooming activities will help to create a new generation of users who find gambling an attractive and familiar online activity.

Gaming for Cash

As was discussed, gaming is considered to be an activity that requires skill, whereas gambling is a game of risk. Gaming is considered an activity that is appropriate for minors, whereas gambling is supposed to be restricted to adults—who presumably have a greater ability to control their potential addiction. In countries such as the United States, Web sites are legally restricted from offering online gambling in which the gambler has to risk some amount of money. But there are no restrictions against Web sites offering free online gaming activities that can lead to a cash reward.

On many sites, users over the age of thirteen are encouraged to participate in gaming activities for cash or other prizes. With a cash prize as a possible award, teens can be enticed to play the game for hours upon hours. Serious addiction can be the result. While not resulting in financial loss from money wagered, these activities are as potentially emotionally damaging as actual gambling addiction. As was discovered from the research, the ability to engage in extensive play is a primary attraction to gamblers. Web sites want their users to engage in extensive play.

Gambling

Although it is illegal to operate an online gambling site in the United States, Internet gambling companies made approximately $10 billion in profit in 2005.[2] They're all based on non-U.S. Web sites, but as much as 80 percent of the traffic comes from U.S.

gamblers. This is an example of how the laws of one country have a limited impact on Internet activities.

Many online gambling casinos are hosted on Web sites in countries that have the fewest legal restrictions on gambling. Enforcement of laws to protect minors in these countries is extremely difficult, if not impossible. In a 2002 study of one hundred of such gambling sites, the U.S. Federal Trade Commission found that 20 per cent of the sites had no warning about age restrictions and most had no effective mechanisms to prevent minors from participating.[3]

A U.S. law, enacted in fall 2006, has created a major change in the online gambling environment. This law prohibits credit and debit card companies from transmitting payments to online gambling casinos. The law cuts off the vehicle most used by gamblers to gamble online. Prior to the enactment of this law, any young person with access to a credit or debit card would have been able to find a way to engage in actual online gambling. Given the incredible amount of funds that are at stake and the international nature of the online gambling activities, it is likely that adult gamblers are finding ways around this law by establishing accounts with institutions outside of the United States. This law probably has made it far more difficult for U.S. teens, who likely do not have significant expertise in international banking, to accomplish such financial transactions.

Teens who reside in other countries likely have the ability to use a credit or debit card or some other vehicle for transferring funds electronically online to engage in actual gambling.

Prevention and Intervention

Parental values and behavior around gambling are a strong influence on child behavior. Evaluate your own values and clarify the values that you will seek to impart to your child on this issue.

Excessive involvement in online gambling is likely to be grounded in underlying social or emotional difficulties and could lead to more extensive problems. If by engaging in online gambling—risk-free or not—your child is seeking to avoid dealing with other areas of life that are causing stress, addressing the underlying concerns is of greatest importance. If your child is more "at risk" to begin with, proactively seek to limit his or her involvement in sites that include gambling-like games.

When you are establishing which sites you consider appropriate for your younger child to use, look closely for the kinds of game activities described earlier to see if the site has "gambling 101" kinds of games. Depending on your child and your personal values regarding this issue, you may prefer not to choose this kind of a site for your child, to choose the site but request that your child avoid any "gambling 101" games, or to use these games as a teachable moment to educate your child about the risks of excessive gambling activities. Children who are not "at risk" to begin with likely are not at risk from these online gambling games. Children who are "at risk" may be. Determine whether the site is awarding points and if those points are used to establish social status on the site. If so, your child could begin to participate in "gambling 101" games for social status purposes—a behavior that is equivalent to adult problem gambling.

On sites offering cash, the financial rewards may be a motivating factor for many teens. All they have to do is play online and they have a chance of winning money. What could be so bad about this? It is never too early for teens to learn that while these activities may provide a form of entertainment if enjoyed in a responsible way, neither gaming nor gambling should ever be considered a vehicle to earn money. If you find that your child is participating in online games for the purpose of earning money, and that he or she expresses the need for money as a motivating factor, provide some other, healthier opportunities for him or her to earn some additional funds.

If you are not a U.S. resident and your child has a credit or debit card or is able to transfer funds electronically, be sure to periodically check the statements to determine whether this card is being used to engage in actual gambling. Also, pay close attention to your own credit and debit card statements.

If you feel your child has a pre-gambling or actual gambling problem, seek professional assistance.

·29·

Tag, I Got You

HACKING AND
COMPUTER CRIMES

Wesley has always been fascinated with computers. His parents have long since given up on trying to figure out what he is doing. Wesley spends countless hours at the computer. If he is not on the computer, his head is in a tech manual—which he actually understands. Wesley hangs out with a few other computer "geeks" at school. They spend their time at school in the computer lab. Wesley and his friends have been trying to figure out how to penetrate the school district's main server—for no reason in particular, just to see if they can. They have gotten some good tips from other teens who love trying to penetrate computer systems.

Hacking is a widespread phenomenon on the Internet. In the early years of computer technology, there was a "Robin Hood"-like admiration for hackers—those technically sophisticated young people who could successfully penetrate the computer security of major corporations and government agencies. Some of today's technology industry leaders were involved in hacking activities when they were younger.

There are many reasons why individuals, teens or adults, "hack" computer systems. Most hackers believe that access to computers should be unlimited—for those individuals who have sufficient technical expertise to penetrate a computer system. They believe that hacking is ethically acceptable unless the hacker commits theft, vandalism, or a breach of confidentiality. Most consider it appropriate to seek to penetrate computer systems because this enhances their understanding. Some claim that enhanced computer security is their motivation. They reason that if they can break into a system, the computer industry will be forced to address that breach by coming up with better security systems. Others claim that hacking is an appropriate form of social activism, and that their actions are intended to improve society. Most hackers have a high distrust of "authority." When some hackers successfully penetrate systems, they leave a technical "calling card" to signal to other hackers that they penetrated the system first. "Marking one's territory" is a common activity of many male animals. This is a rather interesting manifestation of this apparently innate desire.

Hackers have labels for different types of hackers: "white hats," "gray hats," "black hats," and "script kiddies." The first three names reflect a perception of a range of motivations. Beginning teen hackers are called "script kiddies" because they do not have sophisticated understanding of the technologies and are merely running "scripts" provided by others. Other hackers who seek to penetrate but do no other harm refer to themselves as "hackers" and the malicious individuals who do harm as "crackers." Law enforcement officials do not see these distinctions as clearly as hackers do—and regularly prosecute hackers, as well as the more malicious crackers.

There is a vast hacker subculture online. Hackers frequently join up with a group of other hackers online. These hacker groups function in a manner similar to other online groups or communities. They share hacker tools, brag about computer exploits, and discuss computer vulnerabilities and penetration techniques. Sharing information is an important social norm. Some groups are informal and others are more organized and stable, and have strong group cohesiveness. Some groups have dedicated Web sites and communication vehicles and even host conferences.

A significant number of hackers are teens and young adults. Most are male. Teens have been raised with computers and are comfortable and confident exploring computer systems. Teen hackers present significant concerns, however, because they are using technologies that can cause harm, though they frequently are unaware of the true capabilities of these technologies or the extent of harm they can cause. Many are not fully aware of the implications of their hacking or are unconcerned about the consequences of their actions, which can include criminal prosecution. They perceive that they are invisible and that their actions will not be detected or punished.

For many teen hackers, the driving motivation to engage in hacking likely is both explorational and social. Some teens are strongly motivated to know everything there is to know about computers and how they work. Hacking is also a way to become an accepted member of an online group. Some teens with advanced computer skills fit the image of the "techie geek." For these teens, who might lack skills in social relationships, membership in an online hacker group can be emotionally fulfilling. Once the hacker becomes a member of a group, his or her driving motivation is likely to be establishing social status. The more computer systems you have penetrated and information you can share, the higher your status within the group.

Hacking has transformed in recent years from a form of computer skills development or social rebellion to a widespread criminal phenomena. Organized crime and other criminal elements have embraced hacking to accomplish other criminal purposes, which include breaking into computer systems for the purpose of "hijacking" those systems for the transmission of spam, pornography, or other material. There is emerging concern that some younger hackers are receiving "mentoring" from more sophisticated hackers who clearly have criminal intent.[1] The criminal elements appear to be taking advantage of the rebellious tendencies of teens. They seek to engage those teens in hacking activities that support their larger criminal ventures. The teens may be totally unaware of how their activities are supporting such criminal activity.

Hacking and Internet addiction are closely related. Many parents appear to be unaware when their child is involved in hacking. They may believe that their child's excessive online engagement in highly technical activities is dedicated to the improvement of computer skills. This may, in part, be the child's motivation. But improving one's computer skills through illegal activity is not a recommended path for today's technology careers.

Encouraging Your Technically Proficient Child

If your child demonstrates high interest and proficiency in the use of computers, recognize that there is a risk that he or she could become interested in hacking. Make sure that you promote positive, career-oriented computing activities.

- Seek to establish a mentoring relationship between your child and an adult computer professional in your community.

- Encourage your child's school to establish a "tech club." School-based tech clubs provide valuable positive learning experiences for technically proficient teens, allowing them to achieve real-life social recognition for their skills and to envision a future as a well-paid technology professional.

- Check into the local community college course offerings and determine whether your child can enroll in advanced computer classes.

- Encourage your child to provide computer services for a nonprofit social services organization.

- Make good use of teachable moments provided by news articles that report on incidents of arrest or conviction of teens or adults for computer crime. Discuss the concerns of computer crime and the significant potential risks.

- Pay attention to what your child is doing online—especially check out which Web sites or online communities your child is visiting. Unfortunately, a highly gifted computer techie likely will be better than most teens at covering online "tracks."

- Set an ambitious goal for your child. It is possible to become a certified network technician during or shortly after secondary or high school. Part-time employment in this field during college surely would be better than working in a fast-food restaurant.

Young people who have advanced technical skills are a valuable resource in our society. Jobs in the technology industry are highly lucrative. If you have a technically gifted child, make sure you keep your child on the path to success.

·30·

Not the Highest Form of Flattery

PLAGIARISM

Rachel spends about three hours per day gabbing with her friends on their favorite social networking site. She has little time for homework, because of her online and other activities. Rachel knew she had a research paper due for her World History class, but the due date always seemed to be sometime in the future. Now the paper was due and she had not even begun. Rachel started searching online for research resources. She quickly found three good papers that addressed the topic she was supposed to write about. Rachel downloaded the papers and cut and pasted paragraphs from these papers into a paper that she submitted as her own work.

When children and teens use the Internet to complete homework assignments, especially school papers, it is possible that they may plagiarize someone else's work. Schools are becoming more sophisticated in finding instances of Internet-facilitated plagiarism and imposing punishment. Most important, for success in college, your child must know how to research and write a good paper without plagiarizing the work of others.

Inadvertent Plagiarism

Students sometimes inadvertently plagiarize. They may not understand how to incorporate the ideas of others into their paper and provide appropriate citation. They may also lose track of their sources as they conduct their research, especially as they "surf" the Web. They may think that "copying and pasting" what others have said is an acceptable practice. Effective skills in research and writing are essential for success in secondary or high school and college. Children and teens who have good research and writing skills will be far less likely to engage in inadvertent plagiarism. With luck, your child's school has a high-quality, systematic approach to teaching all students how to effectively conduct research and write a paper in a way that avoids inadvertent plagiarism.

Online Research Strategy

The following is a research and writing strategy that is adapted to the era of conducting online research.

Keeping Track of Information Resources. Your child should have a systematic way to record the full reference to any document downloaded from the Internet. One strategy to accomplish this is to create a separate folder for a specific writing assignment. Every document that will be used for reference should be downloaded from the Internet and stored in this folder. Also start a word processing document titled "citations" in this folder. Whenever a document is downloaded from the Internet, add citation information to this word processing document—including the URL for the document that has been downloaded and the date it was downloaded. Any information resources for the project that are in hard copy, such as a copy of an article from a book, should be retained in a "real world" file folder.

Note Taking. Open a new word processing document and title this document "notes." Go through each of the information resources.

Either cut and paste or paraphrase the important information from the information resource onto this page. Make sure that each note is one separate idea—one idea only—and is separated by blank lines both before and after the note. It is important to retain the reference to the source of the information or quote and the page this appears on, and to keep track of when material has been cut and pasted or paraphrased. One strategy is to use the initials of the lead author of the article, "P" or "Q" for paraphrased or quoted (cut and pasted), and the page number. In front of each separate note, there would be an indication: JS-P23 (John Smith, paraphrase, page 23) or JS-Q54 (Jane Smith, quote, page 54).

Organizing. Once all of the notes have been gathered, they need to be organized into an outline form. One way to do this is to print out the entire notes document and cut the notes paper so that each separate idea is on one strip of paper. Then sort the slips of paper into separate groups—one topic per group. Next, organize the notes strips within each topic group and staple the notes in that group together. It will be helpful to create a topic title for each group. Then organize the topic groups into a logical sequence. This logical sequence is the outline for the paper. It is very helpful for younger writers to take the step of physically sorting and organizing the notes. More experienced writers can do this electronically. They can open up a new word processing document, then simply cut and paste the notes from the notes document into like groups and then organize the groups. Or they might have a pretty good idea of the outline and start with the outline and input the notes. The key purpose of this step is to organize the information into a logical sequence for writing. Many young writers have great difficulty with this kind of organization.

Writing the Paper. Open a new word processing document for the actual paper. Each section of the paper will contain one or more paragraphs that present the information for each topic—in the logical sequence or outline that was created. During this step, the notes in each group will be turned into written text. It may help to create the outline first. The outline is the topic title for each group, presented in the logical sequence. The key skill necessary to accomplish the actual writing is appropriately paraphrasing, or stating in one's own words, the writings of another. Sometimes your child will want to select a key section of the writing of another to quote directly. Your child should note where material is being paraphrased or quoted and provide a proper citation using correct citation format as approved by the school. Generally, the older your child is, the more precision will be required in citing specific material in the document. After the paper is written, the document that was created in the first step, with all of the information resources, can be set in alphabetical order and included at the end as the citations.

One of the ways in which this strategy is effective is that nothing ever gets lost. If somewhere along the line a specific citation gets lost, your child can simply backtrack to the notes document or the original sources to find the reference. This approach can be adapted to an individual teacher's requirements. A teacher may require that note cards be submitted. The notes document can be formatted and cut into note card size.

There are books available to help guide your child in effective writing. Ask your child's teacher for some recommendations.

Intentional Plagiarism

When students commit intentional plagiarism they are knowingly engaging in academic dishonesty. They understand that submitting material written by someone else as their own work is wrong, and they make the choice to do it anyway. Students may use the Internet as a tool to intentionally plagiarize in several ways:

- Purchase a paper from a site that sells research papers for students to submit as an original work
- Find papers that someone else has posted online and submit this paper as an original work

- Find several papers on the Internet and cut and paste portions of these papers to create a new paper that is submitted as an original work

Attentive teachers usually are able to tell if a paper has been pla-giarized. The writing style is likely to be different from other as-signments completed by the student. Frequently students make obvious mistakes, such as copying and pasting text and failing to change the font or color of text "borrowed" from different Web sites. Or a student may change information at the front of a paper and not even look at the end of the paper to see that there is incrimi-nating evidence of plagiarism.

Teachers can verify plagiarism by searching for a block of words from the paper enclosed in quotes using an Internet search engine. There are also commercial services that provide teachers with the ability to submit all papers and have them reviewed electronically. Students found to have plagiarized can face a variety of sanctions. The sanctions in college generally are more stringent than in sec-ondary school.

Students may engage in intentional plagiarism for a variety of reasons.

- They may lack skills or confidence to effectively write a paper. This factor is similar to the causes of inadvertent plagiarism. To address intentional plagiarism due to lack of skills or confi-dence in writing requires a focus on learning those skills, as discussed under "Inadvertent Plagiarism."
- Some students may simply have a lack of motivation to accomplish quality schoolwork but still have a desire to get a good grade. Students with this attitude will not, obviously, ultimately achieve success in school—or in life. This moti-vation raises key concerns regarding personal values about work and success.
- Many students do not have effective time management. Lack of effective time management—or simply too many demands

on time—can result in the need to complete or find a paper to hand in at the last moment. This is likely the most significant factor involved in incidents of intentional plagiarism.

- Help your child structure time and tasks to effectively complete major writing projects. This may require use of a calendar to track progress steps along the way. It is possible that for any major writing assignment the teacher will be requiring these performance steps, and your task will be simply to reinforce the importance of staying on track.
- Assess the degree to which your child's life has been scheduled or overscheduled with other demands that are interfering with homework. Internet addiction could be implicated in the lack of effective time management.
- If your child is spending too much time surfing, gabbing, and gaming online this may result in the failure to focus sufficient attention on homework, and lead to plagiarism. Obviously, the Internet addiction issues must be addressed.

·31·

I Can Copy and Share Anything on the Internet

COPYRIGHT PROTECTION
AND INFRINGEMENT

Jason likes to use the computer at his grandmother's house. His grandmother does not know that Jason has installed peer-to-peer networking software on her computer. She doesn't like to use the Internet much because her computer seems really slow and she keeps getting lots of pop-up ads whenever she is searching for something online. Jason has downloaded a large collection of popular hits that he makes available for others to download. The Recording Industry of America has just filed a copyright infringement lawsuit against Jason's grandmother—the owner of the computer.

Although still in high school, Angelica is a gifted graphic artist. She has posted some of her work on a social networking profile, giving others the ability to download her graphic designs for personal use. She recently received an email from another graphic artist. This artist is a professor at a prestigious art school. He is now helping Angelica pull together a portfolio to submit for admission to this art school.

Copyright laws balance two important values:

- *The Rights of the Creator.* The person who has created something has the right to say how others can use the creative work. The creator also has the right to seek to obtain income from distribution of the work or copies of that work.

- *The Benefit to Society.* Making sure that creators can receive income from their creative efforts will encourage them to continue to be creative, which benefits everyone. But also, under copyright, some socially beneficial uses of copyrighted material are generally more freely allowed.

Copyright Basics

Copyright laws vary in different countries, although there are many similarities due to international treaties.[1] The following guidance is based on U.S. copyright law and may not be fully applicable in other countries.

Copyright law protects creative works. A creative work may be writing, music, a musical performance, a picture, a painting, software, or other permanent creation. Most people use a copyright notice on their creative work. A copyright notice looks like this: © year of creation, copyright holder's name. But copyright law protects a work even if it is published without a notice.

The owner of a copyright has five rights—the rights to copy, distribute, modify, display, and perform the work. The copyright owner is the one who gets to decide whether to give permission, called a license, for anyone else to do these five things with the work.

A copyright owner can grant a license in a variety of ways. Many times this is done by contract, such as a contract with a publisher. But a license can also be granted with a permission statement on a Web site. For example, the owner of a copyright in a recorded song can post a notice on the Web site that states, "You may freely download this song and distribute it to others for noncommercial purposes." The copyright owner still holds the copyright and can prevent anyone from incorporating the music onto a CD to sell or from modifying it. But the creator has given individuals permission to download and even share the recording with others.

Copyright owners can also choose to give up their rights in a creative work by placing the work in the "public domain." This is done by making a statement such as, "I place this material into the public domain." The other kinds of public domain works are works for which the copyright has expired and works created by government agencies in some countries, such as U.S. government agencies.

Fair Use Exemption

In the United States, a "fair use" exemption to copyright protection was created because of the interest in ensuring that protections granted to creators do not undermine the benefits to society. If someone wants to use a copyrighted work in a way that is considered a "fair use," they can do so without getting permission or paying for rights. Several questions must be considered to determine whether a use of the copyrighted work would be considered "fair":

- How is the copyrighted work being used? It is fairer to use a work for an educational purpose or to review and criticize the work, and less fair to use the work for a commercial purpose.
- What kind of work is being used? It is fairer to use a factual work, and less fair to use a creative work.
- How much of the work is being used? It is fairer to use only a little, and less fair to use a large amount.
- How will the use affect the market for the work or the potential income the creator expected to receive from the work? It is fairer to use a work in a way that does not hurt the copyright holder financially, and less fair if the copyright holder could expect payment for such use.

As you can tell from these questions, "fair use" is a balancing process. The person who can best help you and your child understand "fair use" is your school librarian. Generally, most of the uses your child will make of copyrighted work for school projects that are not posted online or shared outside of the classroom will be considered to be "fair use." It is also generally acceptable to make one copy of a work to be used for educational purposes—such as making a copy of an article that is used to write a research paper. Many other countries also have provisions that will allow for the free use of copyrighted material by students and researchers for education and research purposes.

The fair use exemption also allows the use of copyrighted material for comment or criticism. It is considered important in a democratic society to allow people to copy a work created by another in order to allow for review or criticism of that work. This is an important way in which knowledge is expanded or concerns are raised. Many other countries also allow use of copyrighted material for comment and criticism purposes.

Copyright in the Information Age

The Internet is creating major changes in the underlying structure of the way in which creators interact with publishing companies and the people who enjoy their creations. Prior to the Internet, creators generally had to license their creative works to publishing companies for distribution. Now it is possible for some creators to form direct relationships with their consumers.

But these technologies also make it much easier to create and disseminate unauthorized copies of someone else's copyrighted work. Once a creative work is provided in electronic form, it is exceptionally difficult to control what others do with that work. Sometimes people think that just because they can make copies without getting caught and punished, that it is all right to do so. Other people think it is okay to make copies because everyone else is doing this.

Help your child understand that it is not okay to use other creative works in a way that is not fair to the person who created the work. One way to communicate this message is to help your child think about how it might feel if someone else "ripped off" his or her own personal creation.

The Internet and other technologies are also causing significant tensions related to copyright protection, the creative process, and who owns or should have the right to control what. Major copyright holders in entertainment and media industries are trying to find ways to address the financial harm they are suffering because the ease with which people can make copies has led to significantly greater infringing behavior. But some of these companies also appear to be seeking even greater, more exclusive, control over copyrighted works—control that shifts the balance away from a consideration of fair use and the benefits to society.

Alternatively, some creators believe in a more collaborative and expansive distribution of creative works. Some creators are collaborating in promoting this approach through a concept called "Creative Commons." More information about this is available at http:// creativecommons.org. Essentially, the approach fostered by the Creative Commons allows creators to choose which of their rights to allow to others, under what circumstances. For example, a creator may allow others to copy and distribute for noncommercial purposes only. Or another creator may choose to allow people to modify the work, as long as the original creation and copyright ownership notice remains with the work.

The Creative Commons approach really does not change the basic provisions of copyright law. It just provides a coordinated way for people to share their creative works more efficiently and effectively. One significant advantage of this approach is that it uses the Internet to more effectively provide creators' works directly to their audience, without the need for an intermediary publisher.

The Creative Commons is a great place for young people to go to find material they can legally incorporate into their own creative works. For example, if your child wants a photo of a "dragonfly" to silkscreen onto a T-shirt to give to a friend, an image likely can be found on the Creative Commons Web site that can be used in this manner.

Copyright Guidance

The basic copyright guidance that children should be taught is that it is appropriate to make copies of materials created by others if, and only if

- The materials are in the public domain (see earlier definition).
- General permission has been granted for the kind of use your child wants to make of the material—with a notice on the work or on the Web site providing the work.
- The use is considered "fair use" in the United States (see earlier definition), or under other use privileges that are available under the copyright laws of other countries. This includes making a single copy of a work for use in an educational project.
- Specific permission has been obtained from the creator. If the creator has a Web site with an email address, your child can send an email to request permission for a proposed use of that person's creative work.

If these conditions are not present, then it is not appropriate for your child to make copies of, distribute, modify, display, or perform a work found on the Internet.

Copyright Infringement and Peer-to-Peer Networking

Many people, including teens, are illegally downloading copyrighted music, movies, games, and software through peer-to-peer networking. Peer-to-peer networking is an Internet technology that allows users to make files that are on a portion of their computer available for others to download. Unfortunately, many of the files that are available for download through peer-to-peer networking are files that contain copyrighted creative material for which no permission has been given to distribute. Most of these materials are commercially distributed entertainment and media products.

The owner of the computer can be held financially liable for copyright infringement accomplished through peer-to-peer networking. So if your child has, even if unknown to you, downloaded peer-to-peer networking software on a computer owned by your family and is using this technology to illegally download copyrighted material, you can be held liable. In the United States, both the recording industry and the movie industry are filing such lawsuits. Use of peer-to-peer networking also presents the possibility of the spread of "malware," including spyware, viruses, and worms, as well as pornography.

There are now many Web sites that allow legal download of entertainment media for reasonable prices. Providing children and teens with the opportunity to use their own funds to pay for copyrighted entertainment media is not only a good way to teach appropriate respect for copyright, it is also can be a much more cost-effective solution than constantly having to take the family computer for servicing to remove nasty "malware" or having to deal with mistakenly downloaded pornography, or even to have to fight off a lawsuit.

Teen Creations

As children are now producing and posting creative works on Web sites, they should also pay attention to their own copyright interests. On many Web sites that allow people to post pictures, graphics, and videos, the terms of use agreement specifically provide that upon posting material, the creator is granting permission for the Web site to do anything it wants with the material—with no obligation to compensate the creator of the work. Your child should think twice about giving away the rights to any creative work online.

·32·

Security First

PROTECTION AGAINST "MALWARE"

Bob loves playing any form of computer game. He loves to surf Web sites to find gaming cheats, which he downloads onto the family computer. Lately the family computer has been acting strangely. It has become very sluggish, and often programs unexpectedly quit. Whenever Bob or any other family members go online, they can't seem to escape a blizzard of pop-up ads.

These days, computer security is everyone's business. This includes all family members who use the computer. Part of being a responsible Internet user is avoiding online activities that jeopardize others or adversely affect the health of the family computer or the financial well-being of the family!

"Malware," which is short for malicious software, includes viruses, worms, Trojan horse attacks, and spyware. Malware is designed to either create havoc or facilitate identity theft or excessive advertising. Malware can cause computer failure, take over computers for the purpose of sending itself on to other computers or facilitate denial-of-service attacks, track online activities to deliver annoying pop-up ads, and obtain personal financial information for identity theft. Key indicators that your machine has become infected with malware include sluggish computer performance, strange files, unusual performance of your browser, lots of pop-up ads, random error messages, and the like. To prevent your computer from becoming infected requires every user to pay attention to security issues.

Computer Security Guidelines

Follow these basic guidelines to help prevent computer security problems and to make sure that if something bad happens, the losses are not extensive.

- Make sure you have installed security software and firewalls on your computer and regularly download updates. A personal firewall will stop uninvited users from accessing your computer and alert you if spyware already on your computer is sending information out.

- Regularly download security updates and "patches" for operating systems and other software. Malware creators are always looking for failure points in popular software. Whenever the producers of software find a failure point, they create a patch. You can download these patches from the company Web site.

- Install an anti-spyware program from a known company that has established independent credibility. Set it to scan on a regular basis. Don't click on links in email or pop-up ads that claim to offer anti-spyware software. Frequently, this action will actually install spyware.

- Disconnect your computer from the Internet when not in use.

- Make sure you are using a secure browser that does not allow the delivery of pop-up ads. Set the browser security to minimize the possibility of inadvertent downloading.

- Regularly back up your computer data on disks or CDs. If your computer becomes infected you could lose all of your data.

Spyware is a form of malware that monitors Internet surfing and is used to send pop-up ads or redirect a computer to Web sites with advertising. Spyware can facilitate identity theft by recording keystrokes that you or your child might use to access financial records. Many sites offer "free techie goodies" including technologies to spice up social networking profiles, games, and the like. Unknown to the users, these little programs also can include all sorts of malware, especially spyware. If your child is downloading files from the Internet, those files can be a major source of concern.

Make sure your child avoids downloading "techie goodies" unless the technology comes from a well-known, reputable site. Before downloading any product from an unknown or questionable source, conduct a search to see if anyone has reported security concerns. Don't install any software without knowing exactly what it is. Take the time to read the license agreement before downloading any software. Sometimes this agreement will indicate an agreement to download spyware—but do not expect this to be in clear language. If the license agreement is hard to find—or difficult to understand—there are more reasons for concern.

Malware can also be transmitted via email attachments. If a friend's computer has been successfully penetrated, the malware could send messages to all of the people in the friend's address book. The message could look like it came from this known friend, when it really did not. Opening the attachment will result in infecting your computer.

Teach your child to be very wary about opening any attachment—especially from a stranger, but also even if the message appears to be from a friend but is not expected or looks suspicious.

A pop-up ad may offer an exciting opportunity—but this generally is just an enticement to click on the link, which can result in the download of some malware. It is best to use a browser that blocks any pop-up ads and to use a browser that is less likely to be subjected to this kind of an attack.

Teach your child to carefully close any pop-up ad by clinking on the close button and to never click on a link that is within the ad itself. Your child should also know to never click on a link in an email message that is from someone unknown or is at all suspicious, even if it is from someone known.

Make sure your child knows how to protect passwords. Following are some password tips:

- Use hard-to-guess passwords. Mix upper case, lower case, numbers, or other characters not easy to find in a dictionary, and make sure they are at least eight characters long.

- Use a unique password for any account established on a financial institution or through which financial transactions are conducted. This way if someone finds out what one password is, they cannot easily access other accounts.

- Never share your password with someone else. Never provide a password if requested to via an email message. You should only have to provide a password once when you first enter a site you are registered on, such as a social networking site. If a pop-up appears that requests your password for a second time, this is likely bogus. Exit the site and reenter. Report the situation to the site.

Peer-to-Peer Networking

Many teens seek to use peer-to-peer, also called P2P, networking to download files and may have installed this software on the family computer without your knowledge or permission. When peer-to-peer software is installed on a computer, it makes a portion of the files on that computer publicly available to anyone in the world who has also installed the same software. Peer-to-peer networking presents significant security concerns, which include the following:[1]

- If installed incorrectly, peer-to-peer software can provide open access for everyone to all files on the computer, including any family financial records.

- Peer-to-peer networking software contains spyware that allows the peer-to-peer company to track all Internet use. The resulting data are provided to commercial advertisers that deliver more pop-up ads and spam.

- Peer-to-peer networking environments are a major source of identity theft technologies that obtain confidential information from your computer and track all keystrokes.

- Malware commonly transmitted via peer-to-peer networking can hijack your computer for other purposes, including sending spam, denial-of-service attacks, and distribution of child pornography.

- The primary use of peer-to-peer networking is transfer of property—music, movies, and software—without paying, essentially theft. Parents can be held legally and financially responsible for the copyright infringement activities of their children.

- A significant amount of pornography and child pornography is being disseminated via peer-to-peer networking, frequently deceptively labeled.

Peer-to-peer technology may provide some benefits to support online collaboration when more appropriate applications or uses are developed. At this stage in its development, it is hard to see any advantages that would justify its presence on a family computer. Make sure your child knows that it is not acceptable to install peer-to-peer networking on a family-owned computer. If you have any suspicions that such software has been downloaded, do a file search of the applications on your computer. You will likely need professional computer services to remove the peer-to-peer software, accompanying spyware, and other forms of malware.

Family Computer Security

The importance of regularly addressing computer security provides an excellent opportunity to hold regular discussions on all aspects of computer use with your family. When you check your computer security, consider doing so in a family meeting. This will provide an excellent opportunity to discuss any other Internet use concerns.

You can also take advantage of your teen's increasing sophistication in the use of technology. Assign your teen the responsibility to keep updated as the family's security expert. This is a job that can provide an incentive for your teen to consider the security implications of online activities.

Given the propensity of teens to want to download "cool" games, software, multimedia graphics, and the like, it is highly probable that malware producers have figured out how to use teen use of the Internet as a conduit for infecting home computers and getting to the parents' financial information. Your teen's unwitting online actions could result in downloading this malware, leading to the theft of personal financial information and resulting identity theft.

Parents of teens should give serious consideration to the need for a two-computer household. One computer could be used for all of the entertainment activities online, including social networking, gaming, and the like, whereas the other computer would be reserved solely for less risky online activity and online financial transactions. Nothing of value should be retained on the entertainment computer, thus allowing a periodic complete wiping of the hard drive to remove any malware. While requiring up-front funds for a second computer, this approach could save money, time, and hassle in the long run. However, if your home computers are connected through wireless and have file-sharing capabilities, make sure that any malware downloaded by one computer cannot be shared with your other home computer.

· 33 ·

Spam, Spam, Spam, and More Spam

UNSOLICITED
(OR UNKNOWINGLY APPROVED)
EMAIL ADVERTISING

On any typical day when Bennett opens his email inbox, he finds messages like the following:

FROM	SUBJECT
Nicholas	Full of health? Don't click
Enterprise	Sign up today and receive $200 free!
John	Any med for your girl to be happy!
Bart	It's Bart :)
Tatiana	Re: Possible meeting
Jesse	End the annoying obesity now
Paul	Stock profiler journal
Gena	What is OEM Software?
Terrence	Earn over $400 monthly
Irina	Still waiting for your reply
Hugh	She wants better sex? All you need

Every Internet user with an email account is, unfortunately, familiar with the problem of spam. *Spam* is the term applied to unsolicited email. This quirky name for unwanted advertising came from a highly popular Monty Python sketch that was first broadcast in 1970. In the sketch, two customers are trying to order breakfast from a menu that includes spam in almost every item. Other customers chime in singing a spam song that builds to an impressive climax. It is unknown who first applied the term *spam* to unwanted advertising, but once applied, the name stuck—to the chagrin of Hormel, the manufacturers of the eatable Spam.

Companies or individuals "harvest" email addresses for use in sending unsolicited email in a variety of ways. They use "spiders," which are search engines, to troll the Internet to find email addresses. The spiders look for the @ symbol and gather the entire email address from this. The harvesters then use these email addresses or sell them in batches to others. Unfortunately, if your teen registers on a social networking site or any other site that allows your child to establish a public presence, this registration will make an email address readily available for such harvesting.

Some of what people consider to be spam is actually commercial email that they have inadvertently or unknowingly agreed to receive. Any time that your child provides an email address online or through an off-line registration form, it is possible that this will result in the receipt of commercial advertising email. If your child has a valued relationship with a particular company, it may be perfectly appropriate for him or her to sign up to receive periodic email messages from that company. Many times these messages include discount coupons or special offers. This is a form of permission marketing. Warn your child to be very wary during registrations of any items that allow your child to "opt in" or require that your child "opt out" from receiving advertising from the site's "sponsors." By "opting in" to this arrangement, your child's email address can legally be provided to many different companies.

As technologies are becoming more mobile and new technologies are developed for Internet use, the spammers are right behind trying to figure out how to spam through these technologies. IM spam, generally called "spim," is an increasing concern. Cell phone spam is also a growing problem.

Many countries have enacted laws that seek to reduce the level of spam. These laws typically exempt what is considered "legitimate commercial advertising"—essentially permission advertising. Typical provisions include the requirement for an "opt out" mechanism in the email message, a valid subject line and header information, and the legitimate physical address of the sender. These laws do not appear to have resulted in a reduction in the flow of spam. Part of the problem is that the Internet is international, so the law has no impact on spam originating on servers in other countries.

One additional problem is the "opt out" provision itself. When companies or individuals that are harvesting email addresses find an address, they have no real way of knowing whether or not the address is valid or currently in use. Many of the spam messages sent out have an "opt out" option. If the message is from a legitimate company, responding to this "opt out" provision will be effective. But if the spam originated from an unscrupulous spammer and you respond to the "opt out" option, all this does is verify your email address as valid. Your email address will then be added to a distribution list of verified email addresses that is sold for a higher amount.

Spam is primarily a nuisance concern. However, a very common item advertised through spam is male sexual enhancement products: "She wants better sex. All you need is here." "Can you satisfy your girl friend?" "Just take a candy and be ready for 36 hours of love." If you have a son, it would be advisable to engage in some prevention conversations related to these products to ensure that the constant receipt of such messages does not interfere with your efforts to raise your child to have healthy, sexual values and personal self-confidence. Specifically address the misperception that these products are necessary for loving sexual activities.

Avoiding Spam and Unwanted Advertising

The following are some strategies that your child can implement to avoid the receipt of spam, or unknowingly approved email:

- Do not provide an email address or cell phone number online, or in any off-line document, unless it is absolutely necessary and it is absolutely clear that your email address or cell phone number will not be provided to others companies for advertising purposes.

- Review all sections of online registration forms or any off-line product or service registration forms. Disallow any agreement to receive email from "others." "Opt out" of statements such as "❏ Please send me promotions and offers from your sponsors," when this appears in any registration form.

- Consider establishing a "throwaway" email account for those times when it is necessary to provide an email address. Use this email address for all online registrations and public communications. If the throwaway email account mailbox gets too full with spam, throw it away and start a new one.

- Do not complete product interest surveys, even if you are offered a prize or opportunity to win something. You naturally have to provide your email address to be notified of the prize—and, if you read the fine-print, this likely will result in the distribution of your email address to advertisers.

- Do not respond to the "request removal" service on the bottom of the email unless you are absolutely sure the message is from a very legitimate company.

- If your email address is posted anywhere online, try to disguise the address in a way that will defeat the email address spiders. Try something like this: usernameatispname. If real people want to send you an email, they will know to reconfigure the address.

- Don't even open email that appears to be spam. Never click on a link in a spam message. This could lead to an inappropriate site or result in the download of malware.

- There is also a variety of technical approaches one can use to reduce the amount of spam received. Internet Service Providers also provide spam filtering services.

·34·

Have I Got a Deal for You

SCAMS AND PHISHING

Colin, a high school senior, received an email from a company that offered assistance in obtaining a college scholarship. "You've been selected by a 'national foundation' to receive a scholarship." "The scholarship is guaranteed or your money back." "We just need your credit card or bank account number to hold this scholarship."

Tiffany has a bank account, which she manages through the bank's Web site. One day she received an email message that appeared to be from her bank. The message indicated that it was necessary for her to update her financial information. Tiffany clicked on the link contained in the message, which took her to a site that appeared to be the same as the Web site from her bank, and she provided her account information, including account number and password.

It is amazing how many people have lost thousands of dollars to Internet scammers or who are now dealing with identity theft because they provided their credit card number on a fake Web site just because someone asked for it. Individuals marketing "get rich quick" schemes or other scams are earning millions of dollars from people who really ought to know better.

Scam operators generally target adults. Children and teens do not have a large amount of financial resources or the easy ability to transfer funds electronically, so it is harder to complete a scam. But a scam artist might attempt to obtain your credit card number from your child. And any teen who has a debit card or credit card or conducts financial transactions online can be the target for a financial sting.

Take the time to educate your child about scams through use of the teachable moments that likely will appear regularly in your email inbox. Do not just toss your most recent "Nigerian scam" message. Create some value out of this message by showing it to your child and discussing the scam techniques that the message incorporates.

The important message to get across to all children and teens is, "There is no such thing as a 'free lunch!' If someone offers you something for nothing or very little, you most likely will lose something and get nothing." Many scams also include an express or implicit threat that unless an action is taken quickly, a valuable opportunity will be lost. Teach your child to be very leery of any message that that implies "act now or you will lose."

Scams

You should know about the basic types of online crime, so that you can properly review any situation with your child and respond accordingly. In the United States, the Internet Crime Complaint Center (IC3) provides a centralized vehicle to receive, develop, and refer complaints related to online crime.[1] The site contains a list of the common Internet scams. Many scams seek a bank account or credit card number. This information is used for identify theft, which is discussed in the following section. The scams that are most likely to entrap teens include the following:

- *College Scholarship Scam.* College scholarship scam operators guarantee or promise scholarships, grants, or fantastic
financial aid packages. They are likely to use high-pressure
sales pitches in which they tell teens and parents that it is
necessary to sign up "right now" or risk losing out on the
"opportunity."

    Some scam operators guarantee that they can get scholar-
ships in exchange for an advance fee and offer a "money back
guarantee." But the conditions necessary for obtaining a refund
are impossible to meet. Others might tell students they've been
selected as "finalists" for awards that require an up-front fee.
Some companies may engage in a form of phishing by seeking
out checking account information or setting up a contract
under which their services will be paid via a small monthly
deduction from this account. There are legitimate companies
that can assist you and your child in finding a scholarship. The
key to recognizing these companies is that they never guarantee or promise that they will be successful. The best source of
guidance and information on college scholarships is the college
and career center at your child's school.

- *Auction Fraud.* If your teen is engaged in purchasing or selling products through online auction sites such as eBay, auction fraud is a clear possibility. There are guidelines on the
eBay site to avoid being stung by an auction fraud. Review
those guidelines in depth with your child. Do not just assume
that because you have read the guidelines that your child
understands what they mean. For each guideline, ask your
child what it means. Make sure you pay close attention to
your child's online financial transactions.

- *Business or Employment Opportunities.* "Earn $3,000 or more
per week spending only a few hours per day. No experience
necessary. Find out more here." Teens who are looking to earn
money could be entrapped by an online offer of a business or

employment opportunity. Unsolicited emails advertising work-at-home opportunities that require "no experience" and offer the prospect of significant earnings for very little work should set warning bells ringing.

- *Investment Fraud.* "An Investor ALERT is being issued starting right NOW. Keep your eyes glued on XYZ!! Explosive pick for our members! Don't get caught in the dust, start watching today because this company could release major news at any time, which could bring the stock up!!" Investment fraud solicitations bear a close similarity to business or employment opportunities. These offers promise fast profits with very little or no risk.

- *Lotteries.* "You are a winner in this lottery [that you never entered]! All you have to do is provide us with your bank account number and we will wire your winnings directly to your account." This scam will result in removal of funds from the bank account and identity theft.

- *Nigerian Scam.* "With due respect and humility, I write to you irrespective of the fact that you don't know me. I have decided to contact you and bestow this trust in you, which I pray you will not ignore. I am contacting you in regards to a most delicate matter. My dear uncle had amassed $25,000,000 in a foreign account before he met a most untimely death. If you can help me obtain these funds, I will be able to reward you most handsomely." This is another scam that will result in removal of funds from the bank account and identify theft.

- *Product Sales.* "$4VE up to +80% on SOFTW4RE NOW" "TOP BRANDS—LOW LOW COST Jewelry * Handbags * Pens * Watches * Neckties * Clutches * Wallets * Visit our site for real photos. Everything comes with a certificate, tags and all the extras, plus a warranty." Responding to an advertisement such as this will result in the receipt of shoddy products, if anything at all, and the likely misuse of a credit card number.

- *Reshipping*. "Earn fast money at home. Your government will not allow us to ship products directly to our purchasers. We need assistance with reshipping. If you will allow us to ship the product to your home address and then reship it to a new address which we will provide, we will pay you $25 per shipment." Responding to this scam could involve your teen in the illegal transfer of products.

Phishing and Identity Theft

Most people think that identity theft is a problem that affects only adults. Nothing can be further from the truth. Young people are also targets for identity theft. Because they rarely worry about or check their credit reports until they are older, an identity theft can go undetected for years and the impact can be quite extensive. Young adults ages eighteen to twenty-five are also significant targets for identity theft.

"Phishing" is a criminal activity that involves attempts to fraudulently obtain personal financial information, such as credit card numbers, passwords used on financial sites, personal identification numbers, and other personal financial data by masquerading as a legitimate, trustworthy business through an official-appearing electronic communication. *Phishing* is short for "password harvesting," but also includes the connotation of "fishing" for financial information.

Phishing is typically carried out through an email message or an instant message. A message appears to be from a legitimate company—perhaps one with which you or your child does business. The message contains graphic images that have been lifted from the actual legitimate company. A typical phishing message will read something like this:

Dear [name of institution] customer,
We recently noticed two or more attempts to log into your [institution name] online banking account from a foreign IP address and we have

reasons to believe that your account was hijacked by a third party with-out your authorization. If you recently accessed your account while traveling, the unusual log-in attempts may have been initiated by you. However if you are the rightful holder of the account, click on the link below and submit the requested information, so we can verify your account. <link>

Please Note: If we do not receive the appropriate account verification within the next 48 hours, your account will remain locked and then suspended. The purpose of this verification is to ensure that your account has not been fraudulently used and to combat the fraud from our community.

Clicking on the link will lead to a fraudulent site that will look identical to the original site of the institution, where the user will be guided to enter financial data, passwords, and the like. When financial identity information has been acquired, the phishers may use it to create fake accounts in a victim's name, ruin a victim's credit, or even prevent victims from accessing their own accounts.

There are many other variations on techniques to obtain financial identity information. Your child could very easily become a victim of phishing, especially if he or she has any financial accounts that are managed electronically, such as on eBay, PayPal, or a personal bank account. Ensure that your child understands how phishing works and how to prevent being duped into providing personal or financial information.

Prevention Strategies

Your child should know never to provide financial information online without your permission or review. Whenever you are involved in a situation with your child that requires providing financial information online, use this opportunity as a teachable moment to go over basic security and privacy protection, as well as to review the overall situation together to determine the potential of scam, phishing, or other fraudulent activity. The next time a phishing email ends up in your inbox or your child's, print it out and discuss how the phishing scam works.

Chapter Thirteen presented a specific list of financial identity information items that your child must know should be protected. Older teens who are conducting financial transactions online must understand how to safely provide financial identity information on legitimate secure sites.

How can you be sure that any financial site or site from which you want to make a purchase is a legitimate, secure site? A recent research study demonstrated that simply looking at the site was not an effective technique.[2] The researchers found that well-constructed phishing sites fooled 90 percent of the participants. Legitimate Web sites use many techniques to establish their credibility and security—and fraud artists can easily implement all of these techniques.

There is one thing that phishers are not likely to be able to accomplish—getting their fraudulent site listed at or near the top of a search engine return. Whenever your child wants to go to a site to conduct a financial transaction, the best safety strategy is to use a search engine. Type the name of the institution or company in the search engine. Review the site description carefully. The site you are seeking likely will be the first one in the list of search returns. If your child will use this site frequently, bookmark it and from thereon use the bookmark to access the site that is known to be the legitimate site. Secure sites are also designated by a URL that begins with <https://>.

If your child receives an email message that really appears to be legitimate from a company that he or she has a financial relationship with, the way to check out the validity of the email is to independently go to the site either by using the bookmarked link or finding the site via a search engine.

Part Five

•

ACCENTING
THE POSITIVE

· 35 ·

Finding the Good Life

BENEFICIAL ACTIVITIES ONLINE

One problem in writing a book such as this one is that the focus is on the negative aspects of the Internet. It's important not to lose sight of the fact that the Internet isn't all bad. Clearly, if your child's use of the Internet is limited to mindless surfing, endless gaming, or inane gabbing, the Internet is likely more harmful than helpful. But there are ways that the Internet can be very beneficial for your child. Here are some thoughts about possible online activities that will enhance your child's well-being—and possibly the well-being of others.

- Foster communication opportunities with family members. The Internet provides an excellent opportunity for your child to develop closer relationships with family members. Encourage your child to share information about life activities with Grandma via email. Or encourage your child to interview family members to create a "family history." Make sure you express clear guidelines about personal information that can be shared with a family member as compared to information that might be shared with others not known to the family. Create a family history social network. Invite all of your extended family to participate, including your grandparents and great-grandparents. Scan in old photos and ask for family stories.

- Your child can make effective use of the Internet to conduct research necessary for school projects. It is necessary that he or she learn how to assess Web site credibility and properly cite sources. Take the time to talk with your child about the information discovered for school projects and seek to involve him or her in a deeper exploration of the material.

- Beyond schoolwork, your child can be encouraged to use Internet resources to explore subjects of personal interest. Is your child interested in dinosaurs? Soccer? Outer space explorations? Egyptian mythology? There are many sites established by science centers and museums that can provide a wealth of information about many different subjects. Start when your child is younger to encourage exploration of this kind of information. If necessary, make an agreement with your teens that a certain amount of time must be spent exploring quality sites every week to earn time for entertainment activities.

- If your child wants to create a Web site or profile on a social networking site, encourage him or her to create a site or profile that showcases personal talents and interests, making sure there is no unsafe disclosure of personal contact information. Encourage your child to treat the profile like a multimedia college application or job application. If your child is an artist, graphic designer, photographer, or musician, encourage the use of the profile to showcase this talent.

- If your child is a member of a team, club, or other organization, encourage a collaborative effort with other members to create a top-notch Web site to profile the activities of the team, club, or organization. The site could be used to coordinate activities, including schedules. The site could also include photos of the members engaging in team, club, or organization activities—be sure to get permission before posting these photos.

- If your child has any political or social advocacy aspirations, encourage the establishment of a site to engage other teens in the school or community to discuss and propose solutions to local issues of importance to teens. Your child also might volunteer for a local nonprofit organization to create or update its Web site.

- Encourage your child to find a way to use the social networking community to organize a social service project—in your own community or on the other side of the world. Does a local homeless shelter need clothes and toys for kids? Does an impoverished village in Africa need books and supplies for a school? How could your child and friends use their social networks to do good for others? Just think of the number of registered users on various social networking sites. If just 10 percent of those users were to start using the social networking sites to coordinate social service projects throughout the world, what a difference this could make!

Most important, make sure your child has a full and active life offscreen. The Internet can bring value to your child's life if, and only if, use of it remains only a small portion of your child's life activities. Don't let your child get sucked into a "life on the screen" and into thinking that this is real life. Real life is also reading books, playing soccer or baseball, enjoying time with friends and family members, going for a walk in the woods, painting a picture, writing a story . . . You get the idea.

Appendix A
Parent-Teen Internet Use Agreement

Chapter Ten provided guidance on how to work with your child to complete this agreement. This agreement can be downloaded from the Cyber-Safe Kids, Cyber-Savvy Teens site at http://cskcst.com.

PARENT AGREEMENT

I agree to help you make safe and responsible choices online. I will respect your growing understanding of safe and responsible online behavior and will help you gain the knowledge, skills, and values to make good choices online.

I agree to pay attention to what you are doing online, so that we can discuss any issues that may arise. I will pay attention to all material that you are posting publicly, including in any social networking site, whether or not privacy features have been implemented. I generally will respect your private online communications, unless I have reason to believe that there are significant concerns.

I will not overreact if you become involved in an online situation that causes concern. I will work with you to mutually review the situation and the choices that were made or need to be made. If I find it necessary to impose restrictions, I will fully explain the reasons for those restrictions and provide a way for you to regain any lost privileges.

Other commitments I make are:

TEEN AGREEMENT

It is my goal to use the Internet in a manner that is safe and responsible. I know that my online actions reflect the kind of person I am. The following are my personal standards for online activities.

I will protect my personal privacy by:

I will protect my personal reputation by:

I will treat others online in the following way:

The kinds of sites and activities I will avoid include:

If I am communicating with someone I do not know in person, the steps I will take to make sure this person is safe are:

If I become worried that someone I am communicating with online is not safe (to me or to other teens), I will:

The following are the steps I will take to keep myself safe if I ever want to meet an online stranger in person.

If I receive a communication from someone that is inappropriate or upsetting, I will:

If someone treats me badly online, including sending repeated inappropriate messages or posting material elsewhere that damages my reputation or friendships, I will:

The amount of time that I will spend online during a typical day is:

The strategies I will use to ensure that my online activities do not interfere with homework and other important tasks are:

If I see material posted online that makes me worried that someone else might be in danger or might cause harm to others, I will:

I will ask you for assistance if:

Other commitments I make are:

_____

Parent's signature   *Teen's signature*

Appendix B
The Cyberspace World

DEFINITIONS OF ONLINE ACTIVITIES AND TECHNOLOGIES

This appendix will provide information on the various Internet and digital technologies and online activities currently available.

One concept that you might hear involves the terms *Web 1.0* and *Web 2.0*. Web 1.0 refers to the style of the Internet when it first was introduced. This version of the Internet included relatively static Web pages for the provision of information, provided by organizations and companies. In the Web 1.0 environment, communication tools, including email, chat, and instant messaging, were used separately from Web sites. In the Web 1.0 environment, access to the Internet was accomplished through a computer with a wire connected to the wall.

Web 2.0 refers to the rapidly emerging Internet epitomized by the social networking sites. In the Web 2.0 environment, everyone has a personal Web page, a blog, or both for the presentation of information that fully integrates a wide range of communication tools. In this appendix, the discrete components of information-provision technologies and communication technologies will be outlined. Readers should understand that these components are merging together on today's Internet Web 2.0.

Hardware technologies include devices that allow users to capture, input, download, upload or post, process, store, and play or show material. In a manner similar to the merger of information-provision and communication tools, all of these technology devices are also merging. In addition, Web 2.0 is mobile and wireless. Mobile computing refers to the ability of an individual to interact with a technology device from any location. Wireless is the means by which communication between devices is accomplished. Using a mobile communications device that fits easily into a pocket and can be used at school, today's teens can instantly access and send email, engage in text messaging, access a Web site, and take and send digital photos. Future technologies will be smaller, faster, more interactive, and more ubiquitous, and will have greater multimedia capabilities.

THE INTERNET

The Internet is a massive network of computer networks. The Internet connects billions of computers throughout the world using a common system or protocol to transfer data. By using the common protocol—computer language—any computer can communicate with any other computer that is connected to the Internet. Sometimes the terms *Internet* and the *Web* are used interchangeably. They are not the same. The Internet is the technical structure. The Web is just one way of accessing and disseminating information that uses the Internet.

INFORMATION PROVISION TECHNOLOGIES

The Web

The Web provides a vehicle to present and access information through the Internet. The Web uses hypertext transfer protocol (HTTP) to transmit data.

Web Pages and Web Sites

Web pages are documents that are on the Web that have been created using hypertext markup language (HTML). Web pages may contain graphics, sounds, text, and video. HTML allows the creation of hyperlinks that provide a connection to another Web page or to another place in the current Web page.

Web sites are a collection of Web pages that are all provided by one specific entity. In the Web 2.0 environment, Web sites also provide access to communication tools. The social networking sites allow their registered users to establish their own personal Web page, also called a profile, on the site.

Every Web page on the Internet has a unique "address" called a uniform resource locator, or URL. A URL starts with http:// for a general Web site or https:// for a secure Web site. On sites that allow individual members to create a Web page or profile, the URL for the specific page or profile is a combination of the site URL with the specific registrant: http://myspace.com/~username. When a Web page links to another Web page, it does so by accessing the URL for the new Web page.

Browsers

Browsers are software applications that are used to connect to different Web pages. Popular browsers are Safari, Foxfire, Netscape Navigator, and Microsoft Internet Explorer. To get to a certain Web page through a browser, it is necessary to input the URL for that Web page into the browser.

Browsers have the ability to record URLs in a bookmark file. If the URL is bookmarked, then it is not necessary to type it into the browser. Bookmarks are an excellent feature to use to establish a set of URLs of sites that you have reviewed and have found to be acceptable for your younger child to access.

Browsers also retain a history file that shows all of the URLs that have been accessed. Most browsers retain histories for a week. It is very helpful for parents to know about history files, because this feature allows you to regularly review the sites that your child has recently accessed. It is possible to erase a history file, but a missing history file is evidence of an attempt to limit your access to important information about online activities.

Search Engines

In addition to typing a known URL or accessing a site that has been bookmarked, the other way to find and get to a Web page is to use a search engine. Popular search engines are Google and Yahoo. To find a Web page that has certain information, it is necessary to type keywords into the search engine. The search engine then provides a search return, which includes short descriptions of Web pages that contain the keywords with a link that will provide direct access to each of these Web pages. Search engines also provide sponsored links to sites that have paid an advertising fee.

ELECTRONIC COMMUNICATIONS

Electronic communication technologies can be used to transmit text and graphic images, including drawings, digital photos, and videos. Electronic communications can be roughly classified in two ways:

- *Synchronous (real time) or asynchronous (delayed)*. Synchronous communications are those in which the participants communicate with each other at the same time. With asynchronous communications, the communication is delayed until a user receives or accesses it. Frequently, when communications are synchronous, the user must take specific steps to preserve the communications. Asynchronous communications are generally preserved or archived in some format.
- *Public or private*. The notion that electronic communications are private actually is misleading. Some communication technologies

can be used in a manner that is ostensibly private, or initially between a limited number of known individuals. But once a message has been transmitted in electronic form, there is absolutely no technology that will prevent the recipient of that communication from sharing it with anyone, anywhere.

The following are common types of electronic communication activities:

Email

Email is short for electronic mail. Email is asynchronous private communication that can be sent to one or many recipients. To send or receive email it is necessary to have an email account and to know the email address of the intended recipient. Email messages are received in a private electronic mailbox that is housed on a server until the recipient goes to fetch the email. Email is provided by the user's Internet service provider (ISP) or through a Web-based email service, such as Hotmail. Email programs have a text editor that allows for the creation of a text message. It is also possible to attach computer files to an email message, including documents and image files. The popular social networking sites have a messages capability that functions like email. For many teens, messaging on social networking sites is their preferred asynchronous, private-communication vehicle.

Instant Messaging, or IM

Instant messaging, or IM, is a synchronous communication system. Instant messaging software allows users to communicate in real time with a specific person or create a custom chat room for a specific group of people. IM can only occur between individuals who have included each other's IM address in their IM "contact" list. When IM addresses have been shared, it is possible for either user to identify when the other user is online and seek to initiate communication. It is possible to save an IM session, but specific steps must be taken to do this. It is also possible to signal to other IM users that you are not to be disturbed, even though you are online. It is possible to block communications from someone through IM.

During the IM registration process, the user creates a user profile. Any other registered user can search these profiles to find and make contacts. Many teens have a large number of IM addresses in their contact list, including many individuals whom they do not know in "real life." The number of IM contacts has become a new measure of one's social worth. Many social networking sites also have IM capabilities.

Chat

Chat is a synchronous communication that is public, but also has the capacity to shift to a private environment that is similar to an IM environment. Chat services are offered by many social networking sites, as well as such services as Yahoo and MSN. Chat rooms generally are established to address a specific area of interest. As with IM, it is necessary for the user to take specific steps to preserve the communications, although the Web site may have some archiving capabilities for public chats. When users enter a chat room, they are identified by their username on the system. Chat rooms may be moderated or unmoderated. From a parenting perspective, the biggest concern about chat rooms is that chat rooms that address topics of interest to young people also attract predators and other dangerous strangers.

A frequent query that is made whenever a new user enters a chat room is "a/s/l," which stands for age/sex/location, information the new user is expected to provide. It is easy and common to lie about such information and generally difficult to ascertain the truth, so it is really quite useless to post the question. Given that many users try out different "personas" online, the response to an a/s/l query can be interpreted as, What is the age, sex, and location of the "persona" the person is pretending to be in the particular chat room, at the particular time?

Email Mailing Lists

Email mailing lists are asynchronous public-communication vehicles. Email mailing lists are distribution lists that individuals can establish within their own email systems or a centralized mailing list for groups or users. The mailing list messages are sent to the individual's email mailbox. Email mailing lists tend to be used more by older Internet users. Young people prefer discussion groups.

Discussion Groups

Discussion groups or boards are another form of asynchronous public communication organized around specific topics of interest. Discussion groups are accessed through social networking and other community Web sites. Discussion groups tend to be the asynchronous public communication environment of choice for teens.

OTHER TECHNOLOGIES OR ACTIVITIES

Blogs, Vblogs, and MBlogs

Blogs are a merger between Web sites and discussion groups. The term blogs is short for "Weblogs." Blogs are online personal diaries or journals.

The owner of a personal blog regularly posts commentary that reflects thoughts and opinions. Frequently, bloggers will solicit and post feedback on their commentary. It is possible to create "blogging rings" that link separate blogs together. To read a blog, one can go to the blog URL or sign up to receive a rich site summary (RSS) feed whenever material is posted to the blog. Podcasting is similar to RSS, but it feeds the content to an iPod or similar device.

Many social networking sites allow their members to create blogs. Frequently, these blogs bear closer resemblance to a discussion group, in which everyone tosses in relatively brief comments. However, with a blog, as compared to a discussion group, the owner of the blog has more control and can remove any posting that the creator deems inappropriate. Vblogs (video blogs) are blogs that feature the dissemination of video images. Mobile logs, known as mblogs or moblogs, can be updated using a cell phone.

Blogs can be sophisticated communication vehicles. Creative teachers are using blogging technology to facilitate classroom discussions and exchange of information and insight. These instructional activities provide a vehicle to teach the principles of responsible blogging.

Peer-to-Peer Networking, or P2P

When peer-to-peer software is installed on an individual computer it makes a portion of the computing capacity and the files stored on the computer available to other individuals throughout the world who are using the same peer-to-peer software. Peer-to-peer networking has some uses in a business and research environment.

There are many reasons to discourage the use of this technology on a family computer. Peer-to-peer networking software is provided for free—but in exchange the software installs spyware, which allows tracking of Internet activity and delivery of pop-up advertising. A significant level of computer crime is conducted through computers that have been compromised through the downloading of "malware," or malicious software, including worms and Trojan horses. This malware takes advantage of the fact that the computer is frequently connected through broadband and remains on. This allows the malware to hijack the computer to send unwanted advertisements or to engage in other inappropriate and potentially illegal activity.

A primary use of peer-to-peer networking is to facilitate the illegal downloading of copyrighted material, including music, videos, and software. A significant amount of pornography, child pornography, and gross images is also disseminated via peer-to-peer networking. Often this material is deceptively labeled.

Image Files

Image files are stored on a computer, cell phone, or personal digital assistant (PDA) and can be disseminated through the Internet or wireless service. Image files all have one of several suffixes—.jpg, .gif, or .tif. Conducting a search of the files on a computer for the files with these suffixes can reveal the files that contain images. This search can allow parents to discover if their child has downloaded or created any inappropriate images.

Text Messaging

Text messaging is the communication of brief messages, generally via cell phones or other PDAs. Although the term implies text only, it is possible to text message images. It also is possible to send anonymous text messages through Internet sites or to forward other electronic communications to a cell phone, which will then appear as a text message.

REGISTRATION-RELATED SERVICES OR DOCUMENTS

Registration Form

To use certain services or to fully participate in an online site or community, it is necessary to register. To register, the user must provide a certain amount of personal information. Information that generally is solicited includes

- Username, which is created by the user and is the identifier for the user on the site
- Email address, which is used to authenticate the registration and to send notices to the person registered
- Age, which is used to determine whether the person seeking registration is of an age that is appropriate for registration on the site and may also be used to determine which kinds of ads are most appropriate to display to the particular user
- Gender
- Location, which may be requested in the form of a postal or Zip code or country and city

There is really no way for the Web site to determine the accuracy of the information provided by the person registering, with the exception of the email address. If a wrong email address is provided, the registration generally is terminated because the person registering must receive and respond to an email in order to authenticate the registration.

Profiles

On many sites, an option is offered to create a user profile. Users may be encouraged to post information in the profiles about their age, location, interests, and activities, as well as online contact information including email, IM addresses, Web sites, and the like. There is no mechanism for the site or service to verify or review this information. Users may also be able to post their picture on their profile, and many teens do. Other registered users or visitors may be able to search these registrations or profiles by any of the categories. Registrations and profiles are a vehicle by which users make contacts with others who have similar interests.

Username

In the course of registration, users create the "username" by which they will be identified through the service or on the site. Some teens have more than one account on a Web site, each with a username and "persona." This allows teens to experiment with different personalities. The username(s) a teen creates often can provide a strong clue about the image the teen wishes to convey on the site or when using the service.

Terms of Use Agreements

Internet service providers, cell phone companies, Web sites, online communities, and providers of the different communications technologies do seek to place some controls on the material and communications posted on their sites or transmitted through their communication tool. The sites and services generally have a document that is referred to as "Terms and Conditions," "Terms of Use," or simply "Terms" that outlines the agreement between the site or service and users. In general, there is a link to the terms of use document on the home page of the site, and during registration, the user must indicate agreement to these terms by checking a box.

Age Limits

For commercial Web sites located in the United States, the Children's Online Privacy Protection Act (COPPA) places severe restrictions on the kinds of personal contact information that the sites can collect from children under the age of thirteen. COPPA also requires parental approval for registration of children under thirteen.

The problem is that there is no accurate way to verify the age of any Internet user who wants to register as another age. Most young people over about the age of ten know that it is possible to lie about their age to register on a site that has an age restriction. Some sites also seek to prevent adults from registering. But adults also know they can lie about their age.

Age Verification

Age verification is a specific process undertaken to verify the actual age of a registrant. Some adult sites have implemented age-verification processes. The companies that provide age-verification services verify the age information provided by the registrant, comparing this information with databases of government- or business-issued identification numbers, such as driver's license and credit card numbers.

It is not possible to establish age-verification systems to determine the age of minors because there are currently no consistent independent government or business identification systems for minors. Further, many parents would have concerns about providing the level of personal contact information necessary about their children to a variety of Web sites to actually validate age.

Privacy Policies

Most sites have privacy policies that outline what information they will gather and how this information will be used. There generally is a link to the privacy policy on the home page of the site.

HARDWARE

Hardware can be classified into several types.

Computing Devices

Computing devices have a large amount of computing and processing power. Computers have the greatest processing power. Some personal digital assistants (PDAs) have a significant amount of processing power. Other digital devices do not have significant processing power.

Image- or Data-Capture Devices

Image- or data-capture devices capture digital images as still images or motion images. The technologies include Web cams, cell phones with camera capabilities, digital cameras and movie cameras, and PDAs.

Content Download and Play Devices

Content download and play devices allow the user to download data from the Internet and play or display the data. Computers were, of course, the original download and capture device. Many PDAs now have similar capabilities with direct Internet access. Other PDAs can download and play data from a computer. MP3 players and iPods can be connected to a computer to download music and text. Some will download and display photos and videos.

Internet Access Devices

Internet access devices are technologies that allow for a direct interface with the Internet. Again, computers were the first such device. Many PDAs now have direct Internet interfacing capabilities, as do some cell phones. Some gaming devices, including the XBox and Play Station 2, also have the ability to interface with the Internet.

Notes

Chapter Four

1. D. Baumrind, "The Influence of Parenting Style on Adolescent Competence and Substance Use, *Journal of Early Adolescence*, 1991, *11*(1), 56–95.
2. Baumrind, "The Influence of Parenting Style," p. 62.
3. Baumrind, "The Influence of Parenting Style," p. 62.
4. Baumrind, "The Influence of Parenting Style," p. 62.

Chapter Five

1. D. Thornburgh and H. S. Lin, "Youth, Pornography, and the Internet," U.S. National Academy of Science, 2002. [www.nap.edu/books/ 0309082749/html].
2. V. Rideout, C. Richardson, and P. Resnick, "See No Evil: How Internet Filters Affect the Search for Online Health Information," Kaiser Family Foundation, 2002. [www.kff.org/entmedia/20021210a-index.cfm].

Chapter Twelve

1. "Marketing to Children: Kids and Tweens Demographic Research Reports," MarketResearch.com. [www.marketresearch.com/browse.asp?categoryid=938& g=1]. Accessed September 29, 2006.
2. "How to Comply with the Children's Online Privacy Protection Rule," U.S. Federal Trade Commisssion, November 1999, [www.ftc.gov/bcp/conline/pubs/ buspubs/coppa.html]. Accessed September 29, 2006.

Chapter Fourteen

1. An additional helpful resource for addressing Internet addiction is K. S. Young, *Caught in the Net: How to Recognize the Signs of Internet Addiction—and a Winning Strategy for Recovery* (Hoboken, N.J.: John Wiley & Sons, 1998).
2. D. Gellene, "Teens' Heavy Cellphone Use Could Signal Unhappiness, Study Finds," *Los Angeles Times*, May 24, 2006.
3. C. Wallis, "The Multi-tasking Generation," *Time*, March 27, 2006. [http:// time-proxy.yaga.com/time/archive/preview/0,10987,1174696,00.html].
4. M. Luciana, H. M. Conklin, C. J. Hooper, and R. S. Yarger, "The Development of Nonverbal Working Memory and Executive Control Processes in Adolescents," *Child Development*, 2005, *76*(3). Summarized in A. Browning, "Teen's Ability to Multi-Task Develops Late in Adolescence," *Medical News Today*, May 18, 2005. [www.medical newstoday.com/medicalnews.php?newsid=24589].

Chapter Fifteen

1. Consumer Reports Webwatch, [www.consumerWebwatch.org/Web-credibility .cfm]. Accessed October 2, 2006.
2. B. J. Fogg, and others, "How Do People Evaluate a Web Site's Credibility?" *Consumer Reports WebWatch*, October 29, 2002. [www.consumerWebwatch.org/ dynamic/Web-credibility-reports-evaluate-abstract.cfm].

3. R. Dhamija, J. D. Tygar, and M. Hearst, "Why Phishing Works," Harvard Engineering and Applied Sciences, 2006. [http://people.deas.harvard.edu/ ~rachna/papers/why_phishing_works.pdf].

Chapter Eighteen

1. A. N. Joinson, "Causes and Implications of Disinhibited Behavior on the Internet," in J. Gackenbach (ed.), *Psychology and the Internet: Intrapersonal, Interpersonal and Transpersonal Implications* (pp. 43–60) (New York: Academic Press, 1998).
2. M. Nisan, "Limited Acceptable Morality," in W. M. Kurtines and J. L. Gewirtz (eds.), *Handbook of Moral Behavior and Development*, Vol. III (Mahwah, N.J.: Lawrence Erlbaum Associates, 1991).
3. A. Bandura, "Social Cognition Theory of Moral Thought and Action," in W. M. Kurtines and J. L. Gewirtz (eds.), *Handbook of Moral Behavior and Development*, Vol. I (Mahwah, N.J.: Lawrence Erlbaum Associates, 1991).
4. E. Erickson, *Childhood and Society*, 2nd rev. ed. (New York: Norton, 1963 [1950]).

Chapter Nineteen

1. Robert B. Cialdini, a professor at Arizona State University, has written an excellent book on this subject: R. B. Cialdini, *Influence Science and Practice*, 4th ed. (Boston: Allyn & Bacon, 2001).

Chapter Twenty-Two

1. This scenario is based on a real, reported incident. H. A. Valetk, "Teens and the Internet: Disturbing 'Camgirl' Sites Deserve a Closer Look," Findlaw Legal News and Commentary, January 23, 2003. [http://writ.news.findlaw.com/commentary/ 20030123_valetk.html].
2. J. Wolak, K. Mitchell, and D. Finkelhor, "Online Victimization of Youth: Five Years Later," Crimes Against Children Research Center, August 2006. [www.unh.edu/ccrc/second_youth_internet_safety-publications.html].
3. D. Finkelhor, K. Mitchell, and J. Wolak, *Online Victimization: A Report on the Nation's Youth*, Crimes Against Children Research Center, 2000. [www.missingkids .com/en_US/publications/NC62.pdf].
4. U.S. Congress General Accounting Office, "Peer-to-Peer Networks Provide Ready Access to Child Pornography: Highlights of GAO-03-351," February 2003. [www.gao.gov/highlights/d03351high.pdf].
5. K. Eichenwald, "Through His Webcam, a Boy Joins a Sordid Online World," *New York Times*, December 19, 2005. [www.nytimes.com/2005/ 12/19/national/ 19kids.ready.html?ex=1292648400&en=aea51b3919b2361a&ei=5090].
6. N. M. Malamuth and E. A. Impett, "Research on Sex in the Media: What Do We Know About Effects on Children and Adolescents?" In D. G. Singer and J. L. Singer (eds.), *Handbook of Children and the Media* (Thousand Oaks, Calif.: Sage Publications, 2001, pp. 269–288).
7. J. Wolak, D. Finkelhor, and K. Mitchell, "Internet-Initiated Sex Crimes Against Minors: Implications for Prevention Based on Findings from a National Study," *Journal of Adolescent Health*, 2004, 35, 424.e11–424 .e20. [http://download .journals.elsevierhealth.com/pdfs/journals/1054–139X/PIIS1054139X04001715.pdf].
8. Associated Press, "Sexual Predators Lose an Outlet," *Wired News*, October 12, 2005. [www.wired.com/news/politics/0,1283,69188,00.html].
9. DatelineNetCrime, "To Catch a Predator," MSNBC.com. [www.msnbc.msn.com/ id/10912603]. Accessed October 4, 2006.

10. R. O'Connell, "A Typology of Child Cybersexpolitation and Online Grooming Practices." Cyberspace Research Unit, University of Lanchester, U.K., 2003. [www.uclan.ac.uk/host/cru/docs/cru010.pdf].

Chapter Twenty-Three

1. This scenario is based on a real reported incident. B. Meadows and others, "The Web: The Bully's New Playground," *People*, March 21, 2005.
2. News Release, "1 of 3 Teens and 1 of 6 Preteens Are Victims of Cyber Bullying," Fight Crime: Invest in Kids, August 17, 2006. [www.fightcrime.org/releases.php?id= 231].
3. J. Wolak, K. Mitchell, and D. Finkelhor, "Online Victimization of Youth: Five Years Later," Crimes Against Children Research Center, August 2006. [www .unh.edu/ccrc/second_youth_internet_safety-publications.html].

Chapter Twenty-Four

1. T. Gutierrez and K. McCabe, "Parents: Online Newsgroup Helped Daughter Commit Suicide," CNN.com, November 11, 2005. [www.cnn.com/2005/US/11/04/ suicide.internet/index.html].
2. "Net Grief for Online 'Suicide'," BBC News World Edition, February 4, 2003. [http://news.bbc.co.uk/2/hi/technology/2724819.stm].
3. N. Hellmich, "On the Web: Thinness Worship," *USA Today*, July 24, 2001. [www.usatoday.com/news/health/2001–07–24-anorexia-sites.htm].
4. J. L. Whitlock, J. L. Powers, and J. Eckenrode, "The Virtual Cutting Edge: The Internet and Adolescent Self-Injury," *Developmental Psychology*, 2006, *42*(3), 407–417. [www.apa.org/journals/releases/dev423407.pdf].
5. National Suicide Prevention Lifeline, "Promotional Materials," U.S. Department of Health and Human Services. [www.suicidepreventionlifeline.org/campaign/ promotional.aspx]. Accessed October 5, 2006.

Chapter Twenty-Five

1. R. A. Franklin, "The Hate Directory: Hate Groups on the Internet." [www.bcpl .net/~rfrankli/hatedir.htm]. Accessed October 5, 2006.
2. National Alliance of Gang Investigators Associations, "2005 National Gang Threat Assessment." [www.nagia.org/PDFs/2005_national_gang_ threat_ assessment.pdf]. Accessed October 5, 2006.
3. K. Oppenheim and others, "Kansas Students Charged in Alleged Plot," CNN.com, April 24, 2006. [www.cnn.com/2006/LAW/04/24/kansas.plot/index .html]; K. Johnson, "Students Had a Hit List, Mayor Said," *USA Today*, April 23, 2006. [www.usatoday.com/news/nation/2006–04 –23-school-plot_x.htm].

Chapter Twenty-Six

1. M. E. O'Toole, *The School Shooter: A Threat Assessment Perspective* (Washington, D.C.: Federal Bureau of Investigation, 2004), 16. [www.fbi.gov/publications/ school/school2.pdf].
2. C. Halcom, "Ex-Student to Face Trial for Threats," *The Macomb Daily*, January 13, 2005. [www.macombdaily.com/stories/011305/loc_osantow 001.shtml].
3. JeffWeise.com, [www.jeffweise.com/profiles.html]. Accessed October 5, 2006. Note: this site provides access to material that reportedly provides access to material that was presumably posted by Jeff Weise and was found and archived after the shooting. There is no source of the identity of the person(s) who have posted the site. Therefore, questions should be raised about the credibility of the site.

4. T. Bahrampour, "Message Is Clear in N.Va.: IM 'Threats' Can Bring Teens Trouble in an Instant," *Washington Post*, May 29, 2005. [www.washingtonpost.com/wp-dyn/content/article/2005/05/28/AR200505 2800913.html].

5. T. Lystra, "Student Charged for Death Threat," *Corvallis Gazette Times*, April 13, 2006.

Chapter Twenty-Seven

1. A. Motluk, "Gaming Fanatics Show Hallmarks of Drug Addiction," NewScientist .com, November 16, 2005. [www.newscientist.com/article.ns?id=dn8327&feedId =online-news_rss20].

2. "Joint Statement on the Impact of Entertainment Violence on Children," American Academy of Pediatrics, American Academy of Child & Adolescent Psychiatry, American Psychological Association, American Medical Association, American Academy of Family Physicians, and American Psychiatric Association, July 26, 2000. [www.aap.org/advocacy/releases/jstmtevc.htm].

Chapter Twenty-Eight

1. The researchers at McGill University, Canada, have an excellent research and information program addressing youth gambling: Youth Gambling International, "Youth Problem Gambling." [www.education.mcgill.ca:16080/gambling/en/problemgambling.htm]. Accessed October 5, 2006.

2. *60 Minutes*, "I-Gaming: Illegal and Thriving," CBS News, November 20, 2005. [www.cbsnews.com/stories/2005/11/17/60minutes/main 1052420.shtml].

3. Federal Trade Commission, "Online Gambling and Kids: A Bad Bet" 2002. [www.ftc.gov/opa/2002/06/onlinegambling.htm]. Accessed October 5, 2006.

Chapter Twenty-Nine

1. Criminal Analysis Branch, "Hackers: A Canadian Police Perspective, Part 1," Royal Canadian Mounted Police, March 14, 2002. [www.rcmp.ca/crimint/hackers_e.htm].

Chapter Thirty-One

1. See the Berne Convention for the Protection of Literary and Artistic Works. [www.wipo.int/treaties/en/ip/berne/trtdocs_wo001.html]. Accessed October 5, 2006.

Chapter Thirty-Two

1. FTC Consumer Alert, "P2P File-Sharing: Evaluate the Risks," Federal Trade Commission, 2005. [www.ftc.gov/bcp/conline/pubs/alerts/sharealrt.htm]. Accessed October 5, 2006.

Chapter Thirty-Four

1. Internet Crime Complaint Center. [www.ic3.gov]. Accessed October 5, 2006.

2. R. Dhamija, J. D. Tygar, and M. Hearst, "Why Phishing Works," Harvard Engineering and Applied Sciences, 2006. [http://people.deas.harvard.edu/~rachna/papers/why_phishing_works.pdf].

About the Author

Nancy E. Willard received a bachelor of science degree in elementary and early childhood education from the University of Utah in 1975, a master of science degree in special education from the University of Oregon in 1977, and a doctor of jurisprudence degree from Willamette University College of Law in 1983. She taught "at risk" children with emotional and behavior difficulties, practiced law in areas of computer law and copyright, and provided consulting services to schools on the implementation of educational technology before focusing her professional attention on issues of youth risk online.

Nancy is director of the Center for Safe and Responsible Internet Use. This center provides resources for educators and other professionals on youth risk online issues. She frequently lectures and conducts workshops for educators on policies and practices related to Internet use in schools and has written numerous articles on this subject. Nancy's book *Cyberbullying and Cyberthreats: Responding to the Challenge of Online Social Aggression, Threats, and Distress* provides educators with insight into the concerns of cyberbullying, plus guidance on how schools can review cyberbullying incidents and respond effectively. This book and other resources for educators are available through the Center for Safe and Responsible Internet Use cyberbullying site at http://cyberbully.org.

Nancy lives in Eugene, Oregon, with her three children, Jordan, Allegra, and Bakul, plus various and assorted two- and four-legged creatures.

Index

A

addiction: gambling, online, 250; gaming, online, 11, 104, 156, 242–244; Internet, 51, 103–108, 156; pornography, online, 156; promotion by advertisers, 80; social networking sites, 104

ads, pop-up, 274–275

advergaming, 86, 90

advertising, youth-oriented Web, 21, 79–90, 143–144

age limits, Web site, 20–22, 312–313

age verification, Web site, 36, 313

amygdala, brain, 132

appearances, manipulation of youth with, 149–150

at-risk youth, Internet and, 155–160, 178, 190

auction fraud scams, 287

authoritarian parenting, children and, 28, 30–31

authoritative parenting, children and, 29–30, 32

authority, manipulation of youth with, 149–150

B

Baumrind, D., 27

"black hats," hacking, 256

blogs, 70, 101–102, 305–306

bomb-making sites, 232–233

bookmarking, Web site, 17

brain development, 131–132

brand loyalty, 79

browsers, Web, 302–303

business opportunity scams, 287–288

C

cached Web sites, 35

"calling cards," hacking, 256

cell phone companies, 166–167

chat, 305

chat rooms, 229

child pornography: peer-to-peer networks and, 182–183; preventing victimization, 185; teen-produced, 9, 185–188

child-safe portals, 17, 33–35

children: email accounts for, 20, 100–101; inappropriate sites, closing, 20; instant messaging (IM) and, 20; online guidelines for, 17–22; reviewing online activity of, 20. *See also* youth

Children's Online Privacy Protection Act (COPPA), 83

civil laws, online behavior, 167–168

clubs, Internet management in after-school, 61–62

college scholarship scams, 287

commercial Web sites, youth-oriented, 77–90

commitments, manipulation of youth with, 146–148

communication technologies: impact on youth, 138–142; protection tools, 36–37; technology savvy of youth, 4

computer security, 13, 167, 183, 276–277, 280

computing devices, 314

Consumer Reports, 114–115

contests, online, 82

cookies, Web, 82